United Nations Fii

MW01597977

This book presents insightful perspectives on the invocation, implementation and application of UN-approved financial sanctions and related issues.

With contributions from academics, diplomats and UN panel experts, Yoshimura offers an analysis of how the UN financial sanctions have evolved, the different roles of various major international actors in agreeing and deploying them, and their success in achieving desired outcomes. It also sheds light on a vital role of Japan in the formulation and deployment of financial sanctions, as the third largest economy in the world with very limited armed forces and a pacifist constitution.

Offering valuable consideration into one of the key implements of international law, this is an essential guide for scholars and practitioners in Diplomacy and International Relations.

Sachiko Yoshimura is professor of International Law and Organizations at the School of International Studies, Kwansei Gakuin University, Japan.

Routledge Advances in International Relations and Global Politics

International Relations as Politics Among People
Hannes Hansen-Magnusson

Mexico's Drug War and Criminal Networks
The Dark Side of Social Media
Nilda M. Garcia

Transnational Labour Migration, Livelihoods and Agrarian Change in Nepal
The Remittance Village
Ramesh Sunam

A Middle East Free of Weapons of Mass Destruction
A New Approach to Nonproliferation
Seyed Hossein Mousavian and Emad Kiyaei

Weak States as Spheres of Great Power Competition
Hanna Samir Kassab

Understanding Mexico's Security Conundrum
Agustin Maciel-Padilla

Exploring Base Politics
How Host Countries Shape the Network of U.S. Overseas Bases
Edited by Shinji Kawana and Minori Takahashi

United Nations Financial Sanctions
Edited by Sachiko Yoshimura

For information about the series: www.routledge.com/Routledge-Advances-in-International-Relations-and-Global-Politics/book-series/IRGP

United Nations Financial Sanctions

Edited by Sachiko Yoshimura

LONDON AND NEW YORK

First published 2021
by Routledge
2 Park Square, Milton Park, Abingdon, Oxon OX14 4RN

and by Routledge
52 Vanderbilt Avenue, New York, NY 10017

Routledge is an imprint of the Taylor & Francis Group, an informa business

British Library Cataloguing in Publication Data
A catalogue record for this book is available from the British Library

Library of Congress Cataloging in Publication Data
Names: Yoshimura, Sachiko, editor.
Title: United Nations financial sanctions / edited by Sachiko Yoshimura.
Description: Milton Park, Abingdon, Oxon ; New York, NY : Routledge, 2021. |
Series: Routledge advances in international relations and global politics |
Includes bibliographical references and index. |
Identifiers: LCCN 2020029448 (print) | LCCN 2020029449 (ebook) |
ISBN 9780367202323 (hardback) | ISBN 9780429260315 (ebook)
Subjects: LCSH: Sanctions (International law) |
Economic sanctions. | United Nations–Sanctions.
Classification: LCC KZ6373 .U55 2021 (print) |
LCC KZ6373 (ebook) | DDC 341.5/82–dc23
LC record available at https://lccn.loc.gov/2020029448
LC ebook record available at https://lccn.loc.gov/2020029449

ISBN: 978-0-367-20232-3 (hbk)
ISBN: 978-0-429-26031-5 (ebk)

Typeset in Galliard
by Newgen Publishing UK

Contents

List of contributors   vii
Preface   xiii

1 UN economic sanctions and financial measures—evolution
   and challenges   1
   SACHIKO YOSHIMURA

2 "Smart sanctions" by the UN and financial sanctions   18
   MIKI HONDA

3 Functions of Security Council subsidiary organs in the UN
   financial sanctions regimes: from the perspective of the law
   of international organizations   34
   RYOSUKE SATO

4 Recent challenges regarding the implementation of UN
   Security Council sanctions   52
   TOMOAKI ISHIGAKI

5 How Japan implements UN financial sanctions   67
   SHUNICHI FUKUSHIMA

6 Implementation of financial sanctions by a state and its
   legal challenges: the case of sanctions-related laws of
   the United States   80
   TAKASHI KUBOTA

7 Financial sanctions implementation by the European
Union—the jurisprudence of the CJEU on the balance
between protections of fundamental rights and effectiveness
of the restrictive measures implementing the UN Security
Council Resolution 1373   96
KAZUSHIGE YAGYU

8 Implementation and enforcement of UN sanctions—the
private sector's key role and evolving standards   111
ALEXANDER DMITRENKO

9 Judicial challenges against UN financial sanctions   120
AKIRA KATO

10 UN financial sanctions against the Democratic People's
Republic of Korea: challenges and proposal for efficient
implementation   134
MAIKO TAKEUCHI

11 UN sanctions on Iran and their financial elements   150
KAZUTO SUZUKI

12 The UN Security Council Resolution 1540 and counter
proliferation financing   166
KIWAKO TANAKA

*Annex I: International and domestic documents
    related to UN financial sanctions (as of March 2018)*   184
*Annex II: Major economic sanctions adopted by the
    UN Security Council under Chapter VII of the
    UN Charter (as of March 2018)*   199
Index   214

Contributors

Alexander Dmitrenko is Head of Asia Sanctions at Freshfields Bruckhaus Deringer Tokyo office. He specializes in advising Japanese and other Asian companies on sanctions, export controls and other compliance matters, including establishing compliance policies and procedures, conducting transactional due diligence and compliance clearance, and conducting internal and regulatory investigations. He regularly publishes and teaches compliance-related topics. Alexander is an adjuct professor (Japan) and is the Chair of the Japanese Committee of the Asian Advisory Board of the Temple Law Centre for Ethics and Compliance. Prior to joining Freshfields Tokyo in 2015, he worked at major international law firms in New York and for a Japanese trading house in Tokyo. He qualified in New York, Russia and England and Wales and registered as a Gaikokuho-Jimu-Bengoshi in Japan.

Shunichi Fukushima is working at EY (Ernst & Young) Strategy & Consulting (EYSC) as an Executive Director since July 2020. Before joining EYSC, he worked for decades at the International Bureau of the Japanese Ministry of Finance, where he managed FATF's mutual evaluations of Japan (2008 and 2019–2020) and conducted numerous economic sanctions programs based on the Foreign Exchange and Foreign Trade Act. He also worked at the International Monetary Fund (IMF) and the Financial Action Task Force (FATF). He became a member of CAMS (Certified Anti-Money Laundering Specialists) in 2014.

Miki Honda is currently a professor in the Department of Global Politics, Faculty of Law, Hosei University. Honda earned a Ph.D. in International Relations from the Graduate School of Asia-Pacific Studies, Waseda University, Tokyo, Japan. Prior to joining academia, Dr. Honda worked as a journalist for *The Japan Times*. Her research interests include United Nations coercive measures under Chapter VII of the UN Charter, and the traditional/non-traditional security studies of the Asia-Pacific regions. Her major publications include *UN Economic Sanctions—Law and Practice* (in Japanese, Toshin-do, 2018; *Complex Emergencies and Humanitarian Response* (Union Press, 2018); "Diversification of Security Concept and Its Influences on UN Security Council Resolution," *The Journal of Asia-Pacific Studies* No.

31 (in Japanese: Waseda University, March 2018); *UN Sanctions and Their Humanitarian Issues: Searching for "Smart Sanctions"* (in Japanese: Kokusai Shoin, 2013); *Long Peace in Northeast Asia: War Avoided* (in Japanese: co-authored, Keiso Shobo, 2012). She is an executive board member of the Japanese Association for United Nations Studies since 2016.

Tomoaki Ishigaki currently serves as Director of the Economic Policy Division at the Ministry of Foreign Affairs of Japan. Since joining the ministry in 1994, he has covered various multilateral and bilateral negotiations ranging from international trade at the WTO, the International Criminal Court, the Arms Trade Treaty to climate change negotiations at COP22 and COP23. He also worked as Counsellor of the Cabinet Legislation Bureau (2013–2016) and Deputy Cabinet Secretary for Public Affairs at the Prime Minister's Office (2018–2020) where he was in charge of international media relations and public diplomacy. He currently oversees Japan's economic diplomacy including G7 and G20 leaders' meetings, WTO and OECD matters, food and energy security, and economic partnership agreements. He is a graduate of Amherst College and studied law at the University of Tokyo before joining the Foreign Ministry. He has written a number of articles on international law, disarmament affairs, and climate change, and taught at Japanese universities on these subjects. They include *Defining the Future by Studying the Past: A Negotiator's Perspective on the Arms Trade Treaty, Japanese Yearbook of International Law*, Vol. 57 (2014)) and *Japan's Proactive Multilateralism: The UN Arms Trade Treaty of 2013* (co-authored with Dennis T. Yasutomo, *Asian Survey* 57(5): 956–979, October 2017).

Akira Kato is Associate Professor of International law at the Faculty of Law, Kindai University, Japan. He obtained an LL.M. and Ph.D. from Kyoto University. His research focuses on UN Security Council sanctions and their conflicts with human rights treaties. His recent publication includes "Kokuren Ho to EU Ho no Soukoku: Radical Tagensyugi no Riron Kozo to Sono Jissenteki Igi" [The Struggle between UN Law and EU Law: the Theoretical Structure and Practical Significance of Radical Pluralism], *Kokusaiho Gaiko Zasshi* [*Journal of International Law and Diplomacy*], Vol. 116 (2018).

Takashi Kubota has been a professor of International Financial Law at Waseda Law School, Waseda University, Tokyo, Japan since 2005. From 1990 to 1998, he worked for the Bank of Japan (central bank) as an economist and legal advisor, and moved to academia in 1998 (as an associate professor at Nagoya University from 1998 to 2004, and at Waseda University in 2004), obtained a Ph.D. (2003, Osaka University), an LL.M. (1996, Harvard University, and 1993, University of Tokyo), and was a visiting scholar at Queen Mary University of London (2011–2012), the University of Melbourne (2000), KU Leuven (2004) and Harvard Law School (1996–1997). His current research includes crypto-assets, financial sanctions, and the global financial regulations. He has published numerous books in Japanese and English, including *International Business Law*, 2nd ed. (Chuokeizai Publisher, 2019), *Practice, Policy and Law of Blockchain* (editor and co-author, Chuokeizai Publisher, 2017) in Japanese, and *International Monetary and Financial Law* (co-author, Oxford University Press, 2010), *Cyberlaw for Global E-Business* (editor and co-author, Information Science Reference, 2007) in English.

Ryosuke Sato is an associate professor in the Faculty of Law, Seijo University, Tokyo, Japan. Before joining Seijo in April 2018, he spent one year as a university lecturer at the College of International Relations, Nihon University, Shizuoka, Japan. He earned a Doctor of Laws from the Graduate School of Law, Hitotsubashi University in Tokyo, Japan, and holds a M.A. in Conflict Resolution from the Department of Peace Studies, University of Bradford, UK. His doctoral dissertation was on the legal problems of United Nations Security Council Authorization under the Chapter VII of the UN Charter. His research interests lie in public international law and laws related to international organizations, especially the United Nations. His current research explores a theory of informal change or transformation of the UN Charter.

Kazuto Suzuki is Professor of Science and Technology Policy at the Graduate School of Public Policy at the University of Tokyo, Japan. He graduated from the Department of International Relations, Ritsumeikan University, and received a Ph.D. from Sussex European Institute, University of Sussex, UK. He has worked at the Fondation pour la recherche stratégique in Paris, France as an assistant researcher and was an associate professor at the University of Tsukuba from 2000 to 2008. He then moved to Hokkaido University until September 2020. He also spent one year at the Woodrow Wilson School of Public and International Affairs at Princeton University from 2012 to 2013 as a visiting researcher. He served on the Panel of Experts for the Iranian Sanctions Committee under the United Nations Security Council from 2013 to July 2015. He has been President of the Japan Association of International Security and Trade. His research focuses on the relationship between science/technology and international relations, including space policy, non-proliferation, export control and sanctions. His recent works include "Iran: The role and effectiveness of UN sanctions" in Masahiko Asada (ed.), *Economic Sanctions in International Law and Practice* (2019), *Space and International Politics* (2011), in Japanese, awarded Suntory Prize for Social Sciences and Humanities), *Policy Logics and Institutions of European Space Collaboration* (2003) and many others.

Hinako Takata is Program-Specific Assistant Professor of International Law at the Graduate School of Law, Kyoto University, Japan. She earned her PhD in 2019 from Kyoto University. Her recent publications include "The Autonomous Status of State Organs in International Human Rights Treaties: Disaggregating the 'State' as a Unitary International Law Entity" *Kyoto Law Review* (forthcoming) (in Japanese) and "Identification of Customary International Law by the International Court of Justice: Some Reflections on Recent Debates,"

Journal of International Cooperation Studies, Vol. 26 (2) (2019) (co-authored with Y. Okada and K. Abe) (in Japanese).

Maiko Takeuchi is a visiting scholar, at the Center for Negotiation and Dispute Resolution Research, Waseda University. She has been serving on the Panel of Experts established pursuant to UN Security Council Resolution 1874 (2009) since 2016, co-authoring the Panel's reports submitted to the Security Council. She joined Japan's Ministry of Defense in 2001. During her career in government, she was appointed to the Embassy of Japan in the Republic of Korea as First Secretary and Civilian Defense Attaché from 2012 to 2016. From 2010 to 2011, she worked on cyber security strategy and communication systems in the Ministry of Defense, and from 2008 to 2010, she worked on strategic trade control as the chief of the research and planning office at the Ministry of Economy, Trade and Industry. From 2004 to 2005, she was appointed to the Cabinet Secretariat for National Security and Crisis Management, where she worked for policy coordination. She holds a Master's degree in Regional Studies East Asia from Harvard University, and a Bachelor of Law from the University of Tokyo. She has written number of articles, including "Smart Language: How to Address an Inherent Weakness Undermining the Implementation of U.N. Sanctions on North Korea" (*International Law Studies*, Vol. 96 (2020)).

Kiwako Tanaka is a senior research fellow of the National Institute for Defense Studies (NIDS), Ministry of Defense, Japan and currently serves as an expert assisting the Committee Established Pursuant to Security Council Resolution 1540 since April 2018. Her main research interests include non-proliferation of weapons of mass destruction (WMD), dual-use technology control, arms transfer and conflict resolution. Prior to joining the NIDS in 2013, she served as an advisor to the Permanent Representation of Japan to the Organisation for Prohibition of Chemical Weapons (OPCW) in The Hague from 2005 to 2008, to the Permanent Mission of Japan to the Conference on Disarmament in Geneva from 2009 to 2011, as well as to the Secretariat of the International Peace Cooperation Headquarters, Cabinet Office of Japan from 2011 to 2013. She obtained a Ph.D. in Public Administration from the International Christian University in Tokyo.

Kazushige Yagyu is currently a professor of International Law and International Human Rights Law at the Faculty of Global and Community Studies, Hiroshima Shudo University, Hiroshima, Japan. He earned a Ph.D. in Public International Law from the Hitotsubashi University in Tokyo; his dissertation was on the direct effect of EU directives in domestic courts of the EU member states. His current research covers the relations of international and national law. He wrote several articles, including "The Consistency of Reviews by the Court of Justice of the European Union Applied to EU Restrictive Measures Including the Implementation of UN Security Council Resolutions," *The*

Hitotsubashi Journal of Law and International Studies 17, Vol. 3 (2018), pp. 115–128.

Sachiko Yoshimura is currently a professor of International Law and Organizations at Kwansei Gakuin University, Hyogo, Japan. She earned a Ph.D. in International Law and Organizations from the International Christian University in Tokyo, Japan; her dissertation was on the legal problems of United Nations economic sanctions. Before joining Kwansei Gakuin University, she was a professor of International Organizations at Hiroshima Shudo University until 2010. She was a visiting fellow at Corpus Christi College and Faculty of Law, Oxford University from 2002–2003, and a research scholar at Ralph Bunche Institute for International Studies, City University of New York from 2018–2019. Her current research spans a broad range of areas of UN economic sanctions, international law, and organizations. She has published numerous books, book chapters, journal papers, and commissioned reports, including *The Legal Problems on the United Nations Economic Sanctions* (Kokusaishoin Publisher, 2003), *Economic Sanctions by the United Nations Security Council* (co-chair, a research commissioned by the Ministry of Foreign Affairs, Japan, 2007), and *International Law* (co-authored, Kobundo Publisher, 2017).

Preface

From the time of the League of Nations, financial sanctions were utilized as a measure of collective security. At the time of the League of Nations and the initial period of the United Nations practice, financial sanctions were regarded as supplements to the trade embargoes; however, currently, the importance of the financial sanctions emerged as asset freeze is regarded as a powerful and desirable measure under the auspices of "smart sanctions." Compared with trade embargoes and other forms of economic sanctions, financial sanctions are unique in many ways, such as, the necessity of private-sector involvement and sophisticated techniques for implementation. With reference to unilateral and other types of financial sanctions, this book mainly analyzes the financial sanctions decided by the United Nations from the perspectives of invocation, implementation, and application.

Adding several experts as new authors, this book is, basically, the English version with necessary modification and adjustment of the same title originally published in Japanese by Toshindo Publisher (Tokyo, Japan) in 2018. Starting from the general description and history of the United Nations and the other financial sanctions (Chapter 1), this book first deals with the invocation sphere at the United Nations, with the chapters focusing on "smart sanctions" issues (Chapter 2), the United Nations Security Council subsidiary organs (Chapter 3), and Non-Allied Movement nations' views (Chapter 4). Then this book moves to the analysis of the implementation sphere focusing on the major world economies, with chapters on Japan (Chapter 5), the United States of America (Chapter 6), and the European Union (Chapter 7). Chapters on the financial sanctions applications follow, by describing the role and compliance of private actors (Chapter 8) and symbolic judicial cases (Chapter 9). Finally, case studies on the United Nations financial sanctions against North Korea (Chapter 10) and Iran (Chapter 11) come, with the concluding chapter on the United Nations 1540 Committee and Counter Proliferation Financing (Chapter 12).

Upon publishing the book in English, the editor and authors realized the considerable deficit of as well as the earnest requests for information and research outcomes regarding Japan in relation to economic sanctions. Therefore, in this English version, regardless the issues dealt with, every chapter author attempts to touch upon certain elements in Japan, one of the biggest economies in the world and thus the influencing power to achieve the goals of United Nations financial sanctions.

The flamework of this study is developed through the vigorous discussions at a series of research seminars and workshops on United Nations financial sanctions, funded generously by the Suntory Foundation. I greatly appreciate the continuous support of the foundation, and enthusiastic participants. I am also grateful of Katsuji Shimoda, the President of Toshindo Publisher, who recognizes the importance of this study and made the original publication in Japanese possible. Finally, I am greatly indebted to (former) graduate students, Takayoshi Miyoke, Miho Sakai, Yutaro Oda, Yusuke Mizuno and Hinako Takata, who contributed significantly to the development of this study.

Sachiko Yoshimura
Hyogo, Japan
June 2020

1 UN economic sanctions and financial measures—evolution and challenges

Sachiko Yoshimura

Introduction

The Preamble of the Charter of the United Nations (UN) proclaims, "We the peoples of the United Nations determined to save the succeeding generations from the scourge of war ... to unite our strength to maintain international peace and security ... have resolved to combine our efforts to accomplish these aims." And Article 1 of the UN Charter stipulates that the UN takes "effective collective measures for the prevention and removal of threats to the peace, and for the suppression of acts of aggression or other breaches of the peace ..." to achieve its purpose. The words "economic sanctions" do not appear in the UN Charter, but non-military "collective measures" can be regarded as economic sanctions.[1]

Economic sanctions as coercive measures had been utilized long before the UN was established. Financial sanctions, a subset of economic sanctions, are also invoked by the UN Charter to achieve collective security. Today, financial sanctions are more targeted with the involvement of many actors. They will urge different kinds of economic sanctions to be used citing technological progress and transaction complexity.

This chapter first follows the institutionalization of economic sanctions and describes the difference between unilateral and UN economic sanctions from the perspective of international law. Next, an overview of the UN economic sanctions mechanism and practice of financial sanctions will be explored. Lastly, the issues with UN financial sanctions from the standpoints of invocation, implementation, and application, with the necessity of reexamination of UN financial sanctions will be discussed.

Economic sanctions and collective security

What are economic sanctions?

International Sanctions, edited by the Royal Institute of International Affairs in 1938, defines sanctions in international affairs as "action taken by members of international the community against an infringement, actual or threatened, of the law."[2]

A study by Hufbauer, Schott, and Elliott demonstrated the use of non-military coercive measures to change the policy of targets in ancient Greece.[3] Later, economic sanctions were utilized as a tool of warfare, for example, the Berlin Decree and the blockade of Britain by Napoleon.[4] In the twentieth century, when the Covenant of the League of Nations and later, the UN Charter, forbade engaging in war and restrained or limited nations from using the "threat or use of force," economic sanctions became an institutionalized instrument at the disposal of these international organizations.

Today, unilateral economic sanctions, which a state (or a group of states) decides to impose on another state, and UN's economic sanctions as a means of collective security are invoked collaterally.[5] The economic sanctions invoked by a group of states or by international organizations of limited membership (such as the European Union) are termed "organized unilateral sanctions," and are different from the economic sanctions enforced by the UN.[6]

Economic sanctions and their institutionalization

Historically, economic sanctions were utilized by a state or a group of states to wage war on the enemy's economy, or as a means to respond or coerce a policy change by the target nation.[7] However, after World War I, economic sanctions were institutionalized by the League of Nations, as a way to achieve peace by a collective security system.

The Preamble of the Covenant of the League of Nations proclaimed, "The High Contracting Parties [*sic*] ... achieve international peace and security by the acceptance of obligations not to resort to war ..." And Article 16 (1) of the Covenant stipulated,

> Should any Member of the League resort to war in disregard of its covenants under Articles 12, 13 or 15, it shall *ipso facto* be deemed to have committed an act of war against all other Members of the League, which hereby undertake immediately to subject it to the severance of all trade or financial relations, the prohibition of all intercourse between their nationals and the nationals of the covenant-breaking State, and the prevention of all financial, commercial or personal intercourse between the nationals of the covenant-breaking State and the nationals of any other State, whether a Member of the League or not.

At the League, economic sanctions were the primary tool to achieve collective security. After witnessing the dramatic scale of destructive power during World War I, more use of non-military measures for dispute settlement was decided. With advantage of interdependency among states, economic sanctions for inducing policy change in target nations came to be seen as more useful, as a natural corollary.[8] Woodrow Wilson's philosophy, "A nation that is boycotted is a nation that is in sight of surrender. Apply this economic, peaceful, silent, deadly remedy and there will be no need for force," resonated throughout the process of creating the League of Nations.[9]

The UN, as well as the League of Nations, considers economic sanctions as one of the measures to achieve collective security. Theoretically, institutionalized economic sanctions are more effective than unilateral sanctions, because of the number of countries that participate in UN economic sanctions.

Difference between unilateral sanctions and sanctions imposed by UN

At present, both unilateral and institutionalized economic sanctions coexist, and are sometimes invoked at the same time on the same target country. But, from the perspective of international law, unilateral economic sanctions and UN sanctions are two different things.

In 1979, at the discussion of the Draft Articles on Responsibility of States for Internationally Wrongful Acts, the International Law Commission (ILC) suggested that the word "sanctions" be used only for mandatory measures by international organizations, and should be distinguished from other measures. At first, Special Rapporteur Robert Ago suggested "Legitimate application of a sanction" as the title of an article on preclusion of international wrongful acts by states, stating "the term 'sanction' should not be understood in too narrow or too broad sense." Other members, though, dissented on the use of the word "sanctions." They were of the belief that the use of the term "sanctions" should be limited to indicate coercive measures adopted by international organizations, and not be applicable to the measures of an individual state.[10] In the end, Special Rapporteur Ago agreed to replace the word "sanctions" with "retaliatory measures" or "countermeasures."[11]

In the text adopted in 2001, the Draft Articles on Responsibility of States excludes the word "sanctions." Instead, the term "countermeasures" is used in the equivalent article that Special Rapporteur Ago proposed,[12] and Part Three Chapter II of the Draft Articles provides the object, obligations and conditions for states to take such actions.

Kazuhiro Nakatani states that, unilateral economic sanctions have a narrower scope in legality under international law compared with sanctions imposed by the UN. He describes, whereas UN sanctions taken in accordance with law of international organizations can derogate from the conditions of legality to be permitted as countermeasures, it is harder for the unilateral sanctions to be legitimate since each state imposing the coercive measures uses its own discretion.[13]

UN economic sanctions and coercive measures

The League of Nations and financial sanctions

As described, Article 16 of the Covenant of the League of Nations lays out the system of economic sanctions. However, in 1920, the International Blockade

Committee was established to consider aspects of economic sanctions.[14] The League Assembly followed and adopted a resolution in 1921, stipulating that each member state has a duty to determine whether the Covenant is violated or not, and sanctions invocations shall be limited.[15] Consequently, economic sanctions under the League became a decentralized and weak instrument.[16]

The League did impose sanctions only once, and it was against Italy for invading Abyssinia in 1935. The Assembly set up the Co-ordinating Committee to determine the sanction measures and the implementation mechanism,[17] and it decided on five areas for sanctions: 1) ban on exports of arms and ammunition, 2) coercive financial measures, 3) ban on imports from Italy, 4) embargo on certain exports to Italy, and 5) organization of mutual support.[18]

Proposal II by the Co-ordinating Committee was devoted to the financial sanctions imposed by the League. Member states were requested to refrain from the transactions, such as, 1) all loans and subscriptions to or from the Italian government, any public authority, person, or corporation in Italy, 2) all banking or other credits and execution to lend to the Italian government, any public authority, person or corporation in the Italian territory, 3) all issues of shares or other capital flotations and subscriptions in the Italian territory.[19]

At that time, financial sanctions were regarded as supplements of trade embargoes, and they had been invoked to deprive "Italy of purchasing power abroad." But Italy perceived the financial sanctions seriously, and even before the League's adopting the coercive actions, she took preventive measures to minimize damage. For example, she ordered Italian residents to register "all holdings of foreign exchange or other credits held abroad" and asked "all such privately held assets … to be handed to the Bank of Italy or other banks."[20]

Despite such efforts, Italy's creditworthiness plummeted for fear of expected impairment by the financial sanctions.[21] After the sanctions were imposed, Italy was forced into harsher economic conditions by the decline in creditworthiness of the Italian lire, the decrease in gold reserves, and an unfavorable international balance of payments.[22] The financial sanctions of the League did inflict financial damage on Italy.

It is true that the overall economic sanctions imposed by the League against Italy could not play the crucial role, since oil and other materials were excluded from the embargoes, and member states of the League did not act in concert. Consequently, in 1936, Italy annexed Abyssinia and economic sanctions imposed by the League ended.[23] In this case, financial sanctions attracted less attention compared to trade embargoes. But now, similar actions are taken by states and corporations under UN financial sanctions, such as restriction of transactions to avoid further risks.

The UN Charter and economic sanctions

The UN was officially established in 1945 with the wisdom gained from the system and the experience of the League of Nations. According to the UN Charter, all members of the UN shall refrain from the threat or use of force (Article 2 (4)). It further provides that UN member states "confer on the Security Council primary responsibility for the maintenance of international peace and security" (Article 24 (1)).

In Chapter VII, the UN Charter stipulates economic and military sanctions as measures for collective security. According to Article 39, the Security Council has the power to

> determine the existence of any threat to the peace, breach of the peace, or act of aggression and shall make recommendations, or decide what measures shall be taken in accordance with Articles 41 and 42, to maintain or restore international peace and security.

The coercive measures based on Article 41 regarded as economic sanctions, are stipulated as follows:

> The Security Council may decide what measures not involving the use of armed force are to be employed to give effect to its decisions, and it may call upon the Members of the United Nations to apply such measures. These may include complete or partial interruption of economic relations and of rail, sea, air, postal, telegraphic, radio, and other means of communication, and the severance of diplomatic relations.

When the Security Council is of the opinion that such non-military coercive measures "would be inadequate or have proved to be inadequate, it may take such action by air, sea, or land forces … " including demonstrations and blockade (Article 42). The coercive measures based on the following articles of the UN Charter are supposed to be the military sanctions by the UN.

Article 25 of the UN Charter provides that the UN member states agree to accept and carry out the Security Council decisions. By including this provision, the implementation of the Security Council decisions, including economic sanctions, become the duty of the member states. In addition, the UN Charter stipulates that it has to ensure that the non-members "act in accordance with these Principles so far as may be necessary for the maintenance of international peace and security" (Article 2(6)). By this provision, the UN requests non-members to comply with the decisions of the Security Council to prevent the creation of loopholes when economic sanctions are imposed.

The Covenant of the League of Nations provided for mutual support among members "in order to minimize the loss and inconvenience resulting" from the economic sanctions implementation (Article 16(3)). The UN Charter follows, prescribing that a state "with special economic problems arising from the carrying out of" economic sanctions "shall have the right to consult the Security Council" (Article 50). Thus, the UN attempts to ensure that states not omit the implementation of economic sanctions for the fear of economic losses they might encounter.[24]

Organs and competence of UN economic sanctions

UN economic sanctions are designed to plug the deficits of the League of Nations collective security system, and the Security Council is liable to determine the measures for maintaining international peace and security. It is composed of five permanent members and ten non-permanent members "elected for a term of two years" based on geographical distribution (Article 23 (1) (2) of the UN Charter).

The voting system at the Security Council is—one country, one vote. Currently, the decisions "shall be made by an affirmative vote of nine members including the concurring votes of the permanent members" for "all other matters" besides procedures (Article 27 (2) (3)). The decisions on economic sanctions are categorized as "all other matters," and at least nine affirmative votes including those from the permanent members are necessary. The word "veto" does not appear in the UN Charter, but a negative vote by a permanent member indicates the power of veto.

In addition to the Security Council, the General Assembly often adopts resolutions on economic sanctions or measures. However, the General Assembly can only "make recommendations with regard to such principles to the Members of the United Nations or to the Security Council or to both" (Article 10). Therefore, the resolutions adopted by the General Assembly, usually, are not legally binding like the Security Council decisions.

Financial measures on economic sanctions and their characteristics

Practice of UN economic sanctions

The analysis of the UN Charter drafting process shows that military sanctions were supposed to play a greater role in the UN collective security system.[25] However, the very first coercive sanction requested at the Security Council was a non-military measure. In April 1946, Poland brought to the attention of the Security Council a problem with Franco's Regime in Spain which was "due to international frictions,"[26] and proposed a draft resolution to call upon "all Members of the United nations who maintain diplomatic relations with the Franco Government to sever such relations immediately" in accordance with Articles 39 and 41 of the UN Charter.[27] Unfortunately, the draft resolution was rejected by seven negative votes of the Security Council, including those of permanent members.[28]

After that, the Security Council could not make decisions on economic sanctions until 1966, when it imposed partial embargoes against Southern Rhodesia. During the Cold War era, it could not function as expected at the time because of political discord. Apart from a series of sanctions imposed on Southern Rhodesia,[29] the Security Council could decide only on an arms embargo against South Africa in 1977.[30]

Instead, after the end of the Cold War, the Security Council dramatically increased decisions on economic sanctions. In August 1990, just after Iraq invaded Kuwait, the Security Council quickly adopted Resolution 661, imposing a total embargo against Iraq under Chapter VII of the UN Charter.[31] From this occasion onward, the Security Council successively imposed mandatory sanctions on the Former Republic of Yugoslavia (FRY), Somalia, Libya, Liberia, Haiti, Angola (UNITA), Rwanda, Sudan, Sierra Leone, the Federal Republic of Yugoslavia (Serbia and Montenegro), Afghanistan (Taliban, Al-Qaida, ISIL (Da'esh)), Ethiopia and Eritrea, the Democratic Republic of Congo (DRC), Côte d'Ivoire, Syria (Hariri suspects), Lebanon, the Democratic People's Republic of Korea (DPRK), Iran, Guinea Bissau, the Central African Republic, Yemen, South Sudan, and Mali.[32] These sanctions regimes decided by the Security Council varied due to the change of targets and scope of sanctions, categorization of targets with different procedures, and sanctions imposed on the same target for different reasons after a previous set of sanctions were lifted.

In 2001, the Security Council adopted Resolution 1373, which determined denial of financial transfers to terrorists and persons who engage in terrorist acts.[33] In 2004, Resolution 1540 banned the transfer of weapons of mass destruction to non-governmental entities.[34] For these sanctions regimes, it is not the Security Council or other UN organs but each member state which has to decide the sanctions designations with domestic implementation of coercive measures.[35]

Through UN practice, the General Assembly and the Security Council often have been adopting non-military coercive measures as non-binding "recommendations." Such distinction is mainly the result of the politicking among the Security Council members, or more broadly, the member states of the UN.

For example, the Polish government requested the Spanish issue to be discussed at the UN General Assembly after the Security Council rejected the call for economic sanctions.[36] In December 1946, the General Assembly adopted a resolution to request severance of diplomatic relations between the Franco regime of Spain and all UN member states.[37] Since then, for decades, the General Assembly has adopted several resolutions on economic sanctions, notably the sanctions against South Africa under the apartheid regime.[38]

Financial measures of UN economic sanctions

As described above, both the Security Council and General Assembly have adopted resolutions with economic sanctions clauses. But what are the kinds of financial coercive measures used?

The original and the most common measures are bans on financial transactions, such as remittances,[39] and freezing of assets.[40] In the early stage of UN sanctions, the scope of targets was rather limited, such as the freezing of assets owned by the government. In recent years, the sanctions targets have been expanded considerably to include the assets privately owned by individuals who are responsible for the imposition of sanctions.[41] The scope of "assets" to be frozen has also expanded in recent years. At first, the targets to be frozen were limited to "any funds," so as to denote just financial assets,[42] but currently, the word "asset freeze" can include not only financial property but also other resources of every kind.[43] The UN economic sanctions have shifted from total embargoes to targeted sanctions, and it has, in part, caused an enlargement in the number of targets and the diversification of measures used.[44]

Another financial coercive measure is the ban on funds transfer. In the early stage of UN sanctions, the applicable ban was limited to the transfer of funds and investment provisions to the Southern Rhodesian government and enterprises.[45] Recently, more detailed measures have been invoked, as exemplified by the UN financial sanctions against DPRK, including prohibition on opening financial offices and establishing joint ventures, termination of ownership interest and correspondent banking relationship, limitation on bank accounts, and repatriation of individuals who work for a DPRK financial institution.[46]

Besides these, the UN Security Council has also been imposing finance-related coercive measures. Upon sanctions imposition against Southern Rhodesia, it resolved to prevent "the right to use any trade name or from entering into any franchising agreement involving the use of any trade name, trade mark or registered design."[47] For the sanctions against DPRK, a ban on financial services and transfer of bulk cash and gold, prohibition on work authorizations for DPRK nationals, repatriation of all DPRK nationals earning income overseas, and prevention of insurance or re-insurance service to vessels had been imposed.[48] The Security Council also called upon member states to undertake appropriate measures to prohibit Eritrea from collecting "Diaspora tax" from Eritreans living outside Eritrea.[49]

Along with the Security Council decisions, resolutions adopted at both the UN Security Council and General Assembly as recommendations often contain measures relating to finance. Measures include various kinds of services, such as forbidding insurance companies from covering flights, vessels, individuals, and air or shipping cargo bound for the sanction targets.[50] The Security Council also called upon member states to apply the Financial Actions Task Force (FATF) recommendations and guidance in relation to the sanctions against North Korea.[51]

Kimberly Elliott has pointed out that financial sanctions are more effective compared to trade embargoes. Since sanctions are easier to impose and difficult for targets to escape from, financial market reactions can accelerate the effect of sanctions, and financial restrictions influence purchasing power. With analyzing the evolution of UN financial sanctions, she found that, originally, members paid more attention to stem the future "flow" of public or private sector finance, but now, they also target existing wealth "stocks," such as bank accounts or other types of assets, and foreign investments that influence enterprise activity as well.[52]

Smart sanctions and the Interlaken Process

At present, the reigning policy of UN economic sanctions is "smart sanctions"— arms embargo, assets freeze and travel restrictions. Since total or comprehensive sanctions targeting particular geographical areas and smart sanctions targeting particular individuals and entities are different in many ways, international conferences with the various sector personnel took place in the 1990s to discuss how UN economic sanctions should be.

The international conferences initiated by the Swiss government in 1998 and 1999, called Interlaken Process I and II, devoted themselves to discussing UN financial sanctions.

The Interlaken Process I started off with the definition of basic terms, such as "financial sanctions" and "targeting," and considered other measures such as national legislation, standards to impose financial sanctions, and international compliance. Additionally, the importance of target designation and the specialization and management of financial flows was proposed, with suggestions to use anti-money laundering practices by financial institutions.[53]

At Interlaken II, three working groups were set up to discuss more specialized issues of financial sanctions. Working group 1 dealt with "The Targeting of Financial Sanctions," discussing the technical minutiae of financial sanctions. It proposed the necessity of information on sanctions targets ("know your target"), and information gathering as well as sanction target designation by member states. Tracing money flow by using the inter-bank software was also proposed. The working group further indicated that the internet banking system might influence future sanctions implementation.

Working Group II dealt with "model law." It emphasized the importance of uniform domestic legislation to implement the UN Security Council resolutions and suggested a model law for sanctions implementation based on Article 41 of the UN charter with a penalty for violating sanctions. The model law can be designed to be applicable both for common law nations and continental law nations.

Working Group III was called "Building Blocks and Definitions." It defined the basic terms of financial sanctions, such as "assets" and "funds or other financial resources," to clarify the interpretation and make sanctions more effective. It also suggested a model resolution on "asset freeze" with a "financial services" clause, for all states to prohibit the provision of financial services by any authority, entity, or other persons of jurisdiction.[54]

At Interlaken Process II, various expert reports and proposals were submitted, too. The most notable one would be a paper submitted by then US OFAC Director Richard Newcomb, which compared the UN targeted sanctions with the Specially Designated Nationals (SDN) and Specially Designated Narcotics Traffickers (SDNT) programs by the United States. He suggested that although there are many differences between UN sanctions and unilateral sanctions, the US practice can be applicable to UN economic sanctions.[55]

The Interlaken Process was held at a time when the UN was transitioning itself to "smart sanctions." Many valuable recommendations were made, and some of them were assimilated in the current UN economic sanctions practice. But if more suggestions made at the Interlaken Process were to be incorporated with the commitments, further UN financial sanctions policy options could be realized.

Issues with UN financial sanctions

Issues relating to invoking of UN financial sanctions

The issues on the UN financial sanctions invocation can be divided into problems relating to the actors and the problems relating to the characteristics of UN financial sanctions.

The main actor in UN economic sanctions is the Security Council, and the collective security concept it centers on is different from the original blueprint of general collective security.[56] In other words, the UN Security Council with the Allied Powers of World War II as its permanent members still decides the sanctions impositions, and it is questionable whether such sanctions can be regarded as legitimate. It is necessary for the Security Council to reform its structure and decision-making process due to the enormous changes in the international community since the World War II.

The decision to impose economic sanctions, or financial measures or trade embargoes should also be considered differently. Financial instruments can move assets and resources faster using enhanced technology whereas goods take longer time to deliver.[57] As one of the measures of UN economic sanctions, financial sanctions should be decided on the basis of characteristics and strategic importance. The wording of the resolutions should be clear and articulate so that economic sanctions are implemented strategically.[58]

At the same time, the UN is an intergovernmental organization and was originally supposed to have a state-centered structure. But currently, the targets of economic sanctions have been widened, and include not only states but also various non-governmental actors.[59] In addition, as exemplified by the emergence of cryptocurrency, there needs to be guidelines about the influence of currency not issued nor controlled by a state.[60]

Issues with the implementation of UN financial sanctions I

Measures taken by the UN to ensure implementation: the Security Council subsidiary organs and their activities

From the early stage of UN sanctions imposition, it has become a practice to set up subsidiary organs called "sanction committees" based on the Security Council provisional procedure. The mandates of the sanctions committees are decided by the Security Council resolutions, and often include a variety of tasks, such as, supervision of compliance with sanctions, exemption from sanctions due to the humanitarian or other reasons, management of the states "confronted with special economic problems." After smart sanctions idea became dominant at the UN, the sanctions committees often have to designate the targets of sanctions.[61] Apart from the sanctions committees, Panels of Experts came to be appointed for the purpose of independent investigations into sanctions violations and report submission.[62]

One difficult issue for these subsidiary organs is information gathering on sanctions implementation and violations. The UN is an intergovernmental organization and not a state, and therefore, it cannot conduct investigations in the same way as the police can do based on domestic legislation. Also, the UN does not have its own intelligence gathering unit[63] and, without the cooperation of states, experts and other actors, it becomes difficult to conduct the information gathering at the local level.

Other issues with the UN financial sanctions implementation are the political considerations for setting up subsidiary organs, decision making inside, and the degree of information disclosure.

The Security Council often set up sanctions committees by the same resolution that decides sanctions. But in some cases, the sanctions committees are not established at all or established much later.[64] On the contrary, for Taliban and Al-Qaida (and currently ISIL) sanctions, an additional subsidiary organ named an Analytical Support and Sanctions Monitoring Team was established[65] to strengthen the implementation degree. Such actions by Security Council would demonstrate whether it regards each sanction regime as positive or negative to implement.

Further, the decision making of these subsidiary organs are by consensus, and just one negative vote can prevent finalizing the decisions. It is true that these organs do submit annual or interim reports, but their meetings are usually closed-door affairs. In some cases, reports by the Panels of Experts are not published due to political pressure.[66]

Issues of UN financial sanctions implementation by states and other actors

The UN financial sanctions can be primarily enforced by states by exercising their domestic legislation. While domestic legislation is important to realize the UN sanctions, it is true that not all states have specific laws to implement UN economic sanctions. Certain states apply trade or finance-related legislation, but in reality, such legislation cannot cover all the UN sanctions since the sanctions have been widened to include more targets and measures.[67] Even some UN member states do not legislate nor enforce the appropriate laws due to their domestic situation.

To make UN financial sanctions more effective, it is important for states to take immediate action to implement them, since financial assets can be transferred easily, and the targeted individuals might move to other countries with lax legislation and law enforcement.[68] Consequently, the loopholes of sanctions would be created without proper actions by states. Well-prepared domestic legislation and law enforcement actions are necessary to implement the sanctions decisions fully, but at the same time, not all states have the capacity to react completely.

Additionally, in reality, financial institutions including private entities play a substantial role as "gatekeepers" for financial sanctions implementation. This makes the implementation mechanism different from the one for the trade embargoes, where a state institution engages in sanctions violations by goods exposure and confiscation. Indeed, financial institutions have to bear the costs of constructing necessary systems for sanctions implementation, and human and financial resources expenditure substantially influences the implementation of financial sanctions.

Issues with the application of UN financial sanctions

General application of UN financial sanctions

UN economic sanctions can be effective when domestic measures are applied to the transactions engaged in by public and private sectors. The jurisdiction of domestic measures, such as extraterritorial application of sanctions, is therefore, a challenge.

The issue arising from the conflict of territorial and foreign legal principles, such as the application of domestic law by headquarters to branches and local offices overseas, always comes into question for the imposition of economic.[69] Some domestic measures are applicable when the national currency is used, regardless of where the transactions take place. In such cases, the jurisdiction is widened, and the issues become more complicated.

For the UN financial sanctions to be imposed, it is assumed that these transactions are conducted by institutions certified by their nations, using legal tender, and can be investigated by national institutions and punished for sanctions violations. However, today, there are financial instruments and transactions that were not even conceived of at the time of League of Nations or the UN creation. There are countries where remittances can be made without a record, such as "hawala" transactions, and where remittances using mobile phones are widely used due to the underdeveloped banking system.[70] Moreover, the legal framework on the regulation of the transactions not involving legal tender, such as cryptocurrencies, is still under development. Such circumstances make it difficult for the state to comprehend and intervene in the transactions.[71]

The application of UN financial sanctions on targets

The "listing" of sanctions targets was first started to unify implementations by targeting the same persons or entities, so that smart sanctions could be more effectively realized.[72] However, as the term "targeted sanctions" shows, "listing" came to be known as the designation of sanctions targets, distant from its original intention. Triggered by the Kadi I appeal judgment by the European Court of Justice,[73] the human rights violations of the individuals targeted for sanctions began to be widely discussed.

Facing such criticism, the UN reformed the listing process, and the reasons to be designated as sanctions targets came to be issued when the lists are released.[74] But it is still doubtful whether all UN sanctions regimes consider a uniform application to individuals. The sanctions against Al-Qaida and ISIL (Da'esh) have a delisting procedure by the Ombudsperson, but the focal point of delisting is used for other sanctions regimes. The main purpose of sanctions designations against individuals should be to maximize the effects of economic sanctions, and a more careful consideration is necessary.

Conclusion

After economic sanctions were institutionalized and became one of the measures of collective security by the League of Nations and the UN, their modes have changed. At present, financial sanctions combined with other sanctions measures or by themselves play a more significant role.[75]

Financial and targeted sanctions can impinge on particular individuals and entities, such as high-level governmental officials and policymakers, and inflict less damage on innocent civilians.[76] Therefore, when designed strategically, financial sanctions can be expected to create greater effects.[77] At the same time, financial transactions today are varied, and often difficult to track, which makes sanctions violations investigation more complex compared to a trade embargo.[78] Today, assets have a wider meaning than economic resources, and therefore, the way to implement an asset freeze, which is used frequently as a measure of UN economic sanctions, should fit such an evolution.

Sanctions can be effective only with more sophisticated strategies and ascertainment of market changes and characteristics of each measure. Without these, sanctions can have adverse consequences even though they are designed to be smart. As Arbinda Acharya notes, there are goals which cannot be achieved by states, but can only be achieved by international organizations, such as the UN.[79]

The degree of contribution to international peace and security by the UN will be evaluated on how it can put the "new wine" (financial sanctions) in the "old wineskins" (state-centered collective security system) without tearing the wineskin. In other words, the UN needs to adjust itself and exploit the financial sanctions and their evolution. By analyzing the issues posed by UN financial sanctions, we can solve some of the complicated challenges that UN collective security and the future of international society face.

Notes

1 For example, the committee set up by General Assembly Resolution 377 A (A/Res/ 377A (V), 3 November 1950 Uniting for Peace Resolution) to discuss the collective security and international sanctions is named "Collective Measures Committee." In the report submitted, there are descriptions of financial sanctions, such as the League of Nations' sanctions against Italy and the Allies' sanctions against Axis powers during the World War II. *Report of the Collective Measures Committee*, GAOR Supplement No. 13, A/1891 (1951), pp. 13–14.

2 Royal Institute of International Affairs, *International Sanctions* (Oxford University Press, 1938), p. 16.

3 Gary Clyde Hufbauer, Jeffrey J. Schott and Kimberly Ann Elliott, *Economic Sanctions Reconsidered: History and Current Policy* (second edition) (Institute for International Economics, 1990), pp. 4–5.

4 Makio Miyagawa, *Keizaiseisai* [Economic Sanctions] (Chuokoron Publisher, 1992), pp. 20–25.
5 Miki Honda, *Kokurennni yoru Keizaiseisai to Jindoujyounosyomonndai* [UN Sanctions and Their Humanitarian Issues] (Kokusaisyoin Publisher, 2013), pp. 35–40.
6 Rahmat Mohamad, "Unilateral Sanctions in International Law: A Quest for Legality" in Ali Z. Marossi and Marisa R. Bassett, ed., *Economic Sanctions under International Law: Unilateralism, Multilateralism, Legitimacy and Consequences* (T.M.C. Asser Press, 2015), p. 75.
7 Kern Alexander, *Economic Sanctions: Law and Public Policy* (Palgrave Macmillan, 2009), p. 12.
8 Hajime Okusako, "Guroubarukajidai ni okeru Keizaiseisai wo meguru Rirontekisaikentou" [Theoretical Reexamination of Economic Sanctions in the Era of Globalization] in Mineko Usui, Hajime Okusako, and Takehiko Yamamoto, eds., *Keizaiseisai no Kenkyu* [The Study of Economic Sanctions] (Shigakusha, 2017), pp. 13–14.
9 Hamilton Foley, *Woodrow Wilson's Case for the League of Nations: Compiled with His Approval* (Princeton University Press, 1923), p. 71.
10 *Yearbook of the International Law Commission 1979*, Volume I, pp. 55–63.
11 Ibid., p. 63.
12 Article 22 of the final version of Draft Articles on Responsibility of States is titled as "Countermeasures in Respect of an Internationally Wrongful act."
13 Kazuhiro Nakatani, "Keizaisaisai no Kokusaihoujyou no Kinou to Sonogouhousei" [The Functions and the Legality of Economic Sanctions Under International Law] (3) *Kokka Gakkai Zassi*, Vol. 100, No. 11–12 (1987), pp. 926–940. The UN Security Council imposed economic sanctions on Iran from 2006, but legality was questioned only for the unilateral sanctions against Iran invoked in parallel. See Masahiko Asada, "Kokkasekininnjyoubun ni okeru Taikousochi to Taiirannseisai" [Countermeasures in the Draft Article on the State Responsibility and the Economic Sanctions against Iran], *Kokusaiho-Kennkyuu*, Vol. 5 (2017), pp. 32–69.
14 League of Nations, International Blockade Committee, *Minutes of the Session held in Geneva from August 22nd to 29th, with Annexes*, A. 28 (b.) 1921 (5 September 1921), Annexes 18 and 19.
15 League of Nations, Resolutions adopted on 4 October 1921.
16 Toshiki Mogami, *Kokusaikikouron Kougi* [International Organization] (Iwanami Publisher, 2016), pp. 57–58.
17 For the role and activities of Co-ordinating Committee and related organs, see Sachiko Yoshimura, "Kokuren no Higunnjitekiseisai ni okeru 'Seisaiiinnkai' no Kinoutoyakuwari" [Functions and Role of 'Sanctions Committee' on the United Nations Non-military Sanctions] *Shudo Hogaku* (2000), Vol. 22, No. 1–2, pp. 168–176.
18 *League of Nations Official Journal*, Special Supplement No. 150, pp. 1–12.
19 Proposal No. II, Financial Measures, adopted by the Co-ordination Committee on October 14th, 1935, ibid., p. 4.
20 "Financial Sanctions" in Royal Institute of International Affairs, *supra* note 2, pp. 76–78.
21 Yoshiro Unno, "Kokusairennmei no Taiitariaseisai" [The Sanctions by the League of Nations against Italy] (2), *Gaiko Jihou*, Vol. 1142 (February 1977) pp. 11–12, Royal Institute of International Affairs, ibid., pp. 78–79.
22 Unno, ibid., p. 11.

23 Yoshiro Unno, "Kokusairennmei no Taiitariaseisai" [The Sanctions by the League of Nations against Italy] (4), *Gaiko Jihou*, Vol. 1144 (April 1977) pp. 26–29.

24 For the drafting and codification process of Article 50 of the UN Charter, see Hiroya Toda, "Kokurenni yoru Keizaiseisai—Kensyou Dai 50 Jyou no Igi" [The Economic Sanctions by the United Nations—The Significance of the Article 50] *Hougakuseijigaku Ronkyu*, Vol. 52 (2002), pp. 61–92.

25 Ruth B. Russel and Jeannette E. Muther, *A History of the United Nations Charter: The Role of the United States 1940–1945* (The Brookings Institution, 1958), p. 252.

26 S/32, 9 April 1946.

27 S/PV. 34, 17 April 1946, p. 167.

28 S/PV. 48, 24 June 1946, p. 388.

29 S/Res/232 (1966), 16 December 1966.

30 S/Res/418 (1977), 4 November 1977.

31 S/Res/661 (1990), 6 August 1990.

32 For the overview of the economic sanctions decided by the Security Council, see Jeremy Matam Farrall, *United Nations Sanctions and the Role of Law* (Cambridge University Press, 2007), Mitsubishi Research and Consulting, *Annporiketsugi ni yoru Keizaiseisai* [The Economic Sanctions by the Security Council] (Commissioned Research by the Ministry of Foreign Affairs, Japan, 2013). For current practice of the UN Security Council on economic sanctions, see United Nations Subsidiary Organs HP, available at www.un.org/sc/suborg/en/sanctions/information (accessed 30 December 2019).

33 S/Res/1373 (2001), 28 September 2001.

34 S/Res/1540 (2004), 28 April 2004.

35 There are studies that regard such actions by the UN Security Council as "legislating," and examine whether it is legitimate or not. For example, see Stefan Talmon, "The Security Council as World Legislature" *American Journal of International Law*, Vol. 99 (2003) pp. 175–193, Masahiko Asada, "Annporiketugi 1540 to Kokusairippou" [The Security Council Resolution 1540 and International Legislating] *Kokusaimonndai*, Vol. 547 (2005), pp. 34–64, Ian Johnstone, "Legislation and Adjudication in the UN Security Council: Bringing Down the Deliberative Deficit" *American Journal of International Law*, Vol. 102 (2008), pp. 275–308.

36 *Annual Report of the Secretary-General on the Work of the Organization*, GAOR Supplement No. 1, pp. 2–3.

37 A/Res/39 (I), 12 December 1946.

38 For reactions by international organizations including economic sanctions against South Africa under the apartheid regime, see United Nations Department of Public Information, *The United Nations and Apartheid 1948–1994* (United Nations, 1994).

39 For the ban on remittances to Southern Rhodesia, see S/Res/232 (1966) paragraph 2(b), 16 December 1966, S/Res/253 (1968) paragraph 3(b), 29 May 1968.

40 For asset freeze on the sanctions against Southern Rhodesia, see S/Res/409 (1977) paragraph 1, 27 May 1977.

41 Kazuhiro Nakatani, "Annporiketsugi ni motozuku Keizaiseisai" [Economic Sanctions based on the Security Council resolutions], *Kokusaimonndai*, No. 570 (April 2008), p. 33.

42 S/Res/409 (1977) paragraph 1.

43 S/Res/2270 (2016), 2 March 2016, paragraph 12.

44 Nakatani, *supra* note 41, p. 33.

45 S/Res/253 (1968) paragraph 4.

46 S/Res/2094 (2013), 7 March 2013, S/Res/2270 (2016), 2 March 2016, S/Res/ 2371 (2017), 5 August 2017. For the overview of the financial sanctions against DPRK by the UN Security Council, see Kengo Omori, "Kitacyousenn ni taisuru Kinnyuu Seisaisochi ni tsuite" [On the Financial Sanctions against DPRK], *Chousa to Jouhou*, No. 933 (January 2017), pp. 4–5.

47 S/Res/388 (1976), 6 April 1976, paragraph 2.

48 S/Res/2094 (2013), S/Res/2371 (2017), S/Res/2375 (2017), 11 September 2017, S/Res/2397 (2017), 22 December 2017.

49 S/Res/2023 (2011), 5 December 2011.

50 S/Res/333 (1973), 22 May 1973.

51 S/Res/2270 (2016).

52 Kimberly Ann Elliott "Analysing the Effects of Targeted Financial Sanctions" in Department of Economy, Swiss Federal Office for Foreign Economic Affairs, *2nd Interlaken Seminar on Targeted United Nations Financial Sanctions* (March 1999, Interlaken, Switzerland), pp. 189–193.

53 Swiss Federal Office for Foreign Economic Affairs, Department of Economy, *Expert Seminar on Targeting UN Financial Sanctions* (March 1998, Interlaken, Switzerland), pp. 5–38.

54 Swiss Federal Office for Foreign Economic Affairs, *supra* note 53, pp. 5–90.

55 Richard R. Newcomb, "Targeted Financial Sanctions: The U.S. Model" in ibid., pp. 29–57. For the background of the establishment of OFAC and its brief history, see David Cortright, George A. Lopez, and Elizabeth S. Rogers, "Targeted Financial Sanctions: Smart Sanctions That *Do* Work" in David Cortright and George A. Lopez, *Smart Sanctions: Targeting Economic Statecraft* (Rowman & Littlefield, 2002), pp. 24–25.

56 Vaughan Lowe, Adam Roberts, Jennifer Welsh, and Dominik Zaum *The United Nations Security Council and War* (Oxford University Press, 2008), pp. 13–14.

57 Cortright et al., *supra* note 55, pp. 29–30.

58 Especially in recently adopted Security Council resolutions, there are often lengthy clauses with very complicated content. See, for example, S/Res/2387 (2017) paragraph 5.

59 Okusako, *supra* note 8, p. 14.

60 Hitoshi Okada, Ikuo Takahashi, and Shigeichiro Yamasaki, *Kasou Tuka* (Cryptcurrencies) (Toyokeizaishinpo Publisher, 2015), pp. 18–20.

61 For the functions and roles of the sanctions committees, see Yoshimura, *supra* note 17.

62 The panel of experts was first set up at the time when the UN imposed economic sanctions against Angola (UNITA). For the process of establishment, see Honda, *supra* note 5, p. 263.

63 Lowe et al., *supra* note 56, p. 21.

64 For example, no sanction committee was set up for the sanctions against Lebanon. S/ Res/1701 (2006), 11 August 2006.

65 S/Res/1526 (2004), 30 January 2004, S/Res/2253 (2015), 17 December 2015.

66 Takahiko Yamamoto, "Watasi no Shiten: Tai Kitacyousenn Seisai" [My Opinion: Sanctions against North Korea] *Asahi Newspaper*, 10 December 2011.

67 For example, Katsuhisa Furukawa, a former member of the Panel of Experts for the UN sanctions against DPRK said that Japan could investigate, but could not confiscate the sanction designated ship which requested emergency evacuation from its territorial waters, due to a deficiency in legal grounds. Katsuhisa Furukawa, *Kitacyousenn: Kaku*

no Shikinngenn [North Korea: The Funding Source of Nuclear Power] (Shincyousha Publisher, 2017), pp. 373–382.

68 David Cortright and George A. Lopez, *Sanctions and the Search for Security: Challenges to UN Action* (Lynne Rienner, 2002), 101–108.

69 Alexander, *supra* note 7, pp. 66–87.

70 For example, Yukio Noguchi demonstrates the money transfer system using mobile phones, with the example of M-Pesa in Kenya, where only a few bank branches have been set up. Yukio Noguchi, *Kasou Tuka Kakummei* (Cryptocurrency Revolution) (Diamond Publisher), pp. 121–132.

71 For legal status of cryptcurrency and related domestic legislations, see Okada et al., *supra* note 60, pp. 115–199.

72 Newcomb, *supra* note 55, pp. 117–118.

73 *Kadi and Al Barakaat v. Council and Commission,* Joint Cases C-402/05 P and C-415/05 P, Court of Justice of the European Communities, Judgment of 3 September 2008.

74 For example, the Security Council Resolution 1735 attaches the format to explain the reasons upon the requesting the listing for sanctions targets. S/Res/1735 (2006), 22 December 2006.

75 Thomas Biersteker and Susuna Hudáková point out that UN economic sanctions tend to be combined with other measures, such as the mechanisms of settlement of peaceful disputes. Thomas Biersteker and Susuna Hudáková (translated by Takehiko Yamamoto and Motoumi Mizutani), "UN Sanctions and Peace Negotiations" in Usui, et al., *supra* note 8, pp. 105–125.

76 Honda, *supra* note 5, p. 52.

77 Kimberly Ann Elliott "The Impacts of United Nations Targeted Sanctions" in Thomas J. Biersteker, Sue E. Eckert, and Marcos Tourinho eds. *Targeted Sanctions: The Impacts and Effectiveness of United Nations Actions* (Cambridge University Press, 2016) p. 174.

78 Even the US intelligence agency points out the difficulty to track Al-Qaida's financial resources and Usama Bin Laden's assets due to the complexity of transfer. Arabinda Acharya, *Targeting Terrorist Financing* (Routledge, 2009), pp. 28–29.

79 Ibid., pp. 96–98.

2 "Smart sanctions" by the UN and financial sanctions

Miki Honda

Introduction

Kofi Annan, the former UN Secretary-General, described sanctions as a "vital tool" in dealing with threats to international peace and security and that they are "a necessary middle ground between war and words."[1] Economic sanctions have been favored as a coercive measure by UN members because, compared to other coercive measures such as military action, they are less-costly, more convenient in that they can be tailored to specific circumstances, and authorized more easily by the UN Security Council under Chapter VII of the UN Charter.

Since the end of the Cold War, the Security Council has imposed economic sanctions more than two dozen times to deal with international threats. The objectives of the sanctions vary from ambitious to moderate. Some target the ending of conflicts, reversing aggression, stopping nuclear proliferation and combating terrorism. Others target supporting peace agreements, restoring democracy and protecting human rights.

In the early 1990s, the UN, however, experienced adverse humanitarian consequences that were directly or indirectly induced by comprehensive sanctions and it was realized that sanctions were a vital but imperfect tool. Since then the UN has reconsidered the objectives, measures and supposed consequences of sanctions. In the mid-1990s, the UN shifted away from comprehensive sanctions to more targeted ones that scholars call "smart sanctions." Targeted sanctions should be more effective as they target specific individuals and entities that have primary responsibility for breaching international peace and security, and they should be more humane with the purpose of avoiding or reducing damage to the innocent population of a target.

The objective of this chapter is to analyze the current situation of smart sanctions after about 20 years since the UN first experimented with them. First, I overview the fundamental shifts in the use of UN economic sanctions. Second, I address the problems raised from a human rights perspective by UN sanctions countering terrorism. I deal with the issue at the universal level and inquire into what kind of protection the UN system provides to individuals and entities targeted by UN sanctions. Third, I discuss the movement for reform within the UN that has been building for years in order to respond to emerging legal challenges and political concerns about UN targeted sanctions. I make a modest attempt to evaluate the UN sanctions mechanism for the imposition and implementation of targeted sanctions.

Fundamental shift in the use of sanctions

Known as the "sanction decade,"[2] the 1990s was when the UN Security Council frequently employed economic sanctions that were directed primarily at intra- and inter-state conflicts. These sanction efforts had ambitious goals and their strategic objective was compelling, for example, by reversing the policies of target states. In addition, they were comprehensive in scope and encompassed the totality of a target's economy. However, the sanctions regimes were poorly implemented leading to tremendous economic costs to the target states but often they did not change the political behavior of the leaders of those nations. The economic impact on the states in question also had damaging social and humanitarian effects, leading many political scientists and researchers to question the morality of economic sanctions as policy instruments.[3] As a result, the UN started to reconsider the effectiveness, the strategic measures, and the objectives of sanctions and shifted from comprehensive to targeted ones.

Oudraat analyzes that the fundamental shift in the use of sanctions had three dimensions: strategic objectives, instruments, and focus.[4] The shift in objectives from compellence to deterrence helped improve the record, according to Oudraat, as compellence is inherently difficult.[5] Deterrence is easier because it does not require immediate action from those who are deterring and because deterrence requires no public action by the one being deterred. Deterrence aims to maintain the status quo which is easier than challenging it.[6]

The shift to targeted sanctions was accompanied by more modest and achievable goals such as: discouraging the adoption of threatening policies or behaviors; urging targets to constrain proscribed activities; sending particular signals to targets; asking targets to consolidate the implementation of peace agreements; urging them to defend human rights norms; and, demanding that they prevent the proliferation of weapons of mass destruction. In particular, the fight against terrorism became a top priority for the UN after the 11 September 2001 terrorist attacks in the United States.

The shift contributed to an improved track record of sanction efforts. Targeted sanctions, by virtue of their limited nature, are easier to implement than comprehensive sanctions and political support for targeted sanctions is easier to mobilize since these sanctions target only those directly responsible for dangerous behavior. Accordingly, sanctions efforts were redirected from conflicts to terrorism.

Lessons from adverse humanitarian effects

In the early 1990s, there were three sanctions regimes in particular that were ambitious and broad in scope: the comprehensive sanctions imposed against Iraq in 1990 because of its invasion and illegal occupation of Kuwait;[7] those against the former Socialist Federal Republic of Yugoslavia (FRY) in 1992,[8] in response to its involvement in the war in Bosnia-Herzegovina, and which were extended in 1994 because of FRY's actions against the Bosnian Serbs;[9] and, those imposed on the military junta in Haiti in 1994 because of its reversal of the 1991 election results.[10,11]

In all three cases, the sanctions led to deterioration in the economic and social conditions in the countries concerned but did not lead to changes in the behaviors of the political leaders. As a result of growing concern over the humanitarian impact of comprehensive sanctions, the Security Council stopped imposing them and turned exclusively to the use of financial, diplomatic, arms, aviation, travel and commodity sanctions that targeted the combatants and policymakers who were most responsible for reprehensible policies.

Regarding the poor record of the comprehensive sanctions of the early 1990s,[12] as Oudraat points out, broad international support was lacking, either because of disagreement over the objectives to be achieved or because there was no country that would take the lead.[13] And these sanction regimes resulted in great social and human costs that were politically difficult to sustain over a long period of time. In particular, the use of military force in each case produced worse humanitarian consequences and social turmoil.[14]

Formulating "smart sanctions"

The reasons behind the poor record of comprehensive sanctions fueled the search for targeted sanctions which was led by US-based scholars in the early-1990s.[15] Targeted sanctions, also known as "smart sanctions," usually consist of travel bans, asset freezes, and embargoes or regulations on strategic goods such as diamonds and timber which can be used to purchase weapons by juntas and terrorists. It was only in the late 1990s that the UN started discussions over targeted sanctions. Such discussions were strongly backed by research institutions.

The revision of comprehensive sanctions had been promoted separately by scholars and UN policymakers. But these separate approaches gradually merged through a series of international policy seminars that were organized to assess and refine the notion and scope of targeted sanctions. In order to initiate change, the seminars named the "Interlaken Process" in 1998 and 1999 were organized. This was the first comprehensive attempt to examine the feasibility of targeted financial sanctions. Responding to a call from Annan, the Swiss government brought together representatives from national governments, central bank authorities, the UN Secretariat, various international organizations, the private banking sector and academia to examine the instrument of the targeted financial sanctions.

The first seminar (Interlaken I) in 1998 focused on the specific technical requirements of financial sanctions and identified a number of preconditions necessary for targeted sanctions to be effective: clear identification of the target, ability to identify and control financial flows, and strengthening of the UN sanction instrument.

The second seminar (Interlaken II) in 1999, attended by about 70 participants including state officials, scholars, UN officials, and NGOs, further developed recommendations on the technical aspects of targeted, but also addressed issues arising from differences in implementation of financial sanctions among states. The seminar developed standardized building blocks of language for future Security Council Resolutions, including prohibitions and exemptions. Such language was utilized for the first time by the European Union as part of its implementation of sanctions against the FRY over the issue of Kosovo and was drawn upon by the Afghanistan Sanctions Committee. Standardized language and definitions in the resolutions could contribute to enhanced effectiveness of financial sanctions, through harmonized implementation across national borders. In addition, the seminar examined the basic elements necessary for a legal framework to implement financial sanctions at the national level.

These consist of the freezing of funds or other financial assets and economic resources that are owned or controlled by designated persons or entities. These measures are regarded as preventive in nature and as an alternative to commerce and trade embargoes. And the measures are "smart" in the sense that their negative consequences are limited to the targeted government-related persons and their families. The measure can avoid damages to ordinary people.

In 2000 the German government and the Bonn International Center for Conversion organized an expert seminar called the "Bonn-Berlin Process" to discuss arms embargoes and aviation bans which are regarded as appropriate for smart sanctions as they would result in less harm to innocent people. And during 2001 and 2002 expert seminars named the "Stockholm Process" were hosted by the Swedish government and Uppsala University to reflect on previous seminars and discuss how to ensure that UN members and related actors could implement UN targeted sanctions.[16]

The series of policy seminars were closely related to the mainstreaming of human rights in the UN. The dissemination of universal values such as respecting human rights and promoting democracy under the norms of "Human Security" and "Responsibility to Protect" played an important role in formulating "humane" targeted sanctions. Some western scholars also stressed the necessity of introducing "morality" and/or "ethics" when formulating sanctions quoting the principles of the "Just War Doctrine" when analyzing economic sanctions. Some created new versions of the doctrine to analyze economic sanctions. These revised versions asked UN policymakers to stop and rethink about any unintended consequences that may result from sanctions. All these efforts were attempts to mitigate any adverse humanitarian consequences of sanctions.

Today, UN sanctions are, in general, targeted sanctions yet they still produce unintended consequences. The most common unintended consequences include corruption and criminality (58%), humanitarian consequences (44%), a decline in the credibility and/or legitimacy of the UN Security Council (37%), a strengthening of authoritarian rule (36%), and resource diversion (34%).[17]

Current targeted sanctions

Today, all UN sanctions are targeted sanctions in some way. By isolating violators of international standards and laws, even modest sanctions measures can serve an important symbolic purpose. The threat of sanctions can be a powerful means of deterrence and prevention. The UN non-proliferation sanctions, for example, send signals not only to targeted states such as the Democratic People's Republic of Korea (DPRK) but also to other regimes who may be contemplating violation of their Non-Proliferation Treaty (NPT) commitments.

Sanctions on individuals and entities

Since 1991, the UN Security Council has employed an average of one sanction per year and so far 25 regimes are in place with more than 1,000 designations worldwide.[18] More than 60% of all the targeted sanctions are against individuals and entities.[19]

Sanctions are adopted as one form of diplomatic tool. Sending a strong message is one of the important functions of targeted sanctions. A signal can be sent simultaneously to more than one target which can prevent similar activities by other suspicious individuals or entities.[20] The signaling functions of targeted sanctions include the process of naming, shaming, and/or stigmatizing a target. These are used for the enforcement of prevailing norms such as compliance with NPT obligations, for the negotiation of the operational meaning of norms such as Human Security and the Responsibility to Protect, and for the articulation of a preference in the hierarchy of norms. The UN signals in the form of collective shame can function as a preventive diplomatic tool.

Bierstecker proposes analyzing targeted sanctions as signals from two different aspects: (1) the communication of a message from a sender; and, (2) the context or social domain of its reception by the target.[21] According to Bierstecker, with regard to the communications aspect, a signal must be correctly received by the target just as the sender intended. A signal needs to be clearly articulated, communicated, received and comprehended by the target. The social domain in which the message is received determines whether the signal communicated produces a sense of shame or of stigma in the target.

The UN has used targeted sanctions to name well over a thousand individuals and corporate entities since 1991. A sanctions committee creates a list of the targeted individuals and corporations and travel bans or asset freezes and so on are then imposed against the persons on the list. Nearly half of the total names designated have been added by the Al-Qaida/Taliban United Nations Security Council Resolution 1267 Committee (the so-called 1267 Committee) alone.[22] This was divided into two separate sanctions committees in June 2011. More recently, related to the DPRK's nuclear test on 6 January 2016, the Non-Proliferation Committee has released the list of individuals and entities that are the targets of a travel ban and asset freeze.[23]

The purpose of a UN assets freeze is to disable a target's ability to engage in any financial transactions beyond those exempted for very specific purposes. It authorizes the blocking of any funds or economic resources that are already directly or indirectly owned or controlled by a designated individual, company or other entity and any funds or financial resources that are being made available to a designated individual, company or other entity. It is always a temporary measure and should not lead to confiscation, transfer, degrading of the value of an asset, or other negative impacts.

The types of assets that should be blocked vary from one sanctions regime to another. Assets or financial resources that are deposited in bank accounts are widely considered to be a category of assets that is easier to freeze. However, immovable assets such as real estate holdings, business ownership and shareholdings, proceeds from real estate, and business ownership or other equity or debt investments are rarely blocked.

The intended effects of an assets freeze are to impair the economic freedom, as well as the ability to finance the activities, say, of a terrorist. While the implementation of an assets freeze is an obligation of UN member states, it could not be effective without the full cooperation of banks and other financial service providers, who must accept steep compliance burdens by instituting careful due diligence procedures.

Current financial sanctions by Security Council are imposed in cooperation with Anti-Money Laundering and Countering the Financing of Terrorism (ANL/CFT) promoted by the Financial Action Task Force (FATF) which is the multilateral framework of OECD.[24] Recommendations by the FATF are not legally binding, but have an implementation mechanism to make public states which do not implement the SC Resolutions to secure certain effectiveness. The FATF is the global standard-setting body for anti-money laundering and combating the financing of terrorism (AML/CFT). In order to protect the international financial system from money laundering and financing of terrorism (ML/FT) risks and to encourage greater compliance with the AML/CFT standards, the FATF identified jurisdictions that have strategic deficiencies and works with them to address those deficiencies that pose a risk to the international financial system.

The FATF reaffirms its 25 February 2011 call on its members and urges all jurisdictions to advise their financial institutions to give special attention to business relationships and transactions with the DPRK, including DPRK companies, financial institutions and those acting on their behalf. In addition to enhanced scrutiny, the FATF further calls on its members and urges all jurisdictions to apply effective counter-measures, and targeted financial sanctions in accordance with applicable SC Resolutions, to protect their financial sectors from money laundering, financing of terrorism and the weapons of mass destruction (WMD) proliferation financing (ML/FT/PF) risks emanating from the DPRK.

Listing/delisting process and human rights

For the effect of financial sanctions, the listing measure is taken by the UN. The listing measure was first introduced in the sanctions regime for Angola (the

National Union for the Total Independence of Angola: UNITA). The clearest indication of naming and shaming in the listing was observable in this case when the sanctions committee chair, former Canadian Ambassador Robert Fowler, publicly named the ruling African heads of state that were assisting Jonas Savimbi and UNITA with the purchase of Angolan diamonds in exchange for arms.

The strategic approach by the Angola sanctions regime was evaluated as effective in sending a strong signal and improving the implementation of the regime.[25] One important factor that enhances the clarity of listing and the effect of the signal sent by naming and shaming is the degree of consensus within the Security Council. In this case it was relatively easy for the Permanent Five Members of the Council to reach a consensus because none of the P5 had a particular strategic interest in Angola. Since the Angola case, listing and naming and shaming has been introduced into UN targeted sanctions against other African nations.

When targeted sanctions were first introduced in the early 1990s, the Security Council considered only sovereign heads of state and/or political/military leaders and elites. The Council did not consider the rights of targeted individuals.

The widespread application of targeted sanctions in support of counter-terrorism measures since 2001 has raised the most questions about their potential violation of individual human rights. UN Security Council Resolution 1267 was a measure that was designed to put pressure on the Taliban regime to hand over Usama bin Laden for the attacks on two US embassies in East Africa in August 1998. The resolution was unusual in the sense that it named an individual in the text of the resolution, Usama bin Laden, even though he was technically not initially the target of the sanctions.

A widespread extension of the asset freeze and travel ban on individuals designated as financial supporters of Al-Qaida immediately followed the attacks of 11 September 2001. Bierstecker describes the period from late 2001 through the first half of 2002 as an extraordinary period due to insufficient investigation of targeted individuals. During the period, the names of individuals that the United States proposed were added to the list with little or no questioning or opposition. As a result, many legal issues emerged and the implementation of Security Council targeted sanctions was challenged by individual Member States.[26]

The largest number of designations has been made by the 1267 Committee which, as of 23 October 2009, had designated 504 individual and entities: 397 individuals (255 associated with Al-Qaida and 142 associated with the Taliban) and 107 entities associated with Al-Qaida.[27]

Targeted sanctions are principally intended to be political and preventive measures, rather than punitive ones. Inclusion on a list is not a legal determination but rather a political finding of association with Al-Qaida and the Taliban. A committee does not require evidentiary standards associated with legal prosecutions. Nonetheless, the open-ended nature of their application by UN sanctions committees, combined with the potential violation of elements of due process in their application to individuals, have led to legal challenges about their punitive nature.

Emerging legal challenges and political concerns

The measures implemented through targeted sanctions are under significant and growing challenge. National and regional courts have increasingly found fault with the procedures used for listing designations of sanctions on individuals and entities, as well as with the adequacy of procedures for challenging designations. This is an unintended consequence of UN targeted sanctions. Human rights advocates have criticized the UN, contending that the prevailing UN procedures for making designations violate the fundamental norms of due process. National legislative and parliamentary assemblies also question the authority of their executive officials to implement UN targeted sanctions without their consent. As a result, a number of Member States have found themselves in the difficult position of being forced to choose between contravening the rulings of their domestic courts and decisions of their legislative bodies on the one hand, and their obligations to implement binding Chapter VII decisions of the UN Security Council on the other.

Although the most potent challenges come from the courts, the issue is not exclusively a legal one. There is a political problem associated with the legitimacy, not only of the instrument of targeted sanctions, but increasingly of actions taken under Chapter VII by the UN Security Council. This is a fundamental challenge to an essential instrument of the international community to counter threats to international peace and security.

There is no inherent contradiction between the defense of fundamental human rights and the maintenance of international peace and security. The UN Charter accords primacy to both goals in Article 1 with the statement of the fundamental purposes of the organization. The Eminent Jurists Panel on Terrorism, Counter-Terrorism and Human Rights came to a similar conclusion in its February 2009 report,[28] acknowledging the necessity of countering terrorism, but pointing out the need to do so whilst maintaining human rights standards. A broad international consensus on this point already exists, as manifested by the UN General Assembly's Global Counter-Terrorism strategy which calls upon all Member States not only to undertake measures to counter terrorism, but to do so "in accordance with the Charter of the UN and the relevant provisions of international law, including international standards of human rights."[29] The issue of UN targeted sanctions designations continues to be framed by both policy practitioners and external observers in terms of a trade-off between security and human rights.

The report "Strengthening Targeted Sanctions through Fair and Clear Procedures," known as the "Watson Report,"[30] recommended that the Security Council improve the four principal aspects of due process: notification, access, fair hearing, and effective remedy.

The Security Council has made reforms to improve the fairness and transparency of sanctions regimes since 2006. But legal challenges in national and regional courts, concerns in parliamentary assemblies, and criticism from human rights organizations still continue. The political problem has only grown worse, with criticism expanding beyond measures to counter terrorism to criticism of targeted sanctions in general.

Legal challenges at the regional and national levels

The present study on UN targeted sanctions is focused on financial sanctions on individuals and entities administered by the 1267 Committee. Since most of the other UN targeted sanctions committees have relied on the 1267 Committee's precedents, the tasks and procedures of this Committee are representative of the practices of other sanctions committees.

More than 30 legal challenges to UN Security Council targeted sanctions listings have been pursued in courts worldwide over designations made either by the 1267 Committee or in the context of the implementation of UN Security Resolution 1373.[31] Some of the cases have been withdrawn after individuals were delisted by the 1267 Committee.

For an individual, placement on a sanctions list is relatively easy but removal from the list is much more difficult. While protection ex-ante—particularly the right to be informed and to be heard before interference with a person's rights actually occurs—is practically non-existent, protection ex-post does not yet offer affected individuals or entities an appropriate remedy for effectively challenging, within a reasonable time from their adoption, the restrictive measures imposed against them.[32]

UN sanctions before the European Court of Justice

The most highly visible decision to date was made by the highest court in the European Union, the European Court of Justice (ECJ), which decided in favor of two legal challenges on 3 September 2008 and disaffirmed the European Union regulation implementing UN Security Council Resolution 1267 with specific reference to the two cases. In its judgments in the cases of Kadi and Al Barakaat,[33] the Court distinguished between the imposition of the sanctions by the 1267 Committee and the implementation of the sanctions at the EU level, holding that the latter are bound by fundamental rights when implementing the sanctions, and that they must ensure that the individuals have the right to be informed of the reasons for listing and the right to contest those reasons. The ECJ granted that the EU Regulation implementing the UN listing would become void.

The Court charged that the rights of the defense, in particular the right to be heard and the right to an effective judicial review of those rights were patently not respected. The EU subsequently applied the procedures it typically employs for EU autonomous sanctions, informing the two plaintiffs of the reasons for their designation and giving them an opportunity to respond. Then, the EU Commission decided to re-instate the designations of both.

There was serious concern at the time, however, that if Europe set a precedent by selectively implementing decisions by the UN Security Council acting under Chapter VII of the UN Charter, it would pave the way for other national and regional bodies to do the same. This would mean undermining the ability of the international community to impose and implement targeted measures with consistency across different jurisdictions. Human rights lawyers charge that the implementation of UN targeted sanctions against individuals may violate fundamental human rights, as protected by regional or global conventions.[34]

UN sanctions and national courts

The individuals and entities targeted by UN sanctions should receive adequate protection through the international monitoring mechanisms under existing human rights treaties. At the universal level, Ciampi mentions the necessity of including the Human Rights Committee (HRC), a body created by the International Covenant on Civil and Political Rights, and at a regional level the European Convention of Human Rights.

In 2008, the HRC delivered its opinion related to Nabil Sayadi and Patricia Vinck, both Belgian nationals and residents, and, respectively, the director and secretary of *Fondation Secours International*, the European branch of an Islamic charity based in Illinois, that had been on the Consolidated List since 22 October 2002.[35] According to information provided by Belgium, criminal investigations of Sayadi and Vinck had started but, although they were subject to a travel ban and asset freeze, they were not given access to the relevant information justifying their listing. In February 2005, a Belgian civil court ordered the Belgian state to initiate the procedure to have their names removed from the list. In pursuance thereof, Belgium requested the committee to delist the authors. The criminal investigation was dismissed in December 2005.[36] Kadi reported this matter to the HRC in 2006 and the report was accepted by the committee. And finally in 2009 the names were delisted from the sanctions list by the judgment of the Security Council.[37]

This case is a peculiar one as Sayadi and Vinck were listed on the basis of information provided by their national state, which was later unable to obtain the removal of their names from the list because of the objections of some of the committee members.

For due process against individuals listed due to UN Security Council Resolution 1267, Reich says that the series of policy seminars in early 2002—the Interlaken Process, the Bonn-Berlin Process, and the Stockholm Process—may have been useful for paving the way for such conclusive legal challenges. This is because UN policymakers and scholars strove to develop a legal framework within international law to combine the effectiveness of an approach vested in the UN with respect for fundamental rights.[38]

Growing political concerns among member states

The issue of UN targeted sanctions has now gone beyond legal challenges and has spilled over into parliamentary debates and motions to limit the ability of Member States to implement UN sanctions under certain conditions. The UK

Supreme Court, for example, has raised questions about the authority of the UK government to implement UN targeted sanctions against individuals without parliamentary approval via primary legislation. Germany derided the application of targeted sanctions and other UN member states have indicated a growing reluctance to add names to the lists of individuals and entities targeted by Security Council sanctions because of these concerns. More than 50 Member States have expressed concern about the lack of due process and absence of transparency associated with listing and delisting.[39]

Moreover, the Eminent Jurists Panel on Terrorism, Counter terrorism and Human Rights issued a report in 2009 titled "Assessing Damage, Urging Action" which strongly criticized the listing system as "unworthy" of international institutions like the UN and EU.[40]

The legal issues and human rights concerns are significant but, as the 2009 Watson Report points out, need to be placed in a broader political context. Virtually all of the major legal challenges to date have stemmed from designations associated with efforts to counter terrorism, but not those associated with the enforcement of peace agreements, human rights violations, or nuclear prolif-eration. Global terrorism has been characterized by the UN Security Council as a threat to international peace and security, and targeted sanctions have been imposed against individuals and entities as both preventive and deter-rent measures. The growing negative reaction to targeted sanctions for counter terrorism purposes, however, risks the further erosion of the credibility and future utility of the instrument of multilateral sanctions in general.

Developments and procedural improvements within the UN

The movement for reform within the UN has been building for years. The High Level Panel on Threats, Challenges and Change appointed by Annan noted in 2004: "The way entities or individuals are added to the terrorist list maintained by the Council and the absence of review or appeal for those listed raises serious accountability issues and possibly violates fundamental human rights norms and conventions."[41]

The 2005 World Summit Outcome document called on the Security Council "to ensure that fair and clear procedures exist for placing individuals and entities on sanctions lists and removing them, as well as for granting humanitarian exceptions."[42]

In response, Annan directed the Office of Legal Affairs (OLA) to begin an interdepartmental process within the UN to develop proposals and guidelines to address such concerns. The OLA 2006 report argued that the Security Council must strive to balance its principal duty of maintaining international peace and security with respect for the human rights and fundamental freedoms of targeted individuals to the greatest extent possible.[43]

Based on the OLA analysis, Annan submitted an informal paper to the Security Council titled "Targeted Individual Sanctions: Fair and Clear Procedures for Listing and Delisting," in which he enumerated basic elements to ensure fair and clear procedures.[44]

The establishment of a focal point

The Security Council called for the Secretary-General to establish a focal point within the Secretariat in 2006.[45] The creation of the focal point allows petitioners seeking delisting to submit requests to the Secretariat; the Secretariat then acknowledges receipt of the requests and informs the petitioners on procedures for processing delisting requests, forwards the requests to the designating states and states of citizenship and residence, and informs the petitioners of the sanctions committee's decision. The focal point represents an improvement in providing accessibility for those listed and is expected to ensure that fair and clear procedures exist for placing individuals and entities on lists and for removing them as well as for granting humanitarian exemptions.[46]

Further reform of the 1267 committee procedures

The Al-Qaida/Taliban sanctions regime has demonstrated impressive institutional development in the past ten years. UN Security Council Resolution 1267 contained no provision for delisting in 1999 but today it represents the most procedurally advanced of the sanctions committees with formalized procedures for delisting.

UN Security Council Resolution 1735 contained the Security Council's efforts to improve the fairness and transparency of sanctions regimes.[47] The resolution elaborated minimal standards for the statements of case, provided for the public release of that information, and created a procedure to improve deficiencies in notification. It also included the first measure to require notification of those listed. Another major change found in UN Security Council Resolution 1735 was that the period of the "No Objections Procedure" (NOP) was extended from 48 hours to five working days. This allows more time for a serious review of cases which is important for a fair hearing in the listing process.

Expanded roles of the 1267 committee

The Security Council expanded the 1267 Committee's role in addressing listing and delisting issues through UN Security Council Resolution 1822.[48] UN Security Council Resolution 1822 contained requirements with the potential to drastically change sanctions committee procedures. First, it required a review of all names on the 1267 Consolidated List within two years, and that every designation should be reviewed at least every three years. Second, it required the development of narrative summaries for all listings on the committee website and an explanation for the inclusion of each name on the list.

The workload associated with the 1822 review has been extraordinary for the committee members, national governments, and those states responsible for the most designations. Reviewing states are asked to indicate if the listing remains appropriate; if not, a delisting request is submitted according to the guidelines. After replies are received from the reviewing states, information is circulated to the committee members and the monitoring team for one month to review. However, the Watson Report points out that initial progress was slower than previously hoped for due to the significant workload and delays in getting necessary responses from Member States.[49]

Appointment of an Ombudsperson

In order to create a clearer and fairer delisting procedure, UN Security Council Resolution 1904 established the system and roles of an Ombudsperson.[50] The Ombudsperson, appointed by the Secretary-General, should be an eminent individual of high moral character, impartiality and integrity with high qualifications and experience in relevant fields, such as law, human rights, counter-terrorism, and sanctions. The Office of the Ombudsperson receives requests from individuals and entities seeking to be removed from the Consolidated List. The ombudsperson makes recommendations in consultation with Secretary-General to the Security Council on appeals regarding committee decisions on delisting. The person is expected to perform these tasks in an independent impartial manner and shall neither seek nor receive instructions from any government. Any final decision on delisting is made by the committee.

Conclusion

The Security Council has engaged in a continual process of self-assessment and reform of its practices with regard to designations, exemptions, and delisting; as indeed it has since the first introduction of targeted sanctions in the mid-1990s. The Security Council has adopted UN Security Council Resolutions 1730, 1735, 1822, and 1904.

Procedural changes to date generally address concerns about notification and improved accessibility, but there have also been improvements in providing elements for a fair hearing. The 2009 Watson Report points out that a completely fair hearing in advance of a designation is virtually impossible given the nature of targeted financial sanctions in particular. However, there have been improvements with regard to providing elements of a fair hearing, notably with regard to periodic review, extending the NOP, transparency, and most significantly, efforts to improve the quality of statements of case.[51]

Individuals and entities targeted by the Security Council have the right to be informed of those measures and to know the case against them; they have the right to be heard within a reasonable time by the relevant decision-making body; and, the right to review by an effective review mechanism. These elements, along with a regular review to mitigate the risks of violating the right to property and related human rights, represent the first articulation by UN officials of minimum standards of procedural fairness.

In order to protect the human rights of targeted individuals, the UN needs to work together with international human rights monitoring bodies such as the

UN Committee of Human Rights and the European Court of Human Rights. In relation thereto, there is no clear answer as to whether these bodies are capable of protecting the rights of targeted individuals and entities when national as well as other international institutions have failed to do so.

It is too early for us to judge the UN's reforms in the reviewing mechanisms of targeted sanctions but, unless the Security Council overcomes legal challenges and growing political concerns over listing/delisting mechanisms, basic human rights cannot be guaranteed in the international community.

Notes

1 Kofi Annan, *In Larger Freedom: Towards Development, Security and Human Rights for All* (United Nations, 2005), para 109.
2 This name comes from the book edited by David Cortright and George A. Lopez called *The Sanctions Decade: Accessing UN Strategies in the 1990s* (Lynne Reinner Publishers, 2000).
3 For example, Joy Gordon, "A Peaceful, Silent, Deadly Remedy: The Ethics of Economic Sanctions," *Ethics and International Affairs*, Vol. 13, 1999, pp. 123–150; John Mueller and Karl Mueller, "Sanctions of Mass Destruction," *Foreign Affairs*, Vol. 78, No. 3, (May–June 1999), pp. 43–53; Thomas G. Weiss, David Cortright, George Lopez and Larry Minear, *Political Gain and Civilian Pain: Humanitarian Impacts of Economic Sanctions* (Rowman and Littlefield, 1997).
4 Chantal de Jonge Oudraat, "Economic Sanctions and International Peace and Security," in Oamela Aall, Chester Crocker, and Fen Osler Hampson (eds.), *Leashing the Dogs of War: Conflict Management in a Divided World* (United Sates Institute of Peace, 2007), pp. 335–355.
5 Ibid.
6 Ibid.
7 S/RES/661, 6 August 1990.
8 S/RES/757, 30 May 1992.
9 S/RES/941, 23 September 1994.
10 S/RES/917, 6 May 1994.
11 Miki Honda, *Kokuren niyoru keizaiseisai to jindojyo no shomonndai—sumāto sankushon no mosaku*[*UN Economic Sanctions and Humanitarian Issues—Searching for "Smart Sanctions"*], Kokusai-shoin, 2013.
12 For example, Pape, Robert, "Why Economic Sanctions Do Not Work," *International Security* 22, No. 2, Fall 1997; Kimberly Ann Elliott, "The Sanctions Glass: Hall Full or Completely Empty?" *International Security* 23, No. 1, Summer 1998.
13 Oudraat, supra note 4, pp. 335–355.
14 Some scholars describe the situation worsened by military force as "genocide." For example, Geoff Simon, *Imposing Economic Sanctions: Legal Remedy or Genocidal Tool?* (Pluto Press, 1999); George Lopez, "Economic Sanctions and Genocide: Too Little, Too Late and Sometimes Too Much" in Neal Riemer (ed.), *Protection Against Genocide* (Praeger, 2000).
15 Fourth Freedom Forum (Indiana, US) and the Joan B. Kroc Institute for International Peace Studies (Indiana, US) are known as pioneers in searching for smart sanctions. David Cortright and George A. Lopez initiated the research.

16 Peter Wallensteen, Carina Staibano, and Mikael Eriksson, *Making Targeted Sanctions Effective: Guidelines for the Implementation of UN Policy Options* (Uppsala University, 2003).

17 *SanctionsAPP*, The Graduate Institute Geneva, Graduate Institute of International and Development Studies at www.sanctionsapp.com (Accessed 12 February 2019).

18 *SanctionsAPP*, p. 4.

19 About 62%, 628 of 1,015, entail sanctions against individuals designated by the UN Security Council. (*SanctionsAPP*), p. 4.

20 For example, Thomas Bierstecker, "UN Targeted Sanctions as Signals: Naming and Shaming or Naming and Stigmatizing?" in Richard H. Friman (ed.), *The Politics of Leverage in International Relations: Name, Shame, and Sanction* (Palgrave Macmillan, 2015).

21 Bierstecker, supra note 20, pp. 166–167.

22 S/RES/1267, 15 October 1999.

23 S/RES/2270, 2 March 2016.

24 www.fatf-gafi.org/home/ (Accessed 20 February 2019).

25 For example, David J.R. Angell, "The Angola Sanctions Committee," in David M. Malone (ed.), *The UN Security Council: From the Cold War to the 21st Century* (Lynne Rienner Publishers, 2004), 195–204; Anders Möllander, "UN Angola Sanctions: A Committee Success Revised," Department of Peace and Conflict Research (Uppsala University, March 2009), p. 9.

26 Thosman Biersteker and Sue Eckert, "Addressing Challenging to Targeted Sanctions: An Update of the 'Watson Report,' " October 2009 (UNO Academia, The Graduate Institute, Geneva Centre on Conflict, Development and Peacebuilding, Watson Institute), p. 7.

27 Ibid., p. 7.

28 "Assessing Damage, Urging Action" issued by the Eminent Jurists Panel on Terrorism, Counter-terrorism, and Human Rights (International Commission of Jurists. 16 February 2009), pp. 113–117.

29 Measures to eliminate international terrorism, A/RES/63/129, Distr. 15 January 2009.

30 *Strengthening Targeted Sanctions Through Fair and Clear Procedures* ("Watson Report") by the Graduate Institute, Geneva Centre on Conflict, Development and Peacebuilding, Watson Institute, March 2006. The report was made an official document of the UN General Assembly and the UN Security Council, A/60/887-S/2006/331.

31 S/RES/1373, 28 September 2001.

32 Annalisa Ciampi, "Security Council Targeted Sanctions and Human Rights" in Fassbender, Bardo (ed.), Securing Human Rights?: Achievements and Challenges of the UN Security Council, Oxford University Press, 2011, pp. 105–106.

33 For an analysis of the Kadi case, see, Albert Posch, "The Kadi Case: Rethinking the Relationship between EU Law and International Law?" *The Columbia Journal of European Law Online*, Vol. 15, 2009.

34 *Watson Report*, supra note 30, pp. 17–18.

35 The names were also placed on the lists appended to the European Union Council Regulation (27 January 2003) and a Belgium ministerial order (31 January 2003).

36 For further information on the Sayadi case, see Helen Keller and Andreas Fischer, "The UN Anti-terror Sanctions Regime under Pressure," *Human Rights Law Review*, 2009.

37 SC/9711, 21 July 2009.

38 Johannes Reich, "Due Process and Sanctions Targeted Against Individuals Pursuant to Resolution 1267 (1999)," *Yale Journal of International Law* 33, 505, 2008.

39 *Watson Report*, supra note 30, pp. 10–11.

40 Ibid.

41 *Report of the High-Level Panel on Threats, Challenges, and Change, A More Secure World, Our Shared Responsibility*, 1/59/656, para. 153, 2 December 2004.

42 UN General Assembly Resolution 60/1, 2005 World Summit Outcome, para. 109.

43 Bardo Fassbender, "Targeted Sanctions and Due Process: The Responsibility of the UN Security Council to Ensure that Fair and Clear Procedures are Made Available to Individuals and Entities Targeted with Sanction under Chapter VII of the UN Charter," 20 March 2006, Study Commissioned by the United Nations Office of Legal Affairs, Office of Legal Counsel, 7–8. See also Fassbender, Bardo, "Targeted Sanctions Imposed by the UN Security Council and Due Process Rights," p. 3 *International Organization Law Review* 437, 449 (2006).

44 Letter dated 15 June 2006 from the Secretary-General to the President of the Security Council, informal paper entitled, "Targeted Individual Sanctions: Fair and Clear Procedures for Listing and Delisting." Proceedings of 5474th Meeting, S/PV.5474, New York 22 June 2006.

45 S/RES/1730, 19 December 2006. This became operational as of 27 March 2007.

46 *Watson Report*, supra note 30, pp. 12–13.

47 S/RES/1735, 22 December 2006.

48 S/RES/1822, 30 June 2008.

49 *Watson Report*, supra note 30, pp. 16–17.

50 S/RES/1904, 17 December 2009.

51 *Watson Report*, supra note 30, pp. 23–28.

3 Functions of Security Council subsidiary organs in the UN financial sanctions regimes

From the perspective of the law of international organizations

Ryosuke Sato

Introduction

Background and problems

Unilateral sanctions and UN sanctions differ with respect to some legal characteristics. While unilateral sanctions can be implemented in isolation, UN sanctions must be conducted collaboratively, namely by the UN and the Member States as a pair. More specifically, the process of UN sanctions consists of decision-making by the UN and implementation by the Member States. Accordingly, one of the distinctive characteristics of UN sanctions is the indispensability of any organizational engagement in the entire process of sanctions on the international level.

UN sanctions regimes have developed remarkably since the end of the Cold War, transforming from comprehensive to "smart sanctions" or "targeted sanctions" by limiting the target's *ratione personae* and *ratione materiae*, in order to enhance the positive effects and mitigate the unintended negative repercussions of the sanctions.[1] Moreover, both the sufficient and reliable information related to the sanctions targets and the appropriate listing of them for sound sanctions implementation have played a key role in enhancing the effectiveness of targeted/smart sanctions.[2] However, such sanctions can still have unintended negative consequences in their implementation. Nevertheless, it should be noted that the development of post-Cold War sanctions regimes has co-occurred with the institutional and functional development of subsidiary organs, as regards increasing the number of organs and expanding their assigned tasks and delegated powers. Therefore, this chapter focuses on the activities and functions of subsidiary organs in the UN sanctions regimes.

Methodological approaches

In analyzing the subsidiary organs from the legal aspects, first, it is useful to invoke an administrative legal framework. For example, Japanese administrative law can be classified into three different systems according to the criteria of objectives and characteristics. *Gyōsei Soshiki Hō* (law on administrative organizations) relates to the establishment, abolition, structure, powers, and so on of an administration. *Gyōsei Sayō Hō* (law on administrative activities) relates to all the activities aimed at achieving legitimate objectives of an administration. *Gyōsei Kyusai Hō* (law on administrative remedy) provides relief to people who are inconvenienced by administrative activities.[3]

Needless to say, an easy and simplistic analogy to domestic administrative law can be detrimental because the international legal order has a heterogeneous structure compared to domestic legal orders. However, it can be assumed that such a classification is still helpful for analyzing the structure and activities of international organizations inclusively and legally, as Yokota pointed out.[4] Therefore, this chapter's approach is grounded in a certain administrative legal framework modified and adapted as below.

First, the *institutional law of international organizations* (*institutional law*) means "a generic term of law relating to the establishment, continuation, modification, dissociation, status, and powers, and so on, of international organizations and one relating to the establishment, revision, abolition, names, powers, structure, and procedures, and so on, of their internal bodies, and one relating to all other personal and material aspects comprising international organizations and their internal bodies."[5] Based on this framework and the scope of this chapter, there can be assumed points of controversy: the legal rationale, or the Security Council's competence to establish, oversee and control subsidiary organs as well as delegate powers to them, and the extent of and criteria for exercising delegated powers of them.

Second, the *operational law of international organizations* (operational law) means "a generic term of law relating to the regulation of any activities undertaken by international organizations for the purpose of achieving their legitimate goals and objectives, and one which regulates other actors through these activities."[6] Based on this framework and the scope of this chapter, we can assume the overall and certain particular points of concern. The overall points of concern are issues to do with the extent of powers or limitations under Chapter VII related to the decision on and implementation of sanctions, and the effectiveness of the sanctions regime. The particular points of concern are issues designating the roles and functions of subsidiary organs. However, it should be taken into consideration that the problems inherent in UN sanctions may not only be related to the construction and implementation of the collective security system, but also to any legal relationship between the UN and the Member States. While the relationship between the UN as a body that carries out sanctions and the States as the target is positioned under *operational law*, their relations as collaborative actors are also positioned under *institutional law*.[7] It may be said that there are problems related to the UN Charter framework, which extends over *institutional law* and *operational law*. The UN collective security system comprises military and nonmilitary measures. The effectiveness of the latter depends on States' political will and capacities to implement sanctions domestically. That is to say, the nonmilitary measures are institutionally characterized by "the centrality of decision-making" and "the decentrality of implementation." Thus, it is questioned how the system secures said centrality and decentrality. Based on the extent and the objective of this chapter, there could be discussion of how those functions and roles of subsidiary organs may influence the imposing of obligations on States (Article 25 and 48) or the controlling of their actions (the limitation of their discretion).

From the perspective of *remedial law of international organizations* (*remedial law*), which Yokota has never mentioned, we could raise an issue about the engagement and functions of subsidiary organs in providing remedy for the injuries or damages caused by international sanctions regimes.

The points mentioned thus far are generally conceivable as those of related to the *law of international organizations*, which is a bundle of norms concerning the structure and activities of international organizations as well as being contained substantially in the constituent instruments.[8] Hence, this chapter examines the functions and roles of subsidiary organs in UN (especially financial) sanctions, keeping in mind the viewpoint of Japanese administrative law, within the framework of the *law of international organizations*.

The purpose of this chapter is to analyze the phase of invoking UN financial sanctions: the decision-making related to the invocation, modification, and termination, and so on of the sanctions, and the exercise of powers related to the said phase. The matter of how to reduce or relieve any human rights abuses that occur in the process of putting sanctions into practice is mainly a problem of implementation and application, not the invocation, of sanctions. Therefore, I will reserve this matter for another chapter of this book. The terms "centrality" and "decentrality" are referred to as concepts related to the allocation and location of the State's sovereignty or power.

Legal status of Security Council subsidiary organs

First, the legal status of subsidiary organs established by the Security Council can be described from the viewpoint of *institutional law*. Subsidiary organs, in general, "may be created by the constituent instrument or under powers granted expressly or implicitly by the constitution." Such powers are exercised in the case of it being "necessary for the discharge of the functions of the organization" or "essential for the performance [of] its duties or appropriate for the fulfilment of the stated purposes of the organization."[9] The UN Charter contains the relevant clauses (Article 7 (2), 22 and 29), and thereby, under Article 29, the Security Council "may establish such subsidiary organs as it deems necessary for the performance of its functions." The functions and powers of subsidiary organs are subject to the constituent instruments concerned or are determined by their principal organs. Further, there are some constraints based on legal principles, such as *Nemo dare potest quod non habet*. For example, "functions of subsidiary organs cannot go beyond the functions of the international organization concerned as defined in its constituent instrument." Moreover, "functions of subsidiary organs are dependent on the scope of powers of the related principal organ or organs."[10] That is to say, these are limitations related to the legal theory of the "delegation of powers."[11]

Generally speaking, principal organs may delegate some of their functions and powers to subsidiary organs. However, such delegation would only be possible if "such a delegation would be allowable in the light of the objectives and balance of interests reflected in the constituent instrument," and if it did not amount to an increase in obligations imposed on the Member States. Specifically, no more functions or powers may be delegated to subsidiary organs than what principal organs possess *per se*. Also, principal organs cannot delegate their own functions or powers to other organs if in doing so they delegate away their responsibility.[12] However, it is difficult to say that the principle of *Nemo dare potest quod non habet* is, in fact, effective for limiting the delegation of powers in the context of the Security Council. That is, it naturally follows, under the framework of flexible/teleological interpretation according to the purposes and objectives of the constituent instruments, that the scope of powers to establish "subsidiary organs as it deems necessary for the performance of its functions" becomes very broad.[13]

Nevertheless, as the corollary of delegation, principal organs (the parent) remain responsible for the actions of subsidiary organs (the agent) to perform their tasks.[14] That is why subsidiary organs are usually required to report periodically to their principal organs, which can thereby oversee and control the former.[15] Subsidiary organs are expected to support the related principal organs in carrying out their missions. But those roles are confined to being subordinate to the related principal organs even if their support is indeed regarded as substantial and essential to the activities of the international organization concerned. Therefore, the corollary of such a subsidiary or subordinate position is that decisions and conclusions taken by subsidiary organs are not binding on the related principal organs, except for the case of a judicial organ established by a principal organ, such as international administrative tribunals confirmed in the *Effect of Awards Case*.[16]

Second, the legal status of such subsidiary organs can be described from the viewpoint of *operational law*. In the UN sanctions regimes, the Security Council determines not only the invocation of the sanctions but also the contents of measures and the methods of implementation and leaves it to the Member States to realize the measures. Then, subsidiary organs are involved in both decision-making and implementation, albeit the extent and manner of involvement are different as follows: The decision-making related to sanctions includes the determination under Article 39 of the prerequisite for invoking the sanctions, through the decision on the sanctions themselves and the contents of measures under Article 41. Moreover, it also includes the modification and abolition of the sanctions. The Security Council usually stipulates the establishment of subsidiary organs in its resolution. While these organs have never engaged in the determination of and the decision on sanctions before they were established, they do play a role in judging the modification and any change in the contents of measures. One of these roles is the management of the listing (drafting, maintaining, and delisting). This management function is also related to the phase of the implementation of sanctions because States lead to apply the sanctions measures against the targets on the list.

The engagement of subsidiary organs in the phase of implementation exemplifies the monitoring of Member States' implementation of sanctions measures, the examination of the effects of the sanctions, and the investigation and determination of a violation. There is no doubt that the said activities in the phase of implementation are also engaged in the phase of decision-making, taking into account the possibility of modifying or changing the contents of the sanctions measures, which may result from investigation and confirmation by the subsidiary organs. This is a notable leap forward in the engagement of subsidiary organs in the phase of implementation in the recent cases of sanctions. To be specific, the Security Council has come to establish other organs than the sanctions committees, such as the bodies of experts, monitoring organs, and the Ombudsperson. As mentioned regarding "the centrality of decision-making" and "the decentrality of implementation" above, it can be assumed that centrality enhances not only the phase of decision-making but also the implementation if the extent of the discretion conferred to subsidiary organs is large and binding on States' decision-making in the phase of its implementation.

From the point of *remedial law*, the substantial remedy system (e.g., compensatory system) and the procedural remedy system (e.g., revocation and annulment) are assumed. Needless to say, the first target of remedy by international organizations is deemed to be the Member States if the logic of domestic administrative laws is followed. Assuming further at the international level, it could possibly be that the target includes the individual victims. On this point, there has been no such subsidiary organ playing the role of the substantial remedy so far, even if the targets were States or individuals. The UN Compensation Commission established by Security Council Resolution 687 is not an organ related to administering UN sanctions measures but to processing claims for damages or injuries caused by Iraq's invasion and occupation of Kuwait.

However, there is an organ possibly relevant to the procedural remedy. When economic difficulties are incurred as a result of sanctions undertaken by the Security Council, the affected State, not the targeted one of the sanction, has a right to consult the Security Council. When the Security Council receives requests for assistance from the State based on Article 50, the sanctions committee sometimes examines the requests and presents its recommendations to the Security Council.[17] Furthermore, there is a possibility in the case of human rights abuses caused by the sanctions that the Ombudsperson, which has relevant powers to receive the petitions of individual victims and manage the delisting, is regarded as the procedural remedy.

Development of financial sanctions regimes

From comprehensive sanctions to "targeted" sanctions

The first sanctions in the framework of international organizations were imposed on Italy under the League of Nations. Moreover, the measures prohibiting financial transactions and so on as part of sanctions against Italy were also the first financial sanctions. Concerning a regime, the League Assembly established the Co-ordinating Committee and the Committee of Eighteen. The Committee of Eighteen forwarded the findings of matters to the Co-ordinating Committee, which thereafter recommended to League Member States the sanctions measures to be taken. Adopted by the Assembly, the sanctions thereby finally came into effect.[18] In a way, this can be said to be a budding linkage with some subsidiary bodies with international sanctions regimes.

In the era of the UN, sanctions against Southern Rhodesia were imposed under Security Council Resolutions 232 and 253, which also included financial sanctions prohibiting investment and remittance. Since then, the Security Council has imposed approximately 30 sanctions regimes. As of August 2019, there were 14 regimes in operation: Somalia;[19] ISIL (Da'esh) and Al-Qaida (ISIL/Al-Qaida); Iraq (Resolution 1518); Democratic Republic of the Congo (DRC); Sudan (Resolution 1591); Hariri's assassination (de facto inactive); North Korea; Libya (Resolution 1970); the Taliban (split from the Al-Qaida sanctions regime by Resolution 1988); Guinea-Bissau; the Central African Republic; Yemen; South Sudan; and Mali. Except for the case of Guinea-Bissau, 13 other sanctions regimes contain financial sanctions. Also, all of the 14 regimes established sanctions committees, and 11 regimes in total have bodies of experts and monitoring bodies for supporting the committees' missions.[20] This shows how important the introduction of financial sanctions[21] and the existence of subsidiary organs[22] are in the UN sanctions regimes.

As the Iraq sanctions (Resolution 661) exemplify, which targeted the assets of the Iraqi government but not those owned personally by Saddam Hussein and his family, the Security Council has not imposed targeted sanctions against individual financial assets *ab initio*.[23] Rather, the Security Council has developed a mechanism of designating individuals or groups as sanctions regime targets over time.[24] First, the Security Council issued a list of individuals targeted by Resolution 917 in the case of Haiti, initially but on a recommended basis, strongly urging the Member States to freeze targeted assets. Regarding a binding resolution, in the case of sanctions against the National Union for the Total Independence of Angola (UNITA) instituted by Resolution 1173, the Security Council decided on Chapter VII measures, including the freezing of the funds and financial resources of "UNITA as an organization or of senior officials of UNITA or adult members of their immediate families." Then, the Security Council imposed asset freezing on Taliban leaders in Resolution 1333, for the purpose of further strengthening the mandatory financial sanctions against the Taliban regime under Resolution 1267. The remarkable point in the UNITA and Taliban cases is the additional establishment of subsidiary organs other than a sanctions committee. The first case in which a panel of experts was established by the Security Council was regarding the UNITA sanctions regime, and also the first case of the establishment of a committee of experts by the Security Council was the Taliban/Al-Qaida sanctions regime.[25] Therefore, it may be said that the evolving transformation of sanctions measures into "targeted" ones has followed the development of subsidiary organs in the sanctions regimes.

The role of subsidiary organs in sanctions regimes was generally limited until around the mid-1990s. The Southern Rhodesia Sanctions Committee, for example, lacked the power to inspect cargo *in situ* and its own independent sources of information. As a result, the Committee could not help but rely on information provided by the Member States and then accept their findings as final.[26] Moreover, the Secretariat also "lacks the administrative capabilities and resources necessary to plan, implement, and monitor [targeted financial] sanctions,"[27] and thus it has played a very limited role in the UN sanctions regimes.[28] Generally, it was in the state that "it lacks a sustained capacity to develop and maintain a list of targeted individuals and companies, and it is unable to ensure the cooperation of Member States in freezing assets and interdicting transactions."[29] Therefore, it may be said that the Security Council has attempted to enhance the institutional capacity of the sanctions regimes for reacting to such a situation, through the development of subsidiary organs, since around the year 2000 when targeted measures were being actualized.

Development of subsidiary organs in financial sanctions regimes

The Security Council has established not only sanctions committees but also a variety of other subsidiary organs under the UN financial sanctions regimes in the post-Cold War era. This means that "the task of sanctions monitoring, which was traditionally undertaken by the Security Council's sanctions committees, is increasingly being delegated to independent bodies of experts,"[30] not to the representatives of Member States.

Sanctions committees[31]

The sanctions committee is a subsidiary organ established by the Security Council for the purpose of administering sanctions regimes. The committee is subject to supervision and control by the Security Council and obliged to report to it. The committee is comprised of the Member States of the Security Council and has taken a limited role only as a monitoring function in the Cold War era sanctions regimes. However, recent developments show that the Security Council has delegated more powers to the committee, which thereby may take a substantial role in administering the sanctions. The functions of the committee include monitoring, reporting, and administering a list of the targets, such as listing, delisting, and exempting.[32] As the committees are *ad hoc* entities, their mandates may vary quite markedly.[33] While it is thus difficult to evaluate evenly the functions and tasks of the committees, their recent functional developments have been apparent in the improvement in monitoring effectiveness and the administration of the lists.

First, with regard to enhancing the efficacy of monitoring, the committee has come to be delegated, for example, the drawing up of rules for monitoring sanctions (the former Yugoslavia[34]); promulgating, announcing, and updating guidelines to facilitate the implementation of sanctions (almost sanctions regimes); investigating reports of sanctions violations (UNITA[35]); assessing reports from the panel of experts and Member States regarding the implementation of sanction measures (Sudan);[36] examining and taking appropriate actions regarding alleged violations (Liberia,[37] the DRC,[38] North Korea,[39] Iran,[40] Libya [Resolution 1970],[41] Yemen,[42] South Sudan,[43] Mali);[44] and sending a field mission led by the chairperson of the committee or visiting the countries himself/herself (UNITA,[45] Yemen,[46] the DRC,[47] Sudan,[48] North Korea,[49] Liberia,[50] Côte d'Ivoire,[51] Libya [Resolution 1970],[52] the Taliban [Resolution 1988],[53] the Central African Republic,[54] South Sudan,[55] Somalia,[56] ISIL/Al-Qaida).[57] As far as the collection of information relevant to monitoring sanctions implementation is concerned, it can be said that the functions of the committees have been much more developed than the previous ones short of examining or verifying information.

While the committee has played a supervisory role that involves receiving and examining the reports of other subsidiary organs (UNITA,[58] Somalia),[59] it has come to assume: for example, seeking the cooperation of States neighboring a target state (Somalia),[60] consulting with regional organizations/arrangements on ways to strengthen the implementation of measures (UNITA,[61] Sierra Leone),[62] assisting States in tracing and freezing funds subject to sanctions (Liberia),[63] and making recommendations to the Security Council on ways to strengthen the effectiveness of the sanctions measures and/or on ways to limit any unintended effects of those measures on a civilian population (Liberia,[64] Côte d'Ivoire,[65] North Korea).[66] Moreover, as mentioned above, the committee sometimes examines requests for assistance from a third state that has incurred economic difficulties arising from the sanctions, and then recommends measures to the Security Council (Iraq [Resolution 661],[67] Libya [Resolution 748],[68] the former Yugoslavia,[69] Haiti),[70,71] which may be a limited function in the context of *remedial law*.

Second, regarding administration of the list, almost all the committees have the powers of drafting and maintaining the list and considering an exemption from it for humanitarian reasons and so forth. Moreover, the committee sometimes designates financial resources to be targeted (ISIL/Al-Qaida).[72] Such delegation of the power of administering the list from the Security Council to the committees has drawn attention not only to the occurrence of human rights abuses against the targeted individuals but also to the role of the committees in a form of "secondary normative power."[73]

Bodies of experts[74]

The Security Council has come to establish bodies of experts for investigating the implementation of sanctions, which take the forms of groups, committees, teams, and panels. Generally speaking, the bodies have a short-term mandate to act within a few weeks or months. In many cases, the Security Council requests that the Secretary-General set up the bodies or nominate the members. A body is obliged to report to the Security Council as one of its subsidiary organs.

The bodies are mainly in charge of collecting information relevant to violations of sanctions and sometimes involve employing not only their delegated powers of visiting a site for more effective information-collection (Sierra Leone)[75] but also investigating sanctions violations and possible links to those violations,[76] and conducting a follow-up assessment mission (Liberia).[77] Some bodies are even assigned to identify parties that aid and abet violations and to recommend measures to end such violations and to improve sanctions implementation (UNITA).[78] Others make recommendations on actions that the Security Council, the sanctions committee, or the Member States may consider to improve implementation of the measures (North Korea,[79] Libya [Resolution 1970]).[80] In some cases the Security Council has acted upon the panel's recommendations (Sierra Leone).[81]

Concerning administration of the list, the panels provide the committee with information relevant to the potential designation of individuals and entities (the Central African Republic,[82] Yemen,[83] South Sudan,[84] and Mali)[85] and report on sources of financing for the illicit trade of arms (Liberia).[86] Related to information gathering, the bodies have cooperated with UN peacekeeping operations. For example, the group of experts in the DRC sanctions regime is mandated to examine and analyze information gathered by the United Nations Mission in the Democratic Republic of Congo (MONUC), and exchange with MONUC information that might be of use in the fulfillment of its monitoring mandate.[87] In the case of the Côte d'Ivoire sanctions regime, the group of experts did the same as in the DRC case vis-à-vis the United Nations Operation in Côte d'Ivoire (UNOCI) and the French force.[88] Furthermore, there is the case of the Liberia sanctions regime in which the Security Council requested the United Nations Mission in Sierra Leone (UNAMSIL) and UNOCI to assist the sanctions committee and the panel of experts by giving any information relevant to the implementation of measures to the committee and the panel.[89]

Monitoring bodies[90]

The Security Council has established monitoring bodies, such as a monitoring mechanism or a monitoring team, in addition to bodies of experts, for monitoring sanctions implementation. Such bodies also have a short-term mandate in general, but indeed tend to operate for a longer term than the bodies of experts. Monitoring bodies are required to report to the Security Council, through the sanctions committee. The functions vary from just collecting additional information on allegations of sanctions violations as an organ succeeding the bodies of experts (UNITA),[91] to making recommendations based on its field-based investigations to the committee (Somalia),[92] as well as playing a more effective role than a monitoring one.

The Taliban/Al-Qaida (ISIL/Al-Qaida, at present) sanctions regime includes a monitoring mechanism comprising a monitoring group and a sanctions enforcement support team, and a monitoring team as an organ that follows. The monitoring mechanism is mandated to observe the implementation of measures, to offer assistance to the Member States bordering the territory of Afghanistan under Taliban control and other States to increase their capacity regarding the implementation of measures, and to collate, assess, verify wherever possible, report, and make recommendations on information regarding sanctions violations.[93] The monitoring team is mandated to submit comprehensive reports to the committee on the implementation by States of measures, including specific recommendations for improved implementation of measures and possible new measures,[94] as well as reporting on listing, delisting, and exemptions, to analyze reports submitted by States to the committee, to assist the committee in preparing its oral and written assessments to the Security Council, and to work closely and share information with the Counter-Terrorism Committee's (CTC's) Counter-Terrorism Executive Directorate and the 1540 Committee's group of experts to identify areas of convergence and to help facilitate concrete coordination between the three committees.[95]

Office of the Ombudsperson

The Office of the Ombudsperson, which was established by Security Council Resolution 1904 and whose mandate was made robust by Resolution 2368, is a subsidiary organ of the Security Council with delegated powers for delisting, although those are limited to the ISIL/Al-Qaida sanctions regime. In particular, the Ombudsperson is mandated to gather information and to interact with the petitioner, relevant Member States, and organizations with regard to the delisting request; to present a comprehensive report to the sanctions committee that contains his/her recommendation to the committee on the request; and to answer committee members' questions regarding the request in the process of the committee's discussion. The committee may overturn the recommendation of the Ombudsperson under certain circumstances, which has not happened to date.[96]

However, the Focal Point for Delisting, which the Security Council requests the Secretary-General to establish within the Secretariat in Resolution 1730, is mandated to receive delisting requests from petitioners other than those whose names are inscribed on the ISIL/Al-Qaida Sanctions List. By definition, however, the Focal Point is not a subsidiary organ.

Some observations from the perspective of the law of international organizations

Now I attempt to observe such developments of subsidiary organs' functions and activities from the perspective of the *law of international organizations*.

First, it is contentious, from the point of *institutional law*, whether said developments of subsidiary organs can alter or have altered the legal relationship between the principal organ and the subordinate organ related to the delegation of powers, in other words, whether there, in fact, any illegal delegation occurred like the delegated powers overriding the powers of the delegating organs. According to a report published by the Security Council Report (SCR), said developments are evaluated in this way: "while they do not have formal authority to make binding decisions, in practice sanctions committees have been delegated substantial tasks, including monitoring, reporting, managing exemptions, and managing designation lists."[97] Certainly, the Security Council sometimes takes action following the recommendations of the sanctions committee or the panel of experts. And the recommendations of the Ombudsperson regarding delisting have never been overthrown by the committee or the Security Council. However, it is appropriate to understand, from a legal point of view, that said powers of the subsidiary organs are nothing but restrictive.[98]

While the committee has played a substantive role in administering the list, there are some cases, for example, in which the Security Council directly decided on the designation of individuals as the sanctions target.[99] With regard to listing, the Security Council usually specifies the designation criteria (listing criteria) in its resolutions, and the committee creates and maintains the list under the criteria.[100] From the legal perspective, there has been no material change to the fact that the Security Council retains the power of final decision vis-à-vis the committee's activities. Therefore, it appears that the relationship of delegation between the principal organ (the Security Council) and the subordinate organ (the subsidiary organs) has not been transformed.

Second, the points related to *operational law*, as stated above, can be divided into problems of decision-making and those of implementation. Subsidiary organs comprising the sanctions regime may substantially influence the process of rectifying the sanctions measures invoked by the Security Council, including the listing management, which may be sorted as those of decision-making. It can be said that there are now more contributions made toward improving the effectiveness of sanctions compared to during the Cold War era. In the context of those related to implementation, there seems to be some development in the expansion and improvement of a monitoring system for putting the sanctions into effect, on the one hand. For example, the ability to collect information has been enhanced, including a site visit, which was not undertaken in the Cold War era. It is also expected that the development of actors involved in activities such as collecting information and determining violations may increase the effectiveness of sanctions implementation, by not only the sanctions committee, which is comprised of the representatives of governments and faces some problems of politicization, but also bodies of experts comprised of persons independent of the governments.

On the other hand, the practice of leaving the task of sanctions monitoring to independent actors, not to the UN itself or the Member States, raises several questions regarding the points of governance and accountability of UN sanctions regimes.[101] In any case, it should be evaluated more carefully how much influence these developments of subsidiary organs have on the effectiveness of sanctions.

Third, from the viewpoint of the Charter framework, which intersects with *institutional law* and *operational law*, there will be discussion points regarding the legal relationship between the UN and the Member States. The points also mean, in other words, whether or not there is any influence on the centrality of decision-making and the decentrality of implementation. Evaluated appropriately, it is necessary to pay attention to not only the problems related to the obligations of sanctions implementation imposed on States but also those concerning the extent of States' discretion in the sanctions regimes. That is, the implementation of any effective sanction is empirically unexpected owing to a large extent of discretion regarding decision-making or implementation left to States, even if said obligations imposed by Security Council resolutions are binding. Therefore, the next section examines the problem of the extent of discretion.

Thus far, subsidiary organs have expanded their functions related to offering assistance to States and monitoring the implementation of sanctions measures by them, as exemplified by the sanctions committees and the bodies of experts having been empowered to visit a site, determine sanctions violations, and review implementation reports. It can be said that the UN itself has developed a kind of "administrative" or "centralized" institutional structure.[102] As a result of the said development, it is understandable that the extent of discretion left to the States has been diminished. As for the listing management, it can be said that "the Security Council nominally identified the targets of these measures or created a UN centralized procedure for such identification."[103] Certainly, in the early years of commencing the listing, there were practices that, as the Security Council "left to individual states to decide which individuals will be placed on the sanctions list, with the effect of obliging all states to apply sanctions to that individual" "the Council effectively approved a unilateral determination by states," which some scholars problematized as undermining the centrality of decision-making by the Security Council.[104] However, the designation of individuals/entities that States have determined should be placed on the list is no longer automatically accepted by the committee. It is likely that this shift has occurred due to the specification of designation criteria (listing criteria) in each Security Council resolution and the issue of committee guidelines that clarify the application process for States (e.g., the necessary use of the standard forms for listing, the requirement of providing a detailed statement of case in support of the proposed listing, including supporting evidence or documents), the listing process for the Committee (e.g., the clarification of designation procedures, the coordination and cooperation with interested States, the Secretariat and regional or international organizations such as INTERPOL, the publication of a narrative summary of reasons for listing), and so on. Namely, "with the listing regime, the Security Council, although not imposing upon States specific ways to comply with sanctions, greatly reduces their margin of appreciation, since they can determine neither the material nor the personal scope of the sanctions."[105]

Under the UN sanctions regimes, in general, Member States have discretion in sanctions implementation. The Security Council resolution imposes on States overall objectives and methods of sanctions implementation, and thereby the uncertainty inherent in the process of embodying them into practice unavoidably engenders some discretion at the States' hands. The wider an uncertain part of sanctions implementation becomes; the more discretion States have. The narrower the uncertainty becomes, the less they have, or the more such discretion is approximate to a kind of ministerial act. The latter is a case in point, which we can see in the development of UN financial sanctions regimes. Moreover, it can be said that it depends largely on the institutional and functional development of subsidiary organs whether States' discretion is diminished or is approximate to a ministerial act in practical terms.

However, such development, which *may* produce the impression that "UN sanctions regimes are close to the administration" or that "the UN system is controlling the entire process of sanctions directly" for us, does not always mean some changes happened in, for example, the legal relationship between the UN and the Member States, and the relationship of delegation between the principal organ (the Security Council) and the subordinate organ (the subsidiary organs). Furthermore, the legal status of States under the UN sanctions regimes has not undergone considerable change by said development. Member States have never become a "subordinate organ" of the Security Council and the committee in a legal sense. If there was an internationally wrongful act of a State that was obliged to implement sanctions measures without any room for discretion, the said act might be attributable to the UN under the framework of responsibility in international law.[106] However, this is not the same situation as that of a State acting through the sanctions regimes being legally regarded as a subordinate organ of the UN. It is not the case that quasi-Article 43 agreements have been concluded between the Security Council and the States, and that they thereby have contracted to enforce sanctions or been explicitly delegated the powers that the Security Council has originally possessed. Also, the Security Council resolutions have not been regarded as having a direct effect on the domestic legal order of States, and there is no change in the structure of sanctions implementation, which necessitates national legislation for bringing into force the obligations imposed by resolutions.[107]

In conclusion, the UN Charter framework regulating the sanctions regime has not been transformed legally. Rather, it seems that institutional and functional developments based on the said framework have diminished Member States' discretion or made it similar to a ministerial act in a practical sense. This should not be regarded as transforming the "decentrality of implementation" in a legal sense, albeit having a politico-practical impact on the UN collective security system judging from enhancing the effectiveness of sanctions.

Conclusion

The effectiveness of UN sanctions is dependent on the extent to which Member States implement those measures, even if States are legally obliged to execute them under the UN Charter. The effects of sanctions might be reduced if States neither cooperated in the sanctions regime nor implemented those measures sufficiently, or if responsible persons such as the political leaders of targeted States slip through the net of sanctions successfully. To that end, the UN itself and nongovernmental organizations have proposed to close sanctions loopholes and thereby enhance the effectiveness of sanctions implementation.[108] On this point, making sanctions more effective necessitates a legal obligation to implement sanctions on the part of States to be secured effectively by institutional capacity-building in the UN. The expansion and improvement of institutional capacity-building have certainly been remarkable in the evolving transformation of sanctions regimes into "targeted" ones. Also, such a development has been connected with some attempts to mitigate the unintended negative repercussions of the sanctions. Stated differently, institutional capacity-building has also been seen in the UN, such as the expansion of the functions of subsidiary organs relating to delisting and the establishment of the Ombudsperson, for the purpose of avoiding the inhumane impact of sanctions.

Through these developments of institutional capacity-building, the Security Council or subsidiary organs have visited sites, determined sanctions violations, and reviewed implementation reports, on the one hand, and have issued many guidelines and set standards for ensuring the fairness and appropriateness of administering the sanctions list, on the other hand. Moreover, the Security Council has published, through the report of an informal working group, the recommended guidelines, criteria, and best practices to be based on their decision-making and implementation by the actors concerned in the sanctions regimes.[109] Formerly, some development was conceived as the expansion of a kind of "administrative function" in counter-terrorism sanctions regimes such as the ISIL/Al-Qaida regime and the CTC.[110] At present, it may be said that the functions and roles of UN-targeted financial sanctions regimes have taken an administrative turn entirely.[111] However, such a transformation into "administrative function," if any, should not be regarded as an appropriate development on the grounds that *remedial law* functions are still undeveloped in the UN sanctions regimes. From the perspective of the *law of international organizations*, to sum up, these developments are as follows: the expansion and improvement of organization (e.g., the establishment and development of subsidiary organs) has occurred under the framework of *institutional law*; the reinforcement and evolution of the framework of *operational law* (e.g., the enhancement of effectiveness followed by institutional and functional developments of the sanctions regimes) has been attempted thereby; and the beginning of efforts to conform to *remedial law* (e.g., coping with requests for assistance from a third state that has incurred economic difficulties arising from the sanctions, and ameliorating the delisting process) have come into view.

Needless to say, comprehensive examinations and reviews are necessary, not only from the viewpoint of invocation but also from those of implementation and application, to evaluate the legal/practical implications of such developments appropriately.

Notes

1 Alain Pellet and Alina Miron, "Sanctions" in *Max Planck Encyclopedia of Public International Law* (http://opil.ouplaw.com/home/EPIL, accessed on 5 August 2019), para. 28.

2 For an overview of listing, see e.g., Security Council Report (SCR), "UN Sanctions" No. 3 (25 November 2013), pp. 8–12 (available at www.securitycouncilreport.org/sanctions/, accessed on 5 August 2019); Lisa Ginsborg, "UN sanctions and counter-terrorism strategies: moving towards thematic sanctions against individuals?" in Larissa van den Herik, ed., *Research Handbook on UN Sanctions and International Law* (Edward Elgar Publishing, 2017), pp. 73–104.

3 Jiro Tanaka, *Yōsetsu Gyōseihō Shinban* [Administrative Law, new edition] (Kōbundō, 1972), pp. 51, 149, 337.

4 Yozo Yokota, *Kokusai Kikō no Hōkōzō* [Legal Structure of International Organization] (Kokusaishoin, 2001), pp. 57–70.

5 Ibid., p. 58. On this point, the definition of "international institutional law" in Schermers and Blokker's book can be regarded as almost the same. See Henry G. Schermers and Niels M. Blokker, *International Institutional Law: Unity within Diversity*, 6th revised edition (Martinus Nijhoff, 2018), pp. 4–5.

6 Yokota, *supra* note 4, p. 66.

7 Ibid., pp. 63–64.

8 See e.g., Tetsuo Sato, *Evolving Constitutions of International Organizations: A Critical Analysis of the Interpretative Framework of the Constituent Instruments of International Organizations* (Kluwer Law International, 1996).

9 Chittharanjan Amerasinghe, *Principles of the Institutional Law of International Organizations*, 2nd revised edition (Cambridge University Press, 2003), pp. 139–140.

10 Ibid., p. 141.

11 See Danesh Sarooshi, *The United Nations and the Development of Collective Security: The Delegation by the UN Security Council of its* Chapter VII *Powers* (Oxford University Press, 1999).

12 Schermers and Blokker, *supra* note 5, pp. 181–192; Amerasinghe, *supra* note 9, pp. 140–141.

13 On this point, see e.g., Prosecutor v. Tadić, Case IT-94-1-AR72, Appeals Chamber, 2 October 1995, para. 38.

14 Schermers and Blokker, *supra* note 5, pp. 185, 192.

15 Beate Rudolf, "United Nations Committee and Subsidiary Bodies, System of" in *Max Planck Encyclopedia of Public International Law* (http://opil.ouplaw.com/home/EPIL, accessed on 5 August 2019), para. 9.

16 Amerasinghe, *supra* note 9, pp. 140–142.

17 August Reinisch and Gregor Novak, "Article 50" in Bruno Simma *et al.*, eds., *The Charter of the United Nations: A Commentary*, 3rd edition (Oxford University Press, 2012), pp. 1389–1396.

18 Jeremy Farrall, *United Nations Sanctions and the Rule of Law* (Cambridge University Press, 2007), pp. 54–55.

19 This committee had been called the Somalia and Eritrea Committee since the adoption of Resolution 1907 in 2009. However, after Resolution 2444 (2018) had terminated the Eritrea sanctions regime, the Committee's name was changed to "Security Council Committee pursuant to Resolution 751 (1992) concerning Somalia."

20 UN Security Council Subsidiary Organs HP, www.un.org/sc/suborg/en, accessed on 5 August 2019.

21 David Cortright, George Lopez, and Elizabeth Rogers, "Targeted Financial Sanctions: Smart Sanctions That Do Work" in David Cortright and George Lopez, eds., *Smart Sanction: Targeting Economic Statecraft* (Rowman & Littlefield Publishers, Inc., 2002), p. 23.

22 The establishment of subsidiary organs is not indispensable (e.g., the case of the 1054 sanctions regime against Sudan). See Farrall, *supra* note 18, pp. 353–357.

23 David Cortright and George Lopez, "Introduction: Assessing Smart Sanctions: Lessons from the 1990s" in David Cortright and George Lopez, eds., *Smart Sanction: Targeting Economic Statecraft* (Rowman & Littlefield Publishers, Inc., 2002), pp. 10–11.

24 Cortright, Lopez and Rogers, *supra* note 21, pp. 35–36.

25 Jeremy Farrall, "Should the United Nations Security Council Leave It to the Experts? The Governance and Accountability of UN Sanctions Monitoring" in Jeremy Farrall and Kim Rubenstein, eds., *Sanctions, Accountability and Governance in a Globalised World* (Cambridge University Press, 2009), p. 200.

26 Vera Gowlland-Debbas, *Collective Responses to Illegal Acts in International Law* (Martinus Nijhoff, 1990), pp. 614–617.

27 Natalie Reid, Sue Eckert, Jarat Chopra, and Thomas Biersteker, "Targeted Financial Sanctions: Harmonizing National Legislation and Regulatory Practices" in David Cortright and George Lopez, eds., *Smart Sanction: Targeting Economic Statecraft* (Rowman & Littlefield Publishers, Inc., 2002), pp. 66–67.

28 In recent years, the Secretariat has developed its support to the Security Council in the design, implementation, and evaluation of the sanctions regimes. However, the need for strengthening its budgeting and staffing on sanctions has still been recognized. See e.g., Security Council 8018th meeting, S/PV.8018, 3 August 2017, pp. 3–5.

29 Cortright, Lopez and Rogers, *supra* note 21, pp. 36–37.

30 Farrall, *supra* note 25, p. 191.

31 See also Farrall, *supra* note 18, pp. 147–157.

32 SCR, *supra* note 2, pp. 6–7.

33 Farrall, *supra* note 18, pp. 148–149.

34 S/RES/820, 17 April 1993, para. 22(a).

35 S/RES/1202, 15 October 1998, para. 14.

36 S/RES/1591, 29 March 2005, para. 3(a)vi.

37 S/RES/1343, 7 March 2001, para. 14(b).

38 S/RES/1533, 12 March 2004, para. 8(b).

39 S/RES/1718, 14 October 2006, para. 12(b).

40 S/RES/1737, 23 December 2006, para. 18(c).

41 S/RES/1970, 26 February 2011, para. 24(h).

42 S/RES/2140, 26 February 2014, para. 19(h).

43 S/RES/2206, 3 March 2015, para. 16(i).

44 S/RES/2374, 5 September 2017, para. 9(g).

45 S/1999/644, 4 June 1999 and S/1999/829, 28 July 1999.

46 Guideline of the committee for the conduct of its work (hereafter cited as "Guideline") (resolution 2140), para. 12(e).

47 "Guideline" (resolution 1533), para. 12(e).

48 "Guideline" (resolution 1591), para. 12(e).

49 "Guideline" (resolution 1718), para. 14(e).

50 S/2002/83, 18 January 2002, para. 15.

51 S/RES/1572, 15 November 2004, paras. 9–10 and S/2005/790, 15 December 2005.

52 "Guideline" (resolution 1970), para. 12(e).

53 "Guideline" (resolution 1988), para. 16(c).

54 "Guideline" (resolution 2127), para. 15(e).

55 "Guideline" (resolution 2206), para. 13(e).

56 S/RES/1474, 8 April 2003, para. 8 and "Guideline" (resolution 751 and 1907), para. 14(c).
57 S/RES/1333, para. 16(f) and "Guideline" (resolution 1267, 1989 and 2353), para. 16(d).
58 S/RES/1374, 19 October 2001, para. 4.
59 S/RES/2060, 25 July 2012, para. 15.
60 S/RES/954, 4 November 1994, para. 12.
61 S/RES/1221, 12 January 1999, para. 9.
62 S/RES/1132, 8 October 1997, para. 9, 10(h).
63 S/RES/1532, 12 March 2004, para. 4(c).
64 S/RES/1343, para. 14(g).
65 S/RES/1572, para. 14(f).
66 S/RES/1718, para. 12(g).
67 S/RES/669, 24 September 1990, preamble.
68 S/RES/748, 31 March 1992, para. 9(f).
69 S/RES/843, 18 June 1993, para. 2.
70 S/RES/917, 6 May 1994, para. 14(g).
71 Farrall, *supra* note 18, p. 144.
72 S/RES/1267, 15 October 1999, para. 6(e).
73 Pellet and Miron, *supra* note 1, para. 40.
74 See also Farrall, *supra* note 18, pp. 147–157.
75 S/RES/1306, 5 July 2000, para. 19(a).
76 S/RES/1343, paras. 19(a)(c).
77 S/RES/1395, 27 February 2002, para. 4, S/RES/1458, 28 January 2003, para. 4 and S/RES/1478, 6 May 2003, para. 25(a).
78 S/RES/1237, 7 May 1999, paras. 6(b)(c).
79 S/RES/1874, 12 June 2009, para. 26(c).
80 S/RES/1973, 17 March 2011, para. 24(c).
81 Farrall, *supra* note 18, p. 167.
82 S/RES/2399, 30 January 2018, para. 32(f).
83 S/RES/2140, para. 21(a).
84 S/RES/2206, para. 18(a).
85 S/RES/2374, para. 11(a).
86 S/RES/1731, 20 December 2006, para. 4(a).
87 S/RES/1533, paras. 10(a)(f).
88 S/RES/1584, 1 February 2005, paras. 7(a)(f).
89 S/RES/1521, 22 December 2003, para. 23.
90 See also Farrall, *supra* note 18, pp. 174–180.
91 S/RES/1295, 18 April 2000, para. 3.
92 S/RES/1519, 16 December 2003, paras. 2(c)(f).
93 S/RES/1363, 30 July 2001, paras. 3–4.
94 S/RES/1526, 30 January 2004, para. 8.
95 S/RES/1617, 29 July 2005, Annex I, paras. (c)(d)(e)(m).
96 Office of the Ombudsperson HP, www.un.org/sc/suborg/en/ombudsperson, accessed on 15 November 2018.
97 SCR, *supra* note 2, p. 7.
98 Andreas Paulus, "Article 29" in Bruno Simma *et al.*, eds., *The Charter of the United Nations: A Commentary*, 3rd edition (Oxford University Press, 2012), p. 999.
99 S/RES/1672, 25 April 2006, para. 1 and S/RES/1737, para. 12 and Annex.

100 SCR, *supra* note 2, pp. 8–10.

101 Farrall, *supra* note 25, pp. 191–214.

102 Nico Krisch, "Article 41" in Bruno Simma *et al.*, eds., *The Charter of the United Nations: A Commentary*, 3rd edition (Oxford University Press, 2012), pp. 1326–1327.

103 Pellet and Miron, *supra* note 1, para. 28.

104 See e.g., Alexander Orakhelashivili, *Collective Security* (Oxford University Press, 2011), p. 212.

105 Pellet and Miron, *supra* note 1, para. 46.

106 See e.g., Report of the International Law Commission, A/66/10, pp. 107–108 (Art.17 commentary (7) and (13)).

107 Krisch, *supra* note 102, p. 1325.

108 Mary Ellen O'Connell, "Debating the Law of Sanctions," *European Journal of International Law*, Vol. 13 No. 1, pp. 67–68.

109 S/2006/997, 22 December 2006.

110 Shuichi Furuya, "Kokusai Terorizumu ni taisuru Kokuren Anpori no Taiō—Rippouteki Gyōseiteki Kinou no Kakudai" [UN Security Council Reaction to International Terrorism: The Expansion of Legislative and Administrative Functions] in Shinya Murase, ed., *Kokuren Anpori no Kinō Henka* [Changing Functions of the UN Security Council] (Toshindo, 2009), pp. 41–55.

111 Pellet and Miron, *supra* note 1, para. 42.

4   Recent challenges regarding the implementation of UN Security Council sanctions

Tomoaki Ishigaki[1]

Introduction: overview of UN Security Council sanctions and issues at stake

Measures imposed by the United Nations Security Council not involving the use of armed force (often referred to as UN sanctions) were modeled after those used during by the League of Nations.[2] Such measures taken by the UN Security Council range from comprehensive trade bans (similar to the ones introduced during the Second World War) to symbolic ones (such as bans on the movement of people and the severing of diplomatic relations), and are considered the most extensive of the Security Council's non-military measures. Article 41 of the UN Charter provides a non-exhaustive list of measures including the "complete or partial interruption of economic relations and of rail, sea, air, postal, telegraphic, radio, and other means of communication, and the severance of diplomatic relations." However, the UN Security Council introduced few measures during the Cold War due to tensions between the United States and the Soviet Union except for the actions against Southern Rhodesia and South Africa. The majority of sanctions measures taken during the Cold War were by western countries against the communist countries in the eastern bloc.

After the end of the Cold War, the UN Security Council started to introduce sanctions measures more aggressively. One of the most notable examples is comprehensive sanctions by the Security Council against Iraq after its invasion of Kuwait in 1990.[3] The measures against Iraq were a *de facto* trade ban, and they were criticized for inflicting considerable damage to the local citizens as well as neighboring trade partners. Consequently, the Security Council started to look for ways to limit the scope of sanctions yet increasing their impact, especially to the leadership of the targeted country. In such processes so-called targeted sanctions were developed.

All UN Security Council sanctions introduced after the Gulf War are targeted sanctions. Specific modalities of UN Security Council measures have been improved and became more sophisticated as methods of evading sanctions had developed.[4] In the meantime, there has been constant criticism of UN Security Council sanctions, aside from their unintended negative impact. Owing to the composition of the Security Council and its decision-making process, a number of developing member states questioned the legitimacy of UN sanctions. Such criticism, as well as frustration with the Security Council, was expressed by the developing member states of the NAM that comprise two-thirds of UN membership.[5]

The development and sophistication of the sanctions measures introduced by the Security Council pose new challenges to the implementing authorities such as customs and export-import authorities of respective UN member states. The globalization of the international economy has increased and diversified modes of transferring goods and money, thus creating more openings for evading sanctions. Individual and unilateral sanctions introduced by respective UN member states also make the implementation process more complex. While individual sanctions contribute to refining the modalities of UN sanctions measures, improving their effectiveness, they can also complicate the process of implementation by other UN member states which are not legally bound by such unilateral measures. Such unilateral measures can be criticized even more for their lack of legitimacy or universality.

Against such a historical and legal backdrop, this chapter examines the three following points. First, the grounds for criticism of UN Security Council sanctions (UN sanctions) by developing members will be examined from a historical perspective. Second, this section will describe the practical difficulties arising from the improvement and strengthening of UN sanctions measures. Third, this chapter will point out the significance of individual sanctions measures introduced by respective states and the complications they could create in implementing UN sanctions. Several financial sanctions will be used as case studies in this context. The chapter intends to indicate pragmatic ways to enhance the effectiveness of UN sanctions measures while ensuring the legitimacy and ownership of each UN member state.

Constant criticism towards the legitimacy of UN sanctions

The legal basis for UN member states to be bound by the sanctions measures decided upon by the Security Council can be found in Articles 24 and 25 of the UN Charter. Article 24 stipulates the Security Council's primary responsibility for the maintenance of international peace and security, and member states' permission for the Security Council to act on their behalf. Article 25 describes the agreement by UN member states to accept and carry out the decisions of the Security Council. Notwithstanding these explicit legal obligations, it is premature to assume that all UN member states find UN sanctions to be their key priorities and that it is necessary to take proactive measures. For instance, the UN sanctions on Iran's nuclear program, considered a critical security issue of global concern, enjoyed limited engagement by member states. One indication can be found in the relatively modest number of reports submitted by member states on their state of implementing sanctions, even though this reporting was legally obligated under relevant UN Security Council resolutions.[6] The lack of a sufficient level of engagement by UN member states cannot be attributed only to insufficient resources or financial constraints. In fact, the composition and decision-making process as well as the political nature of the Security Council are constant sources of criticism raised by many developing members when arguing about the problems related to UN sanctions.

The notion that a group of particular UN member states are obligating other members to take certain actions and the lack of opportunities for the majority of the membership to be involved in the deliberations of such actions has been regarded as a symbol of unfairness among many UN member states, especially in the NAM. It is therefore not surprising that many developing member states find the Security Council does not properly reflect their views, as they do not have permanent representation there. Such views were constantly expressed by the NAM caucus during the Cold War, presenting a powerful position independent from both the western and eastern blocs.[7] Their views were expressed, for example, on the Rhodesia situation[8] as well as on apartheid in South Africa.[9] In both cases, NAM members demanded robust sanctions to be introduced towards these two countries and criticized the Security Council in failing to do so.[10] Throughout the 1980s, the NAM was reluctant to endorse UN-backed sanctions, except for the measures against South Africa. The NAM held the view that the Security Council was an institution which served the interests of western countries (which they viewed as promoting a colonialist and imperialist agenda).

The negative views held by developing countries towards UN sanctions persisted even after the introduction of targeted sanctions in the 1990s. Their cautious approach was evident in the deliberations at summit meetings of NAM members held every three years. In 1992, when countries were seeking a new international order after the Cold War, the NAM leaders' declaration (usually entitled, "Final Document") stressed the need to find an appropriate balance of power between the Security Council and the General Assembly, and expressed more concern on the political use of the Council by a certain group of states than the efficacy of sanctions.[11] In the same declaration, NAM members also criticized the Security Council for being selective in which issues it decides to address, similar to the criticism towards the Council during apartheid in South Africa.[12]

In contrast, the views of NAM members on the Iraqi invasion of Kuwait are much muted. Even though one of its members was attacked, the 1992 NAM leaders' declaration did not denounce Iraq and simply welcomed the end of hostilities among the parties involved.[13] The subsequent declaration in 1995, issued five years after the beginning of sanctions against Iraq, highlighted the economic damages caused by the UN sanctions imposed on Iraq and neighboring countries.[14] While acknowledging NAM members' internal dynamics and political considerations within the organization, it could be surmised that their views towards UN sanctions remained cautious and critical.

Targeted sanctions have developed throughout the 2000s with more specific methods employed to minimize collateral damages and to cause a more significant impact on the leadership responsible for illicit activities, but many developing members continued to maintain critical and negative views towards UN sanctions. Their viewpoint was reinforced when a series of claims was made at various international judiciaries which ruled that UN sanctions, particularly in the Al-Qaida and Taliban sanctions committee, did not provide due process of law towards individuals named in the sanctions list. When the European Court of Justice and the European Court of Human Rights made rulings in favor of such claims, NAM members incorporated a critical assessment of these courts in their leaders' declarations. The NAM summit documents stated that due process of law had to be respected, sanctions had to be applied as a last resort and its mandate and time frame should be clearly defined.[15]

NAM members also held critical views towards the expanded scope of targeted sanctions. They argued that the measures imposed to restrict the proliferation of goods, material and technologies related to the development of weapons of mass destruction (WMDs) could hamper the legitimate goals of developing countries to promote their space and scientific programs.[16] Unilateral sanctions introduced by individual states are viewed even more negatively as NAM members argued their lack of legitimacy. NAM members often describe such individual sanctions as the imposition of political will by powerful nations upon the weak.

Through the development of targeted sanctions, the UN Security Council has had some degree of success in reducing the negative economic impact experienced by ordinary citizens and neighboring countries. This success, however, did not have much impact on mitigating the critical views held by many NAM members. The highly political nature of the Security Council and its composition, combined with the newly emerging issue of due process of law and tension with other international norms, did not contribute to enhancing the developing states' confidence in such sanctions. It is therefore premature to assume that the strict enforcement of UN sanctions would be guaranteed especially when many developing members have some reservations about the legitimacy of these sanctions measures.

A number of practical responses have been made to address criticisms of UN sanctions. The responses include enhancing transparency of the decision-making process inside the Security Council regarding resolutions on sanctions, and improvements in the procedure for the listing and de-listing of individuals and entities on the sanctions list.[17] Changing the political nature of the Security Council cannot be easily achieved, and such characteristics may be needed as the Council remains, albeit with criticisms, the primary organ to address issues relevant to international peace and security and mandated to determine any acts of threat and breach. Also, the nature of threats to global security has diversified in recent years, encompassing issues related to climate change and human rights abuses, and there is a growing expectation among the states for the Security Council to take up more issues related to emerging threats. Given such background, a practical approach to enhancing the legitimacy of UN sanctions would be to improve the transparency of decision-making processes for relevant resolutions so that the content and the degree of obligations become more understandable, thus enhancing ownership of the resolutions among non-Security Council members.

This may seem a roundabout path but it could be the most certain approach to addressing the existing criticisms towards UN sanctions which range from the political nature of the Council, to the lack of transparency and due process.

Expanding the scope of sanctions measures and growing challenges of implementation

The targeted sanctions introduced since the 1990s have been improved and strengthened over the years, expanding their scope and developing a more sophisticated approach in identifying possible loopholes for the illicit transfer of goods and money. A notable example of such a development can be found in financial sanctions as the Security Council needed to respond to the rapidly globalizing economy that diversified methods of financial transactions. In accordance with UN Security Council resolutions, UN member states are obligated to introduce wide-ranging financial regulations to enforce sanctions measures. As the perpetrators of civil war, or proliferators of sensitive nuclear and missile technologies would try to find new ways to evade sanctions, authorities are in constant need of updating their investigation methods and equipping themselves with new legal mandates to prosecute such illicit activities. With regard to the transfer of funds, for instance, a series of new regulations for UN sanctions has been introduced including the banning of bulk cash transfers or enhanced vigilance towards diplomatic pouches.

In addition to providing new legal mandates to regulatory bodies, the UN Security Council, with assistance from members of the panels of experts on the sanctions committees, has expanded the scope of both groups of people who may be at risk for involvement in illicit activities as well as items that can be used in such activities. First, the scope and categories of regulated groups (such as individuals, organizations, and entities) have expanded over the years so as to effectively curb proliferation activities. For example, scientists whose expertise could be used to develop nuclear weapons or ballistic missiles are required to undergo scrutiny if their knowledge may be transferred to the targeted individuals or entities. Additionally, some private enterprises and financial institutions could face charges as their businesses and financial transactions may benefit from illicit activities by procuring items and funds from the targeted states and entities.

Second, the scope of categories and items identified in targeted sanctions under UN Security Council resolutions has also expanded over the years in order to suppress any activities through which targeted individuals, organizations and entities would transfer goods, materials and money illegally. Goods and materials that can be used to develop nuclear weapons or ballistic missile technologies, for example, are listed in relevant UN Security Council resolutions.[18] They are constantly updated by international regulatory bodies such as the Nuclear Suppliers Group or Missile Technology Control Regime which identify various military and dual-use items (such as carbon fiber) that could be used for proliferation activities. In the meantime, proliferators try to circumvent such regulations by using goods and materials that are slightly below the technical specifications of regulated goods and materials. Monitoring and identifying suspicious activities as well as preventing illicit financial transactions require the political will of respective governments and the technical capabilities of authorities involved. Constant changes and the development of sanctions create practical challenges for the regulatory bodies of member states enforcing the obligations under UN Security Council resolutions.

While newly introduced measures add further challenges to UN member states for effectively implementing UN sanctions, some states continue to face difficulties in implementing conventional sanctions measures such as travel bans since they require a thorough understanding of the specific measures to be taken by relevant domestic authorities. One typical example would be the restrictions on the movement of scientists who could contribute to the development of WMDs and their means of delivery. In the cases of UN sanctions towards North Korea and Iran for their nuclear weapons programs, relevant UN resolutions prohibit the provision of technology to scientists who could contribute to the development of nuclear weapons and missiles. Implementation of such obligations could result in limited access to certain areas of research and studies in nuclear and electronic engineering by scientists of targeted states, as well as exchanges between them and scientists of other UN member states. The legal restriction for limiting access may have practical implications, yet it is not easy to identify who could be involved in the nuclear and missile development programs of the targeted states.[19] In areas of export control, various regulations are introduced by the governments and research institutes of respective UN member states to limit the access of those who are involved in the studies of sensitive technologies, but the application of such regulations has posed various challenges.[20]

Similar challenges occur in the area of export control on goods and materials. In particular, industrial machinery, electronic devices and advanced materials like carbon fiber can be used for both military and civilian purposes. Such dual-use items and materials need to undergo rigorous scrutiny so that they are not transferred to individuals or entities connected to the weapons development programs of targeted states. Determining the technical specifications for such items as well as tracking their end users requires technical expertise that may not be easily available to some developing countries.[21]

While the UN Security Council and member states try to impose effective sanctions measures, the targeted entities devise various methods to evade such measures. This cycle, often called a "cat-and-mouse game," is observed particularly in the area of finance where new modes of financial transfers and networks are constantly being developed, requiring authorities to seek better ways of enforcement. A traditional and most common method of sanctions evasion is to use aliases and front companies (also known as "paper companies") and to make it difficult for authorities to track the illicit flow of money to and from targeted entities. Other approaches include the use of bulk cash, and conducting barter transactions between different types of goods and materials of financial value.[22] It is also said that newly developed methods of sanctions include crypto-currency such as bitcoins[23] and underground banks in order to avoid detection by financial authorities.[24] UN member states need to keep up with the pace of so-called "sanctions busters" who constantly create new methods to conceal their trails.

In addition to the need to respond to the constant development in *modus operandi* of sanctions evasion, UN member states are often faced with constraints in financial, human, and technical resources. This particularly holds true for developing member states. For instance, cargo inspections at seaports only cover 2% to 3% of the total volume of trade in order not to block the free flow of goods and materials in global trade. To compensate for the small number of inspections, a risk management approach is utilized where suspicious transactions are detected by processing and analyzing massive amounts of data related to shipment. The same approach is used to monitor transfers of funds as the regulatory bodies identify elements in the sea of data that draw suspicion based on the information related to the senders and recipients of funds. If the authorities of member states are not equipped with such investigative techniques, they face serious challenges in effectively enforcing the regulations required under UN Security Council resolutions.

Developing member states which face difficulty in effectively enforcing sanctions measures can become the targets of illicit activities as the sanction violators as well as organized crime elements often take advantage of insufficient regulations and lax border control for the transfer of goods and money.[25] Using multiple transactions and forged accounts are typical ways of concealing the footprints of governments, individuals, and entities targeted by UN sanctions. In order to confuse and distract the investigations of regulatory bodies, countries, cities and ports with insufficient monitoring and surveillance are used as points of transshipment and transfer. Some developing member states may not have the necessary situational awareness to prevent their ports and financial institutions from being exploited, not for the sake of attacking them but to avoid detection of illicit measures.

In order to support the developing member states with limited resources, some UN bodies try to provide necessary assistance. For instance, under the framework of UN Security Council resolution 1540 (2004) that obligates member states to take necessary measures to prevent non-state actors from proliferating WMDs, a system exists to facilitate matchmaking between states that need capacity-building with those states that can provide expertise and financial support.[26] Also, under UN Security Council resolution 1373 (2001), member states can seek support to enhance their capacity in counter-terrorism measures.[27] These systems, however, are ad hoc and temporary and not sufficient to meet the requirements of the UN sanctions that are evolving. The means to circumvent sanctions are also constantly changing and some developing member states may not find it critical to adapt themselves to such a changing environment.[28]

Against such challenges, the critical awareness among UN member states is of vital importance so as to understand that vulnerable points will be targeted as potential vehicles for sanction violations. Strengthening the relevant regulations in respective member states could reduce the risks of these countries to become possible targets of illicit transfers and sites for the proliferation of WMDs, thus contributing to their national security. Such strengthening of measures could contribute to their national security environment in a broader sense, as they could promote mitigating risks for regional tension and domestic instability, or, efforts to prevent WMD proliferation could support the sustainable development of their economies. In order to enhance the sense of ownership among UN member states to become more actively involved in implementing sanctions measures, it is essential that they would appreciate the positive impact that sanctions measures would have in the broader context of international security rather than in the individual interest of a single member state.

Relationship between individual sanctions and UN sanctions

Targeted sanctions under UN Security Council resolutions can be supplemented and reinforced by individual sanctions introduced by respective UN member states. At the same time, the measures of those states that proactively introduce more sophisticated and complex sanctions measures could not only strengthen the international framework of sanctions implementation but also complicate the process of the Security Council to introduce further measures.

One of the main objectives of the Security Council in introducing sanctions is to determine acts of human rights violations, civil war or the proliferation of WMDs that threaten international peace and security and to adopt measures that all UN member states can utilize to suppress such acts. Given the political nature of the Security Council, however, there has been a number of cases where key members, especially the five permanent members of the Council, could not agree on the assessment of a situation, let alone the measures to be taken. This happened frequently during the Cold War and it is still observed in situations like the civil war in Syria. In such situations of stalemate, some member states that have more critical awareness of the situation in question would introduce sanctions either unilaterally or in partnership with other interested member states.

Such examples can often be found in financial sanctions. In the cases of nuclear and missile development in North Korea and Iran, the United States, European Union and Japan, respectively, devised regulations to prevent financial flows that benefit the proliferators. The scope of measures introduced was much broader than that of UN Security Council resolutions, encompassing a larger number of individuals and entities as well as items and measures to be targeted.[29]

Such individual sanctions introduced by member states can be useful and effective in strengthening UN sanctions. They not only broaden the scope of measures covered in the overall sanctions but also pave the way for the Security Council to add more measures later when there is less tension and fewer disagreements among Council members. In the case of sanctions against North Korea, individuals and entities originally designated on the sanctions list by the United States, the European Union, and Japan were later included in UN sanctions measures. Furthermore, after North Korea's nuclear and ballistic missile tests, the UN Security Council has often incorporated sanctions measures that have already been introduced by individual member states. As such, individual sanctions measures by member states often serve as precursors to the wider and more comprehensive actions taken by the UN Security Council.

Despite such positive aspects of individual sanctions, they continue to receive criticisms from other UN member states, especially from developing states, as seen in the NAM leaders' declarations since the 1990s. Such individual sanctions are often described as politically motivated and lacking legitimacy as other states were not involved in the decision-making.

Looking at the practical challenges caused by individual sanctions, the measures can add another and different layer of regulations if one member state decides to proactively implement sanctions measures. More specifically, measures required for export control, financial regulations, and restrictions on the movement of people regarding WMD proliferation and human rights violations could differ from UN Security Council resolutions to the cooperation towards member states that introduced additional measures. Such possible differences in the measures could affect practical business transactions such as transshipment or the complicated supply-chain network in the global trade of goods and services. If some member states already face difficulty in taking the necessary actions required under UN Security Council resolutions, they could encounter additional challenges if individuals and companies of the states wanted to conduct business with their counterparts from states where individual sanctions are enforced. A third-party state has no legal obligation to undertake measures required by individual sanctions introduced by another state. Nevertheless, if a company of the third-party state conducts business, especially financial transactions, within the jurisdiction of that state where individual sanctions measures are in place, it will still have to find ways to be in compliance with the financial regulations. As such, even if the third-party does not introduce any additional measures in response to individual sanctions, its entities will have to respond, thus making their compliance policies more complex.

It is often observed and criticized that when individual sanctions are introduced ahead of Security Council resolutions, sanctions evaders would respond by diverting their funds in cases of financial sanctions before the universal measures are adopted by the UN Security Council, thus nullifying the impact of UN sanctions. Such a gap in timing could benefit the violators as it could give them more time to adapt to new regulations before they are introduced worldwide through the implementation of the UN Security Council resolutions. Not only for financial regulations, but the proliferators of sensitive technologies could find other means of acquiring relevant equipment that can be used as substitutes for the restricted items banned under individual sanctions.[30]

Even though there is an increasing number of measures devised by sanctions evaders, it is premature to conclude that UN sanctions have lost their significance. It has been pointed out that the designation of targeted individuals and entities by individual sanctions preceding UN Security Council resolutions may reduce the "element of surprise" which is considered important in not allowing sanctions designees to take countermeasures.[31] However, the impact of the universal application of UN sanctions should not be underestimated. Even if the designated individuals or entities would take countermeasures by using new aliases or front companies, the fact that their names are listed on the UN sanctions list demonstrates the intent of the international community's collective will in stopping the illicit activities of such individuals and entities. UN Security Council resolutions would provide the legal grounds for authorities of respective member states to initiate investigations and enforcement based on the UN Security Council's list even when the listed individuals and entities are using pseudonyms.

The UN Security Council may be criticized for its political nature but such characteristics do not undermine its most universal mandate when compared to individual sanctions measures by respective member states. Given the fact that decision-making at the Council may take longer periods of time, the benefits of the complementary role that individual sanctions plays, as well as its contributions towards the further development of UN sanctions measures, should be duly recognized. As for the practical constraints and difficulties faced by member states in implementing the possible overlapping and competing requirements of the Security Council sanctions and individual sanctions, it would be most beneficial in practical terms to enhance exchanges of information, especially regarding ways to identify the listed individuals and entities.[32] The expert panel that supports the work of respective UN sanctions committees also plays an important role in facilitating the communication between the committee and member states. Their expert analyses on the specific measures that need to be taken to prevent sanctions evasions is of great value to the regulatory bodies of member states. The panel members take part in various forms of discussion ranging from open seminars to more discreet dialogues, and such efforts to better communicate with member states should be encouraged.[33]

Conclusion: prospects for more effective implementation of targeted sanctions

This chapter examined the challenges related to the implementation of UN sanctions while providing an overview of the historical and political developments of targeted sanctions. Targeted sanctions were introduced since the 1990s to reduce unintended economic damages to ordinary citizens and neighboring countries and to have greater impact on the leadership responsible for violating international norms. UN sanctions have developed to limit the scope of measures that could be taken by the leadership and relevant entities involved in illicit activities, yet the scope of items and categories of groups continued to expand to ensure the effective implementation of sanctions measures. Such expansion and strengthening of measures affected both developed and developing member states of the UN since the change called for more robust regulations and enhanced capacities of regulatory bodies. The political nature and dynamics within the Security Council also had a negative effect on forging a sense of ownership and solidarity among member states in the implementation of sanctions measures on occasion. Individual sanctions by proactive member states could create additional burdens on other member states as well as private entities conducting business.

This chapter attempted to provide some practical suggestions for improving such a complex environment surrounding the UN sanctions regime.

The basic trend of the Security Council playing a central role in addressing international peace will remain the same and it will continue to take non-military measures including the use of sanctions. Criticisms towards the Security Council will also continue yet there is little argument that the most effective, non-military measures that can be taken by any UN member state is a collective action initiated by the Security Council. This chapter described how individual sanctions have been met with criticism and skepticism for their lack of legitimacy and political nature. The utility of individual sanctions should be acknowledged, in the absence of collective measures by the Security Council, especially in times of internal disagreement within the Council. In the meantime, the limitations of individual sanctions as well as the continuing criticism of UN sanctions should not be overlooked even with the explicit mandate conferred upon the Council by member states. Continuous efforts by the Security Council to improve its decision-making processes to incorporate the wider views of other UN member states are critical to enhancing the legitimacy of UN Security Council resolutions on targeted sanctions. After the adoption of new UN Security Council resolutions, the Council as well as its sanctions committees and their expert panels need to engage in continuous dialogue with member states. As many member states face various challenges in implementing ever-evolving and complex obligations under UN Security Council resolutions, pragmatic discussions and necessary assistance provided to the implementing authorities are the key to improving the effectiveness of such measures.

Notes

1 The author served at the Permanent Mission of Japan to the United Nations in New York from 2010 to 2013 and worked on the sanction issues related to North Korea and Iran as well as disarmament and non-proliferation matters. The content of the chapter is based on his experience at the time in New York as well as when working at the Cabinet Legislation Bureau of the Japanese Government from 2013 to 2016 supervising treaties and international legal matters. The views expressed in this chapter, however, reflect his personal views and may not represent the view of the Japanese government.

2 The Covenant of the League of Nations stipulates in Article 16 that the measures to be implemented against the states in breach of the covenant can be subject to

> the severance of all trade or financial relations, the prohibition of all intercourse between their nationals and the nationals of the covenant-breaking State, and the prevention of all financial, commercial or personal intercourse between the nationals of the covenant-breaking State and the nationals of any other State.

For an overview of the sanctions measures taken by the League of Nations, see Miki Honda, *Kokuren ni yoru Keizai Seisai to Jindo-jo no Sho-kadai—Smart Sanction no Mosaku* [Economic sanctions by the UN and their humanitarian implications—in search of "smart sanctions"] (Kokusai Shoin, 2013) pp. 37–39.

3 The UN Security Council resolution 660 (1990) adopted after the invasion of Iraq to Kuwait denounced the invasion and called for the unconditional withdrawal of Iraqi forces (S/Res/660 (1990) 2 August 1990). The subsequent resolution 661 (1990) demanded all UN member states to import goods from Iraq and Kuwait and to prevent funds from being transferred to Iraq and Kuwait (S/Res/661 (1990) 6 August 1990). The UN Security Council resolution 678 (1990) authorized all UN member states to take all necessary measures including military actions to realize the withdrawal of Iraqi forces from Kuwait)S/Res/678 (1990) 29 November 1990).

4 Since 1966, the United Nations has established 26 sanction regimes and with the exceptions of sanctions imposed on Southern Rhodesia and South Africa, all of them were introduced after the 1990s. They are: Former Yugoslavia, Haiti, Iraq, Angola, Sierra Leone, Somali, Eritrea, Liberia, Democratic Republic of Congo, Côte d'Ivoire, Sudan (two types), Lebanon, North Korea, Iran, Libya (two types), Guinea Bissau, Central African Republic, Yemen, South Sudan, Mali, ISIL, Al Qaida, Taliban (two types). The list is available at www.un.org/securitycouncil/sanctions/information last accessed on 25 November 2019.

5 The Non-Aligned Movement (NAM) consists of 120 member states and 10 observers, as of 2016. These include 53 states in Africa, 39 in Asia, 26 in Central and South America, and 2 in Europe. In addition, 17 observers and 10 international organizations attend their meetings. With regard to the overview of the NAM, various materials are available but the outline of its history and development described by a NAM member can be found in the material issued by the Foreign Ministry of India, available at http://mea.gov.in/in-focus-article.htm?20349/History+and+Evolution+of+NonAligned+Movement, last accessed on 25 November 2019.

6 As of 2015, among the 193 members of the UN, 106 states have submitted reports regarding their status of implementing the obligations under relevant UN Security Council resolutions on Iran. All of the non-reporting members are developing countries. See Tomoaki Ishigaki, "UN Security Council Sanctions and Developing Member States: Its Acceptance and Effectiveness," *Kokusaiho Kenkyu* [Tokyo Review of International Law] No.4 (2016), pp. 89–92.

7 A number of the NAM summit documents criticize the UN Security Council for imposing the political will of a particular group of member states. For more details, see Ishigaki *supra* note 6, pp. 92–93. The subsequent references to the NAM leaders' declarations (Final Documents) are cited from the database compiled by the Middlebury Institute of International Studies. http://cns.miis.edu/nam/index.php/site/documents?forum_id=5&forum_name=NAM+Summits&doctype_id=7&doctype_name=Official+Documents, last accessed on 25 November 2019.

8 For an overview of the Rhodesia situation from 1965 to 1966, see *Waga Gaiko no Kinkyo* No. 11 (1967) [Overview of Japan's Diplomacy] available at www.mofa.go.jp/mofaj/gaiko/bluebook/1967/s42-2-2.htm, last accessed on 25 November 2019. As for the details of sanctions measures taken by the Security Council towards Southern Rhodesia, see Sachiko Yoshimura, *Kokuren Hi-Gunjiteki Seisai no Houteki Mondai* [Legal Issues Concerning Non-military Sanctions of the UN] (Kokusai Shoin, 2003), pp. 113–121.

9 With regard to the basic facts about the sanctions against South Africa, see Yoshimura, *supra* note 8, pp. 121–128. The NAM leaders' declaration in 1983 (paragraph 53) expressed concern for the lack of comprehensive measures by the UN Security Council and called for members not to support the South African regime. It states:

The Conference expressed deep regret that the Security Council has time and again been prevented from imposing comprehensive and mandatory sanctions under Chapter VII of the Charter. It urged all Governments and international organizations to sever contacts with the racist regime of South Africa. The Heads of State or Government called for a cessation of all assistance to South Africa by the International Monetary Fund and other United Nations specialized agencies, as the granting of such assistance and credits has been used by the Pretoria regime to meet its increasing expenditures on military and repressive purposes directed against the majority population.

Also, the preceding declaration in 1973 explicitly criticizes the United States, the United Kingdom, France and Germany for supporting the apartheid regime as shown below.

[The Conference f]urther condemns the continued economic, financial and military assistance given to South Africa by certain NATO powers, in particular the United States of America, France, the Federal Republic of Germany and the United Kingdom, thereby enabling the government in Pretoria to maintain and reinforce its policy of repression and apartheid.

10 See paragraphs 42–50 of the NAM leaders' declaration of 1979. It calls for the oil embargo on South Africa as seen below.

The Conference called upon all non-aligned oil-exporting countries to prohibit the sale of their oil to South Africa and to institute and/or intensify efforts to monitor the final destination of their oil. The Conference further requested the oil-exporting countries of the Non-Aligned Movement to penalize the oil companies guilty of supplying oil to the racist apartheid regimes.

11 See paragraph 32 of the 1992 NAM leaders' declaration, Chapter 2.
12 See paragraph 33 of the 1992 NAM leaders' declaration, Chapter 2.
13 See paragraphs 29 and 30 of the 1992 NAM leaders' declaration, Chapter 2.
14 See paragraphs 59, 172 of the 1995 NAM leaders' declaration, Chapter 2.
15 See Ishigaki, *supra* note 6, pp. 92–99.
16 See Ishigaki, *supra* note 6, pp. 94.
17 For details, see See Ishigaki, *supra* note 6, pp. 107–112.
18 See, for example, S/Res/2094 (2013) 7 March 2013, and S/Res/1929 (2010) 9 June 2010, on North Korea and Iran.
19 The issue of access to sensitive information at advanced research institutions has been discussed and dealt with in a number of countries including Japan. There was a legal case in Japan where an Iranian nuclear scientist was not permitted to study at a university. See Tokyo High Court Case No. Wa-20511, 2011. The outline of the case can be found at the 20 December 2011, issue of *Nihon Keizai Shimbun* available at: www.nikkei.com/article/DGKDZO37423540Q1A221C1CR8000/, last accessed on 25 November 2019. The scientist and the university later settled the dispute and study was subsequently allowed.
20 With regard to the recent cases of handling sensitive information at universities, see "Oubei Shuyokoku no Anzen Hosho Yushutsu Kanri tono Hikaku Kara Miru Waakuni no Daigaku ni Okeru Kenkyu Katsudo no Seiyaku to Kaiketsu no Houkousei ni tsuite" [The constraints of research activities in Japanese universities and the trend of resolving

them through comparative analysis of security-related export control measures in major European and American countries], *CISTEC Journal* No. 148 (2013)

21 The determination of technical specifications includes not only dual-use items but also military equipment such as firearms. For example, the export control authorities may have to determine if the firearms in question will be used for legitimate purposes of maintaining security and public order, or can be used for human rights violations.

22 See paragraphs 11 and 14 of S/Res/2094(2013) 7 March 2013.

23 Yuji Nakamura and Sam Kim, "North Korea Is Dodging Sanctions With a Secret Bitcoin Stash," *Bloomberg Businessweek* (12 September 2017). Dune Lawrence, "North Korea's Bitcoin Play" *Bloomberg Businessweek* (15 December 2017.) Aatif Sulleyman, "Bitcoin Price Surge May be Helping North Korea Raise Money Amid Heavy Global Sanctions" *Independent* (12 December 2017). Ryan Browne, "North Korea Appears to be Trying to Get Around Sanctions by Using Hackers to Steal Bitcoin" *CNBC. COM* (12 September 2017).

24 See JETRO China and North Asia Division, *2016 Nendo Saikin no Kita-chosen Keizai ni kansuru Chousa* [Research concerning the recent North Korean economy], Japan External Trade Organization (March 2017), p. 81.

25 The case of MV *Everest* identified by the Iran sanctions committee raised awareness of the Nigerian authority which discovered a large amount of weapons on board the ship. See Ishigaki, *supra* note 6, pp. 106–107.

26 See Tomiko Ichikawa, "Tairyo Hakai Heiki no Fuakkusan to Kokuren Anpori no Yakuwari" [Non-proliferation of weapons of mass destruction and the role of the UN Security Council] in Shinya Murase, ed. *Kokuren Anpori no Kinou Henka* [Functional Changes in the UN Security Council], Toshindo, 2019, pp. 63–64.

27 See Shuichi Furuya, "Kokusai Terorizumu ni taisuru Kokuren Anpori no Taiou— Rippo, Gyouseietki Kinou no Kakudai" [Responses by the UN Security Council towards international terrorism—expansion in legislative and administrative functions], Murase, *supra* note 26, pp 47–51.

28 Various reasons can be observed for such a lack of awareness among developing countries. They range from the insufficient recognition that the country can be used as a venue for transshipping illegal goods and materials, to the lack of specific knowledge on their obligations under UN Security Council resolutions.

29 With regard to the sanctions against North Korea, the United States requires in principle that any export to North Korea must be subject to approval. Japan prohibits both imports from and exports to North Korea. The UN Security Council resolution 1718(2006) restricts the export of luxury items to North Korea based on the rationale that such luxury items are used as a means to maintain and strengthen a regime that advances its nuclear weapons and missiles program. UN sanctions are introduced separately from Japan's individual measures of a complete trade ban, but they were both introduced around the same time. S/ Res/1718 (2006) 14 October 2006.

30 John Park and Jim Walsh, "Stopping North Korea, Inc.: Sanctions Effectiveness and Unintended Consequences," *MIT Security Studies Program* (August 2016) at http:// web.mit.edu/SSP/people/walsh/Stopping%20North%20Korea%20Inc_Park%20%20 Walsh_FINAL.pdf (last accessed on 25 November 2019). The key observations of Park and Walsh can also be understood from: Jim Walsh and John Park, "To Stop the Missiles, Stop North Korea, Inc.," *New York Times* (10 March 2016).

31 Kiho Cha and Tilo Stolz Wammes, "United Nations Security Council Sanctions and the Rule of Law: Ensuring Fairness in the Listing and De-listing Process of Individuals and

Entities Subject to Sanctions," *Weatherhead Journal of Diplomacy and International Relations*, Vol. 13 (2012), pp. 133–152.

32 It is often observed that new measures under UN Security Council resolutions are adopted only when a major conflict, a large number of civilian casualties, or major developments like nuclear weapons tests took place. This may result in a time gap where no new measures including the addition to the sanctions list can be made. That may also serve as the time when some proactive states introduce their own sanctions measures. In the meantime, it is equally important for the sanctions committees as well as expert panels to continue analyzing the patterns and cases of sanctions violations and to consider possible additions to the list.

33 The visits made by expert panels to relevant member states as well as seminars for technical experts are of great value to enhance the understanding of the specific contents of UN sanctions measures. Japan annually hosts the Asian Export Control Seminar to enhance the capacity of regional experts and invited most recently in February 2017 representatives from the panel of experts on the North Korea sanctions committee. The overview of the Asian Export Control Seminar can be found at www.meti.go.jp/english/press/2019/0304_005.html, last accessed on 25 November 2019.

5 How Japan implements UN financial sanctions[1]

Shunichi Fukushima

Introduction

This chapter reviews how Japan implements United Nations Security Council Resolutions (UNSCRs) and examines the issues related to Japan's approach to UN financial sanctions. In Japan, UNSCRs do not apply directly as a domestic law. Unlike some other countries, Japan does not have a so-called "United Nations Act," through which UNSCRs become enforceable as a domestic law.[2] In contrast, in Japan, UNSCRs are transposed into existing domestic laws, and competent authorities take equivalent measures in a most appropriate and effective manner.

Economic sanctions are diplomatic tools to make designated persons/countries (targets) cease or suspend certain actions that breach international laws or international orders by imposing burdens on economies or economic activities of the targets.[3] Economic sanctions based on UNSCRs can be divided into three groups based on the object of the restrictions: namely, "human beings," "goods," and "financial resources."[4] The following passages provide an overview of how these three types of sanctions are implemented in Japan.

First, sanctions with respect to the movement of human beings are (i) a prohibition on the entry or transit of targeted persons or (ii) a ban on travel by Japanese citizens to a designated country. These measures are mainly implemented by the Ministry of Justice (MOJ) and the Ministry of Foreign Affairs (MOFA), in accordance with *the Immigration Control and Refugee Recognition Act*.

Second, sanctions with respect to the movement of goods are implemented by restricting the flow of these objects to designated countries or regions. Regarding commodities and products, the ways to restrict such flows are by prohibiting the trade of certain items/goods or a complete embargo. The restrictions regarding commodities, products, or technologies are handled by the Ministry of Economy, Trade and Industries (METI) in accordance with *the Foreign Exchange and Foreign Trade Act* (FEFTA). As a supplementary measure to the trade restrictions, inspections of vessels passing through Japan's territorial waters are conducted by the coast guard (the Ministry of Land, Infrastructure and Transport (MLIT) and the customs (Ministry of Finance, MOF) in accordance with the *Act on Special Measures Concerning Cargo Inspections*, and the *Customs Act*, respectively.

Sanctions on travel of human beings and trade of goods are also implemented by prohibiting aircraft or vessels belonging to the targeted country from landing at airports or entering Japanese ports. These measures are being implemented mainly by the MLIT based on the *Aviation Act* or the *Act on Special Measures Concerning Prohibition of Entry of Specified Ships into Ports*, and the MOJ by *the Immigration Control and Refugee Recognition Act*.

Third, sanctions with respect to the movement of financial resources are being implemented in a variety of forms, but the typical ones are those prohibiting targeted persons from (i) disposing or moving their financial asset in Japan (asset freezing) or (ii) transferring the funds to the targeted persons. The MOF administers these measures based on the FEFTA.

Implementation of UN financial sanctions

Overview

UNSCR 253 (adopted in May 1968) is said to be the first UNSCR that introduced financial sanctions. The resolution prohibited making any investment funds or any other financial or economic resources available to the illegal regime in Southern Rhodesia (today, the Republic of Zimbabwe).[5]

Recent UN financial sanctions have taken a variety of forms in terms of their object, ranging from asset freezing to brand new measures, such as the restriction of financial transfers that contribute to certain prohibited activities (e.g., development of nuclear and missile programs); correspondent banking relationships; and establishing a branch or a representative office and others. Such diversification is one of the dimensions of "smart" or "targeted" sanctions, which is a recent practice of the Security Council.[6] Table 5.1 provides a list of recent financial sanctions by the United Nations and the Japanese laws applied.

A brief history of the FEFTA

The FEFTA is Japan's basic law that comprehensively administers cross-border transactions of financial resources, goods, and technologies. In the context of the FEFTA, "cross-border" is defined as between Japan and foreign countries/territories or between residents and non-residents. The FEFTA covers (i) payments; (ii) capital transactions; (iii) direct inward/outward investment; (iv) service transactions; and (v) foreign trade.

Japan's control over cross-border transactions dates back to 1931 when the *Act on the Prevention of Capital Flights* (APCF) was promulgated. The basic legislative structure of the current FEFTA was formulated after World War II by replacing the APCF with the *Foreign Exchange and Foreign Control Act* (FEFCA, the predecessor of the FEFTA) in 1949.

Under the FEFCA, any cross-border transactions remained under the government's control, and they were prohibited in principle. With developments in the Japanese economy from the 1960s through the 1980s, the tight controls

Table 5.1 Major UN financial sanctions measures

Sanctions measures[1] (prohibited acts or transactions)	UNSCRs	Japanese laws implementing the measures
Movement and alteration of Asset (asset freezing)	1267, 1373, 1718, 2231	FEFTA
Flow of funds contributing to designated activities	1874, 2231	
Provision of financial services (including insurance services)	1874, 2321	
Provision/maintenance of correspondent banking services	2270	
Transfer of precious metals	2270	
Bulk cash transfer to a designated country	2094, 2321	
Supply, sale, or transport of petroleum products	2375	
Procurement of certain items from targets country	2375	
Investment	2375	
Opening and operation of a bank in the designated country	2270	Banking Act[2]
Opening and operating branches of a bank in member country's territory	2270	

1) Only mandatory measures in each UNSCR are listed here. The most updated list of measures currently effective is available at www/mof.go.jp/international_policy/gaitame_kawase/gaitame/economic sanctions/list.html (accessed on December 4, 2019).
2) The Banking Act and its regulations per se do not identify the targeted countries. Opening a bank branch or starting a bank operation is subject to the Prime Minister's permission. The provisions concerning such banking operations are being handled in this permission system.

were gradually eased, and the current system was established following two comprehensive amendments in 1980 and 1998. As opposed to the FEFCA, the FEFTA applies a principle that foreign exchange, foreign trade, and other cross-border transactions are free from restrictions (Article 1), and authorizes a competent minister(s) to introduce restrictions only in certain emergency/exceptional situations in which restrictions are necessary and justified in view of national security or foreign exchange situation in Japan (see Table 5.2).

When the FEFCA was enacted in 1949, it was considered that "stability of the foreign exchange system can be achieved through foreign trade control"[7]; therefore, the FEFCA introduced a system by which transfers of both financial assets and goods are administered by a single piece of legislation. In those days, the government administered foreign exchange reserves and import was subject to authorization based on budget allocations under the Foreign Currency Budget System. With this in mind, a rationale for controlling both foreign exchange and foreign trade in a single law existed at that time. Japan abolished the budget system in 1964 when it became an Article 8 member of the International Monetary Fund. Since then, the regulations on foreign exchange transactions and foreign trade started to follow different paths.

In general, foreign trade in Japan is administered in view of a supply-demand balance of certain goods or the production capacity of certain goods. In the

Table 5.2 Acts and transactions subject to the FEFTA

Acts/Transactions	In principle	Restrictions	Grounds to impose restrictions
Payments (16)	Ex post fact reporting (55)	License (16)	1. For the sincere fulfillment of obligation under treaties or other international agreements
Capital transactions (20)	Ex post fact reporting (55-3)	License (21, 24)	2. To enable Japan to contribute to international efforts to achieve international peace
Service transaction (25)		License (25)	3. To maintain peace and security in Japan 4. Smooth management of the Japanese economy is significantly adversely affected
Outbound direct investment (23)	Prior notification (23) / Ex post fact reporting (55-3)	Order to alter or discontinue the investment (23)	1. Smooth management of the Japanese economy is significantly adversely affected 2. International peace and security are impaired 3. The maintenance of public order is disturbed
Inbound direct investment (26, 27)	Prior notification (27) / Ex post fact reporting (55-5)	Order to alter or discontinue the investment (27)	1. National security is impaired 2. The public order is disturbed 3. The public safety is hindered 4. Smooth management of the Japanese economy is significantly adversely affected
Export/Import of cash and precious metals (19)	Prior notification (19)	License (19)	To assure enforcement of provisions of the FEFTA

(Note) the number in parenthesis is the number of articles of the FEFTA.

meantime, trade control of arms and items that can be diverted to military use in accordance with international regimes established after World War II. The major regimes are (i) the *Coordinating Committee for Multilateral Export Controls (COCOM)* concerning high-technology items; (ii) the *Nuclear Suppliers Group (NSG)* concerning items related to weapons of mass destruction (WMD); (iii) the *Australia Group (AG)* concerning chemical and biological weapons; and (iv) the *Missile Technology Control Regime (MTCR)* concerning missile technologies. With the end of the Cold War, the restrictions based on the *COCOM* were replaced by the *Wassenaar Arrangement (WA)*, where the regulatory regime is fundamentally represented by "catch-all" measures.

In contrast to such export control regimes, no equivalent international regime exists for financial transactions. Export control focuses on the character or nature of individual goods or technologies. It is possible to identify, to a certain degree, specific goods or technologies that could be used for prohibited activities (e.g., nuclear or missile programs) by their nature and usage. In contrast, money has no such color in general. Effective restrictions on financial transactions require the collection and analysis of information, such as the purpose of the transaction or money transfer, the nature of individuals/entities being involved in the transactions, the destination or origin of the money, the ultimate beneficiary of the money transfer and a rationale for the transaction. The process of identifying such risk factors and assessing the magnitude of risk is known as a risk-based approach, which is recognized as a principle of anti-money laundering, countering of financing for terrorists and proliferation of WMD.

Such different paths that regulations on trade and financial transactions have followed in the history of the FEFTA may result from fundamental differences in nature between goods and financial assets. As opposed to trade control, financial regulations are difficult but at the same time dynamic. Considering such fundamental differences between trade and financial transactions, there is an argument in Japan that the FEFTA should be separated into a specific law on trade and finance. Foreign exchange control is abolished, and the linkage between trade and foreign exchange is not as clear and simple as it used to be. Having said this, few urgent and substantive needs to separate chapters of trade and finance into individual laws are recognized in practice.

Types of regulations under the FEFTA

The bulk of the financial sanctions are implemented by applying the FEFTA as shown in Table 5.1. The provisions on payments and capital transactions are mainly applied so as to implement financial measures under UNSCRs.

In the FEFTA, "payments" (Article 16) can be defined as an act of a transfer of payment means such as cash or other acts that have equivalent economic and legal effects to settle claims/debt obligations. Bank remittance is a typical payment form; however, other types such as physical provision/receipt of payment means and set-off of claims (credit) and obligations (debt) are also included in payments.

A "capital transaction" (Article 20) is an act that involves the occurrence, alteration, or extinction of financial claims. Typical transactions are contracts on money deposits, money lending, obligation guarantees, and financial derivatives.

Asset freezing is a measure most frequently used in UN financial sanctions. Although the FEFTA has no concept of "freezing" or "blocking" *per se*, it achieves economic and legal effects equivalent to the asset-freezing measure by imposing an obligation to apply for a license when making payment to/by and capital transactions with the targeted persons.

The license system of capital transactions is mainly used to prohibit a bank deposit contract with the designated persons (i.e., opening a deposit account, withdrawing from a bank account, and transferring money to/from the account belonging to the designated targets), and money lending to the designated persons.

To ensure enforcement of the license system, the FEFTA also has a provision to restrict physical cross-border movement (hand carrying) of cash and precious metals through another license system of the Finance Minister (Article 19). This measure is currently used to prohibit bulk cash transfers to the Democratic People's Republic of Korea (DPRK) in accordance with UNSCR 2094.[8]

In addition to payment and capital transactions, the FEFTA has provisions concerning (i) an acquisition of securities issued by foreign entities (outward direct investment, Article 23); (ii) an acquisition of securities of Japanese entities by foreign investors (inward direct investment, Article 27); and (iii) service transactions between resident and non-resident (provision of labor or benefit, Section 5 of Article 25).

These provisions have not been applied very often to implement UNSCRs, unlike the provisions concerning payment and capital transactions. This is because either direct investments or service transactions accompany and end up with the transfer of funds/money.[9] The types of restrictions and their individual grounds to impose the license obligation are summarized in Table 5.2.

Grounds for license requirement under the FEFTA

The FEFTA provides three grounds to authorize competent minister(s) to impose "license requirements" for payments and capital transactions. The first ground is "when the competent minister[10] deems necessary for the sincere fulfillment of obligations under treaties or other international agreements which Japan has signed" (Article 16). This ground is only applied to implementing mandatory operative paragraphs (OPs) of UNSCRs (i.e., paragraphs starting with "*decides*").

In the meantime, non-mandatory paragraphs of UNSCRs starting with "*calls upon*" are implemented by applying the second ground of the FEFTA defined as "when [the competent minister] deems particularly necessary to enable Japan to contribute to international efforts to achieve international peace." This is often called the "ground of international cooperation."

This second ground was introduced following Japan's bitter experience during the Gulf crisis in 1990. When the Iraqi government led by Saddam Hussein invaded Kuwait on August 2, 1990, the Group of Seven (G7) member countries except for Japan (i.e., Canada, France, Germany, Italy, the United Kingdom, and the United States) spontaneously imposed asset-freezing measures against Iraq and Kuwait in an effort to preserve assets and properties plundered from Kuwait. Because the FEFTA, being enacted at that time, only had the first ground, Japan could not join other G7 members in conducting the concerted asset-freezing measures. Four days later (August 6, 1990) Japan could implement compulsory asset-freezing measures based on a mandatory provision (OP 4) of UNSCR 661. During that period, however, the Japanese government introduced administrative guidance for local financial institutions (FIs) as a substitute. The Ministry of Finance asked FIs to apply *de-facto* asset-freezing measures by conducting enhanced due diligence for transactions regarding Iraq and Kuwait. Given this experience, the FEFTA's second ground on international efforts was added on the occasion of the amendment thereafter.

The ground of international cooperation has become more important and is frequently used, as reflected in recent situations in which the UN Security Council does not function especially when the five permanent (P5) members of the UN Security Council fail to reach consensus (e.g., sanctions against Russia and Syria). In practice, the term "international effort" used to be strictly interpreted, and the provision was applied only when all the G7 members take the same or an equivalent measure. In recent measures against Russia and the DPRK, however, a more flexible interpretation has been applied.

The third ground is provided as "when it is particularly necessary in order to maintain peace and security in Japan" (Article 10, Section 1). The Cabinet may decide measures provided in the FEFTA when they find a certain situation fulfills this ground. This ground was introduced when the FEFTA was revised in 2004 with a proposal of multiparty Diet members in response to an increasing threat posed by the DPRK. This ground enabled a competent minister(s) to impose sanctions without the international framework that the first and second grounds require. This ground is currently applied only to a complete ban on trade with the DPRK.

Measures to ensure enforcement of the license system

No laws would work unless their enforcement is ensured. The enforcement of the license system concerning payments and capital transactions under the FEFTA is ensured in two ways.

The first way is criminal penalties applied to those breaching certain provisions (Chapter 9 of the Act). The second way is the "confirmation obligation" which is imposed on FIs. The FEFTA (Article 17) obliges FIs to confirm whether the customer obtains the license when the payment/transaction needs the license of a competent minister.

This confirmation obligation is imposed on FIs based on the notion that a cross-border transaction ends up with a bank remittance to/from foreign countries or the selling/purchasing of currencies between resident and non-resident. The FEFTA utilizes FIs as a "gatekeeper" to ensure enforcement of the license system. FIs' compliance with this obligation is supervised by both on-site inspections and off-site monitoring (e.g., mandatory reporting requirement and supervision) conducted by the MOF. When the Finance Minister finds an FI not being fully compliant with the obligation, the minister may issue an order to fulfill the obligations (Article 17.2). FIs not properly following this rectification order would be subject to criminal penalties (Article 70).[11]

The FEFTA as basic legislation for UN financial sanctions

As described under section "A brief history of the FEFTA", the FEFTA was originally designed to implement foreign exchange controls and to restrict cross-border transactions, mainly for economic reasons, such as the stability of foreign exchange rates and the maintenance of the equilibrium of the international balance of payments of Japan.

The FEFTA was recognized as a basic law to implement asset-freezing and other financial sanctions in 1999 when the UN Security Council adopted Resolution 1267. The continuous designations of terrorists based on UNSCR 1267 and its successor resolutions made asset-freezing measures one of routine tasks of FIs. UNSCRs concerning proliferation financing, which the UN Security Council adopted intermittently since 2006 further strengthened such measures (e.g., UNSCR 1737 and its successor resolutions concerning Iran and UNSCR 1718 and successor resolutions concerning the DPRK). With these UNSCRs, several individuals and entities were frequently and continuously designated by the UN Sanctions Committee. As a result, the FEFTA came to be recognized as basic legislation to fulfill these obligations.

This was not what the MOF, one of the principal ministries that administers the FEFTA, anticipated at the outset. The MOF considered the asset-freezing measures based on the FEFTA only as a temporary and transitional measure until a more comprehensive legislation exclusively designed for asset-freezing measures is established. In early 2001, representatives from relevant ministries and agencies attempted to explore a new mechanism for implementing asset-freezing measures against terrorists, and they shared the view that comprehensive legislation would be necessary. At the end of the day, however, this discussion did not come to such conclusion, partly because (i) an urgent need existed to promptly respond to asset-freezing measures intermittently designated by the UN or G7 members; and (ii) all terrorists designated at that time were non-Japanese who were highly unlikely to live or hold assets in Japan.

Limitations of the FEFTA

Whenever a new UNSCR that contains decisions on mandatory financial measures is adopted, relevant ministries and agencies led by the MOFA examine the text of the resolution to determine how the provisions can be implemented in Japan. This process involves a comprehensive and thorough review under existing laws and regulations in force, including administrative measures. Since the implementation of an UNSCR is to some extent left to member countries' discretion, this review process always faces a dilemma between compliance with each provision of an UNSCR and challenges arising from the domestic legislation and administrative system. The question is to what extent the provisions of an UNSCR should be domestically implemented. This issue stems from Japan's legislative system in which no UNSCR is directly applicable to the Japanese citizens. Examples of this dilemmas are (i) consistency between the measure(s) that UNSCRs oblige and the legal framework under the Japanese Constitution; (ii) consistency with existing legislations; (iii) the expected level of enforcement (or enforceability); (iv) anticipated burden on FIs and their customers; (v) impact on ongoing transactions (contracts agreed prior to the adoption of the UNSCR); and (vi) a litigation risk posed by those designated persons and others who claim to have suffered loss or damages by the restrictive measures.[12]

In addition, the FEFTA has its own limitations stemming from its inherent nature. Among others, the scope and the enforcement mechanism are critical in relation to the implementation of UN financial sanctions.

Scope

The FEFTA covers financial transactions between residents and non-residents, payments from Japan to foreign countries, and capital transactions denominated in foreign currencies. In the meantime, UNSCRs are applied to all nationals of the member country, and they do not care about the "residency" of the targets or persons conducting transactions with the targets.

While the FEFTA regulates money transfers (i.e., transfer of the payment methods and settlement of credit and debt obligations), the scope of the UNSCRs is much broader: UNSCR 1267 uses the term "funds and other financial resources" (paragraph 4(b)); and UNSCRs 1373 (paragraph 1(c)) and 1718 (paragraph 8(d)) use the term "funds and other financial assets or economic resources."

In 2008, the Financial Action Task Force (FATF) conducted its third round of mutual evaluation of Japan, and they pointed out that the narrow scope of the FEFTA does not fully comply with a FATF Recommendation (Special Recommendation III, today's Recommendation 6) that requires FATF members to fully comply with the financial provisions of UNSCRs 1267 and 1373. To remedy the deficiency, Japan promulgated and enacted the *Act on Special Measures Concerning International Terrorist* in 2014. This new Act authorizes the National Public Safety Commission to freeze assets belonging to individuals categorized as "designated terrorists" by UN Sanctions Committees. The new Act freezes the assets of all nationals in Japan regardless of their residency. It is also applied to securities, precious metals, real estate, automobiles, vessels, and aircraft.

Having said this, UNSCRs' provisions of asset freezing against non-terrorists such as those engaged in the WMD programs of the DPRK or Iran (i.e., proliferation financing) are not within the scope of this Act, and the FEFTA remains applied.

Confirmation obligation

As previously described, the FEFTA obliges FIs to confirm whether customer and transaction fulfill requirements under the FEFTA, but not all cross-border financial transactions are made via FIs. A good example is set-off of credit and debt obligations, which can be completed through a bilateral agreement between a creditor and a debtor.

The FEFTA is applied based on the legal and economic effect of individual payment or transactions rather than the route that money or other payment methods followed. Here is an example (see Figure 5.1): person "A" living in Japan makes a payment to person "B" in the DPRK via person "C" living in the People's Republic of China (China). Although the payment is being made

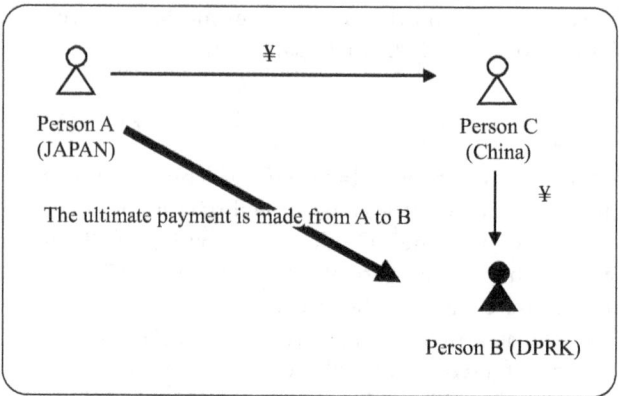

Figure 5.1 The scope of payment in the FEFTA.

via person C's bank account in China, the FEFTA considers that the ultimate payment was made from A to B. In this case, if the payment is subject to the Finance Minister's prior license, person A must apply for a license before making the payment.

If person "A" did not obtain the license in advance, the person would be accused of a breach of the FEFTA. Although the FEFTA's license system applies in this way, this accusation would not be sufficient to fulfill the provision of UNSCRs that aim at proactive restriction of funds provided/transferred to a targeted person(s). In addition, with the recent evolution of "fintech" (new financial services using information technologies), financial transfers without using FIs (e.g., as settlements with crypto-assets and fundraising by way of "crowd-funding") are expected to become ubiquitous, and legislation including the FEFTA needs to keep up with such developments.

In relation to virtual asset, the FATF revised its Recommendation (Recommendation 15) and obliged virtual asset service providers (VASPs) to abide by the asset-freezing measures applied to FIs.[13] While this is innovative progress, this application is based on a hypothesis that virtual asset also travels as wire transfers between banks. In the light that not all virtual assets transfer is conducted via VASPs (i.e., peer-to-peer, or "P2P"), effectiveness of such an approach is questionable.

Concept of the Comprehensive Sanctions Act

Against the backdrop of such limitations, critical views exist on the current way that UNSCRs implemented, such as "the application of existing laws is 'patch-work' and does not efficiently and precisely cover provisions of UNSCRs"[14] or "it is questionable whether the current approach is sufficient to fulfill provisions of non-military measures under Chapter VII of the UN Charter."[15]

At the same time, critics are developing alternative proposals such as "more comprehensive legislation designed to fulfill non-military sanctions decided by the UN"[16] or "a law that authorizes the administrative branch to implement the UN Security Council's decisions on economic sanctions"[17] is necessary.

Additionally, considering the recent trend in which the UN Security Council introduces brand new financial measures, as shown in Table 5.1, responding by amending the existing laws or by adopting a new *special treatment act*[18] whenever a new UNSCR is adopted seems somewhat unrealistic. Such an approach would even impair the framework of Japan's legislative system. The question is how such a comprehensive law or enforcement mechanism could be designed. At least two points should bear in mind: (i) how enforcement can be ensured, and (ii) restrictions should focus on activities or transactions in its substance rather than on types of payment methods used.

As regards enforcement, an independent organ with competent authority and mandate needs to be established. Currently, the MOFA plays a similar role, but the ministry/agency in charge of specific laws takes substantial and exclusive mandate for its implementation, which surpasses MOFA's coordination power. Such a situation in which there is an absence of a commander-in-chief results in a patchwork of individual measures.

As regards the focus of restrictions, measures based on payment methods would not be sustainable as a new payment method continuously emerges, and more importantly, a supervisory organ could differ by payment instrument, which could impair effective coordination.

As such, it would not be too early to consider a law which could be replaced by the current FEFTA, but no comprehensive picture has yet been drawn.

A comparison with the US sanctions system

This section compares the FEFTA with the sanction regime of the United States and attempts to draw lessons for designing effective financial sanctions. The United States implements a variety of sanctions in accordance with UNSCRs as well as unilateral foreign policies. The entire picture can be seen in the Office of Foreign Assets Control (OFAC)'s website.[19] Differences of sanctions programs between Japan and the United States can be seen in various fronts including degree, scope and legislation, but the most significant difference exists in the mechanism for initiating sanctions measures.

Under the US legal system, UNSCRs are incorporated into domestic laws through the *United Nations Participation Act* (UNPA). Section 5(a) of the UNPA refers to Article 41 of the UN Charter and authorizes the President of the United States to implement specific measures accordingly. Unilateral financial sanctions of the United States are based on several statutes, and among others, the *International Emergency Economic Powers Act* (IEEPA) plays a fundamental role in numerous financial sanctions programs.

Under the IEEPA, the US President declares an emergency when he believes there is "a continuing threat to national security, foreign policy, and economy of the United States and a disturbance of the international relations of the United States exists" (Article 1701). With this declaration, the IEEPA authorizes the US President to implement measures stipulated in Article 1702, namely, the prohibition of foreign exchange transactions and asset-freezing. The details of the measures are prescribed in Executive Orders (EO) and regulations implementing the EOs.

A typical feature of the US sanctions regime is that the President first identifies a "threat to the US," and then decides measures to prevent and mitigate the threat. In contrast, such an assessment process is not clearly established in Japan, at least in implementing the FEFTA. While the third ground of the FEFTA (Article 10) is based on Japan's own initiative to apply restrictive measures, it is not necessarily clear: (i) who leads the assessment of the situation concerning peace and security in Japan; and (ii) who decides the rationale for measures responsive to the situation.

Conclusion

Economic sanctions could be punitive to responsible targets in economic terms, but they could also function to protect country (e.g., its economy and financial system) from being abused. This is what is often classed as "economic security."

When it comes to a discussion of national security in Japan, attention is given to issues such as military power or defense equipment rather than its economic fronts. It would be important to bear in mind that national security concerns not only life and death of the national citizens but also much broader issues, including tangible and intangible assets held by the citizens, land or territory of a country, infrastructure, stable economy and sound financial system as a whole.

The current system based on the FEFTA demonstrates that Japan's legal system and its implementation mechanism designed for protection of the national security are insufficient and are still at an early stage. A priority would tend to be placed on "symptomatic therapy" that takes care of immediate impediments as described in section "Limitations of the FEFTA", but defining the national security in Japan's context and identifying its elements should be the first. Redesigning the current approach to UN financial sanctions needs to be considered in this comprehensive picture. One must see the wood for the trees.

Notes

1   In this chapter, "UN financial sanctions" is defined as financial sanctions in accordance with UNSCRs.
2   For example, Australia and Singapore have a law called the "United Nations Act."
3   Hufbauer, Schott, Elliott, and Oegg analyze that economic sanctions have the following policy goals: (i) change target country's policies in a relatively modest and limited manner; (ii) change the target country's regime; (iii) disrupt a military adventure; (iv) impair the target country's military potential; and (v) change the target country's

policies in another major way. Gary Clyde Hufbauer, Jeffrey J. Schott, Kimberly Ann Elliot, and Barbara Oegg, *Economic Sanctions Reconsidered* (Peterson Institute, 2007), pp. 52–53.

4 Types of economic sanctions can be classified in various ways. For example, Farrall first classified sanctions by "a range of prohibitions" (i.e., economic and financial sanctions vs. non-economic sanctions) and then by a range of targets (e.g., single state, multiple states, de facto states, failed states, sub-states, extra-states, and individuals as targets). Jeremy M. Farrall, *United Nations Sanctions and the Rule of Law* (Cambridge University Press, 2007), pp. 106–107.

5 OP.4 of UNSCR 253.

6 Farrall, *supra* note 4, p. 143.

7 Shigeki Ito, Keiji Ono, and Kunio Shoji, *Chūshaku-Tokubetsu-Keihō* [Commentary to Special Criminal Acts], Volume 5.1 (Tachibana-Shobō, 1986) p. 438.

8 OP. 14. Although this paragraph is not considered mandatory, Japan takes a proactive approach.

9 This does not neglect the effects of the restrictions. In the meantime, it should be considered who could possibly regulate at the time of a contract. Unless someone functions as a gatekeeper, the prohibition at the time of the contract has no effect.

10 The competent ministers for the FEFTA are the Finance Minister for provisions on financial transactions and the Minister of the METI for trade-related payments and transactions and technology transfers.

11 The penalty is imprisonment for not more than three years, a fine of not more than 1 million yen, or both.

12 Many UNSCRs have a provision that "no claim shall lie in connection with any contract or other transaction where its performance was prevented by reason of the measures imposed by [this] resolution or previous resolutions" (UNSCR 2270 (March 2, 2016)). It is unclear, however, whether a court applies this provision as a domestic law when it comes to a litigation.

13 FATF Methodology 2013 (Recommendation 15), www.fatf-gafi.org/publications/mutualevaluations/documents/fatf-methodology.html (accessed on December 3, 2019)

14 Masahiko Asada, *Kitachōsen no Kakukaihatsu to Kokuren no Keizai-seisai* [Nuclear Development of North Korea and UN Economic Sanctions], *Ronkyū Jurist* (2016), p. 105.

15 Sachiko Yoshimura, *Kokuren-hi-gunjiseisai no Hōtekimondai* [Legal Issues concerning UN Non-military Sanctions] (Kokusaishoin, 2003), p. 267

16 Ibid., p. 267.

17 Asada, *supra* note 14, p. 106.

18 In Japan, an Act on Special Measures (*Tokubetsu-sochi-hō*) is one of the legislative methods to cover a temporary measure. For example, the Act on Special Measures concerning Cargo Inspections, etc., was promulgated to fully implement cargo inspections requested by UNSCR 1874 (June 12, 2009). Once UNSCR 1874 is terminated, the Act is to be abolished.

19 OFAC, Sanctions Programs and Country Information, www.treasury.gov/resource-center/sanctions/Programs/Pages/Programs.aspx (accessed on November 26, 2019).

6 Implementation of financial sanctions by a state and its legal challenges

The case of sanctions-related laws of the United States

Takashi Kubota

Introduction

This chapter considers the implementation of financial sanctions by a state and its legal issues from the perspective of an international transaction law with the sanctions-related laws of the United States at the center.

What are financial sanctions?

Financial sanctions are a type of economic sanctions where financial penalties are imposed against a state that violated international rules. Financial sanctions do not function well politically unless all five member states of the United Nations Security Council (UN Security Council) are unanimous. Oftentimes the UN Security Council members form conflicting camps with the United States and Europe on one side and China and Russia on the other. A UN Security Council resolution that leads to effective financial sanctions is challenging (many countries refuse to implement the resolution even if it is passed). Conversely, the United States implements many financial sanctions on its own, and often asks Japan to cooperate, against countries with which Japan has a limited relationship as seen from Japan's forced alignment with the United States. Aside from the UN Security Council, there is peer pressure from coalitions of countries, such as the G7 on Financial Action Task Force (FATF) recommendations (peer reviews by member states, public announcement of sanctions by country name) in measures against money laundering and combating the financing of terrorism (AML/CFT).[1] Additionally, even within the United States and Europe, countering laws are directed at each other if there is significant conflict of interests among countries implementing sanctions. For example, the EU activated a countering law that mitigates the impact of the American sanctions on Cuba to the EU region through EU Council Regulation No. 2271 (EC2271/96) in 1996.[2]

Financial sanctions include asset freezing, prohibition of investments, regulations on correspondent arrangements and branch opening by banks, severing financial communications, such as the Society for Worldwide Interbank

Financial Telecommunication (SWIFT), and the removal of foreign banks from the financial markets of countries that violated sanctions. While these are all powerful means of economic sanctions, many issues still remain with respect to their effectiveness. The types of financial sanctions include: (1) sanctions through a resolution by the UN Security Council (United Nations Charter Article 25, Article 41), (2) sanctions without UN Security Council resolutions, or sanctions by a coalition of countries that aim to complement UN sanctions through international cooperation (multi-sanction scheme), and (3) sanctions by a single country. The Iranian case introduced in this chapter is a classic case in which all three types of sanctions have been used.

Contents of this chapter

This chapter first introduces the contents of a book that analyzes the actual state of financial sanctions from the US perspective by Zarate, former deputy assistant to the president, in the first section. Then, a description of domestic laws on financial sanctions with a comparison of US and Japanese laws in the second section. The third section introduces the case of Iranian sanctions, and finally, the fourth section brings together legal issues of sanctions by a state (extraterritorial applicability) and discusses several issues surrounding the effectiveness of financial sanctions, for example, the adverse effects of concentration in US dollars and the impact of blockchain on transactions.

The rationale for financial sanctions by the United States

This section briefly introduces Juan C. Zarate's *Treasury's War: The Unleashing of a New Era of Financial Warfare*,[3] an analysis of financial sanctions used by the United States. The author served as the Assistant Secretary of the US Department of Treasury (Terrorist Financing and Financial Crimes) and as deputy assistant to the president (in-charge of anti-Terrorism and National Security) during George W. Bush's administration and directed financial sanctions against Al Qaida, Iran, North Korea, and so on, after 9/11. He calls it "the hidden war" as the author sees financial sanctions as a new approach to waging war against enemies in the future based on his experiences (see Prologue: "The Hidden War"). In the case of Banco Delta Asia (BDA) in Macau, which had a transactional relationship with North Korea, the United States prohibited any transactions with American financial institutions, and it became de facto impossible for BDA to make payments in US dollars and be able to conduct international financial business. In the financial sanctions against Al Qaida immediately after the 9/11 terrorist attacks of 2001, the first issue for the United States government was to obtain information on bank transactions of sanction targets (useful for sanctions against past terrorist suspects as well as preventing future terrorist attacks), in which SWIFT, the international remittance infrastructure, cooperated. Additionally, the government was able to obtain the cooperation of private banks that handle primary information for financial transactions, as overlooking "suspicious financial transactions" would lead to compromising reputation. The author provides rich, diverse examples, and concludes that, to maintain its influence, it is important for the United States to: (1) retain a hegemonic position on US dollars as the key currency of the world, (2) deal with structural risks of the American economy that was too dependent on investments in China, and (3) secure superiority in cyberspace and construct a national security strategy that suits the current milieu and enhances execution ability by coordinating with private companies. Such an awareness had been shared nearly consistently by US diplomacy up until now. For example, a strong opposition by the United States against the Japanese Asian Monetary Fund framework proposed immediately after the Asian currency crisis and the ensuing debates in the APEC Business Advisory Council[4] shows that both the public and private sectors of the United States are sensitive to movements that could affect the hegemony of US dollars.

The author argues that the exercise of American power and influence in finance—the use of financial isolation from Legitimate Financial System (LFS)—has become the key means for the national security of the United States. The author concludes the book by discussing some considerations for exercising force by the United States in finance in the Epilogue: Lessons from the Use of Financial Power. While they are the personal views of the author, they are, nonetheless, a good point of reference as the views held by a former official of the US government. The considerations discussed by the author are shown below.

Considerations against the financial ecosystem

First, according to the author, the world of international finance forms an ecosystem in which it interacts with regulations and diplomacy, and the effectiveness of the US financial sanctions is maintained by the presence of the hegemonic economic position of American finance and US dollars. Participants in the LFS are rewarded by the United States if they conduct legitimate transactions by following the rules, but they are punished and isolated if they do not follow the rules. This ecosystem is powerful yet fragile. In other words, "legitimate" participants, such as large foreign banks leave the LFS for de-risking if the ecosystem diverges from legal rules and is broadly misused for diplomacy and political persuasion and the possibility of entry by non-legitimate participants increases.

In fact, in the financial sanctions imposed against the BNP Paribas Bank in 2014, the year after Zarate's book was published, there was an active debate among the foreign banks of the US allies on avoiding US dollars, to avoid sanction risks.[5] In the United States, the authorities for financial sanctions (Office of Foreign Office Control or OFAC) aggressively apply extraterritorial financial sanctions and invite concerns over financial supervision (Federal Reserve Board or FRB) from within the United States and abroad. However, it could be assessed positively if, like the author, we assume that the US government has the willingness to self-control. The book also explains how increased sanctions that depend on LFS lead to counteraction from other networks that do not depend on international financial systems, such as the hawala network, a large underground financial network that consists of money-exchange businesses, and so on, in Central Asia and North Africa, and the transactions represented by prepaid cards and cryptocurrencies, such as bitcoin, the counteraction by China and Russia aimed to weaken LFS, and the countries isolated by LFS through sanctions, such as Iran and North Korea, conducting transactions directly with each other, all of which ultimately highlight the complexity of the problem.

So, what should be done to retain the "legitimate" participants in the LFS while isolating the "un-legitimate" participants? According to the author, LFS needs to carefully narrow the target of isolation to only those that can be captured, while LFS should consider the profits from "legitimate" participants, such as large banks while incorporating others as "legitimate" participants by improving the transparency and accountability of transactions by new technologies in finance as well as transactions by developing countries (but isolate those with a low level of transparency). As the development of new financial technologies, such as blockchain is expected to bring about the decline of existing banks, approaches to demarcating the range of "legitimate" participants will be a challenge in future.

Strategic persuasion of American values and construction of LFS by the public and private sectors

Conversely, the author also asserts that a state needs to proactively incorporate private companies and emerging forces, such as financial institutions from the national security perspective to maintain and enhance LFS through the efforts of both the public and private sectors, because nation states are no longer participants with absolute influence in the international political economy. At this point, there are two key elements, the first of which is public persuasion. In other words, this is encouraging private companies from foreign countries to proactively follow the United States by disseminating American values, such as the rule of law, freedom of speech, freedom of the press, respect for human rights, protection of minorities, empowerment of women, free trade, aid for entrepreneurship, secured accountability of the government, and secured transparency of private companies to the world. The second key element is the emphasis on the role of non-states. The author argues that cooperating with non-state forces (US and foreign private companies, etc.) that share American values through strategic persuasion by the US government and exercise global influence through the public and private sectors towards the national interest of the United States is important while private financial institutions serve as the gatekeepers of LFS.

The tone of the author is somewhat self-righteous as it stands on the idea that the United States is righteous and that American values should be uniformly welcomed by private companies in foreign countries, but the national strategy of the US government shares the same sentiment. To be fair, the author also states that "legitimacy" and "reputation" are two sides of the same coin, and at least recognizes that the self-righteous exercise of influence with poor reputation would mean that the United States would lose its legitimacy.

Japan will likely experience an increased number of opportunities in which participation in sanctions is requested due to the need for international cooperation as a US ally while the influence of America's own sanctions is declining in relative terms. The policies of the Trump administration are received poorly at times and are likely to lose the American "legitimacy." With China and Russia as neighbors, striking a balance between promoting bilateral cooperation and participation in a multi-sanction scheme will be a challenge for Japan in maintaining its national interests.

The US laws pertaining to financial sanctions

This section details the US regulations pertaining to financial sanctions through: (1) a comparison with the Japanese laws and (2) the US legal system.

Comparisons with Japanese laws

First, the primary law in Japan on financial sanctions is the Foreign Exchange and Foreign Trade Act (another is the Act on Special Measures Concerning Asset Freezing, etc., of International Terrorists). According to Article 16 Item 1 of the Foreign Exchange and Foreign Trade Act, sanctions can be imposed for contributing to the efforts of the international community.[6] The following is a discussion of the main characteristics of this law against the US laws on financial sanctions.

First, there are differences in the legal systems of the two countries. The Foreign Exchange and Foreign Trade Act in Japan requires international agreements, international peace, and peace and safety for Japan (see Foreign Exchange and Foreign Trade Act Article 16 Item 1), while Article 1701 of International Economic Emergency Powers Act (IEEPA), the primary law for financial sanctions in the United States, notes that financial sanctions can be applied if "any unusual and extraordinary threat ... to the national security, foreign policy, or economy of the United States", and it is difficult for the Japanese law to address the differences in detail. Next, the Japanese Foreign Exchange and Foreign Trade Act takes a sequence of resident vs. non-resident, domestic, foreign, payments, asset transactions, and service transactions, which could encourage the evasion of regulations (e.g. an alien is considered a Japanese resident after six months). Additionally, there are issues in the Japanese law regarding the unclear positioning of actors involved in cyber-attacks and human rights violations, difficulty in freezing of assets other than financial assets (e.g. vessels), absence of governing rules for shutting down communications (SWIFT connection)[7] (the sanctions related to banks are addressed by the Banking Law), and the rigidity of the Japanese law against the flexible legal system of the United States.

Second, there is extraterritorial applicability. Article 5 of the Japanese Foreign Exchange and Foreign Trade Act[8] provides that actions of the foreign branches of Japanese corporations are only partially regulated (every action in the United States and the EU), while as far as the US laws are concerned, the actions of

American corporations are regulated broadly on nationality principle, and extraterritorial applicability applies broadly to regulating the actions by non-Americans outside of the United States (secondary sanctions), such as the cases where foreign corporations use American dollars extraterritorially or aid and abet American corporations. The Comprehensive Iran Sanctions and Accountability and Divestment Act 2010 (CISADA) is one example of secondary regulation. The US government can limit or ban transactions of American banks with foreign financial institutions if they conduct or facilitate significant transactions with Specially Designated Nationals (SDN).

Third, there is the abundance of penalties. While the Japanese laws impose three years in prison and less than 1 million Japanese yen (or less than triple the price of the target object if the tripled price exceeds 1 million yen), the US IEEPA sets the upper limit at 250,000 dollars or double the amount of illegal transactions as civil punishment, whichever is higher: less than 20 years in prison; and less than 1 million dollars in penalty for criminal punishment. Moreover, the OFAC imposes an order to improve business operations and the maximum penalty stipulated by law along with civil penalties and penalties by other federal and state authorities. For example, in the sanctions against BNP Paribas (2014),[9] the United States Department of Justice (DOJ) imposed a fine of 8.9 billion dollars (900 billion Japanese yen) against the French foreign bank for violation of American financial sanctions (funds transferred to clients in Iran and Sudan), and banned the bank for a year from settlement services in dollars in its branches in cities, such as New York. Despite the French president negotiating directly with the US president, severe sanctions were imposed on the bank anyway. Sanctions have also been imposed on many other foreign banks, including HSBC in Britain and Mitsubishi Tokyo UFJ Bank in Japan.

The US legal system[10]

The primary law dealing with financial sanctions is the aforementioned IEEPA (United States Code Vol. 50 Chapter 35), which gives the president the authority to regulate finance, economy, and transactions, such as asset freezing in times of emergency. Apart from IEEPA, there are: (1) other Acts (e.g. against Iran, Iran Sanctions Act of 1996 (ISA), CISADA, etc.), (2) Presidential Decrees (e.g. Order 13622 of 2012 (regulating foreign financial institutions), etc.), and (3) federal regulations (e.g. the Iranian Transactions and Sanction Regulations (ITSR), etc.).

Then there are regulations by OFAC, the main administration. OFAC regulations prohibit all transactions to countries designated as SDN, such as Iran, and freezes their assets, while there is another list other than by country. OFAC regulations are ambiguous on transactions that are intentionally banned, which creates room for various interpretations. According to the OFAC Economic Sanctions Enforcement Guidelines,[11] "involvement with a U.S. Person" is recognized if the transaction is settled in US dollars even if the person conducting the transaction is not a US citizen. It further prohibits indirect transactions (e.g. transactions with an SDN) in addition to direct transactions, prohibits facilitation of actions banned for US Persons (e.g. ITSR560.28), and imposes bans even if the said person does not actually know the violation of sanctions so long as there are reasons to know (existence of information that can be obtained easily through ordinary research effort). Additionally, OFAC regulates corporations where over 50% of the entity is owned by a total of one or more SDNs, while those with less than 50% owned by SDNs where a significant ratio is owned by entities whose executives are SDNs are also regulated. The criteria for penalties include, intentional or reckless actions, recognition of the violation of the law, negative impact on the objective of economic sanctions, management structure, and response after the discovery of violations. While law enforcement is a risk for foreign companies (particularly financial institutions) that are targets of secondary sanctions, suspicion by mass media or the parliament could also damage their reputation, and adjusting to the right level of OFAC regulations has a considerable impact on the management of these companies.

The case of Iranian sanctions

This section introduces the case of Iranian sanctions, which manifest the characteristics of US financial sanctions most significantly.[12] The events are discussed in chronological order as follows.

Discovery of Iran's nuclear program

Iran ratified the Nuclear Non-Proliferation Treaty (NPT) in 1970 and concluded a comprehensive safeguard agreement with the International Atomic Energy Agency (IAEA) in 1974. However, Iran had been conducting nuclear development clandestinely. In August 2002, NCRI, an Iranian dissident group, blew the whistle on the construction of a secret uranium enrichment facility and heavy water reactors in Iran, which attracted the attention of the world. Later that year, Iran admitted that it had begun uranium enrichment in 1991 without declaring it to the IAEA.

Reconciliation policy by Britain, Germany, and France

Britain, Germany, and France (EU3) sought to avoid the exit of Iran from the NPT through a reconciliatory approach, but failed. In October 2002, the foreign ministers of EU3 concluded the Tehran Declaration with Iran (which Iran later de facto broke) and EU3 opposed a plan by the United States in the UN Security Council in November of the same year and the referral was later overlooked. However, in February 2004 it came to light that Iran had obtained nuclear technologies. While EU3 and Iran concluded the Paris Agreement in November of that year, Iran refused to execute the agreements in August of the following year and declared that it has resumed uranium enrichment in January 2006. Considering this development, the IAEA Council reported Iran's violation to the UN Security Council in February 2006. In retaliation, Iran halted every voluntary measure it had promised to IAEA.

The UN Security Council resolution

The UN Security Council made several resolutions. In July 2006, Security Council Resolution 1696[13] demanded that Iran stop all activities related to uranium enrichment and reprocessing, including research and development and obtain validation by IAEA—a demand that Iran rejected. In December of the same year, the UN Security Council passed Resolution 1737[14] that determined that all activities pertaining to every heavy water project, including uranium enrichment, reprocessing, and research activities including R&D must accept validation by IAEA while preventing UN member states from transferring or procuring any item that may contribute to the Iranian nuclear development from Iran. In the same resolution, smart sanctions were employed that utilize approaches, such as a weapons embargo, asset freezing, and a ban on relevant individuals and groups to suppress economic damage to the citizens of the sanctioned country, but the resolution employed only a limited number of such approaches. As a result, the effectiveness of the sanctions was limited. In light of this, Security Council Resolution 1747[15] was passed in March 2007 that put limited entry and passage of relevant individuals and groups and requested all member states to stop financial aid and investment to Iran. More smart sanctions followed through Security Council Resolution 1803[16] in March 2008 and Resolution 1929[17] in June 2010, but the changes in Iranian policies were almost non-existent since the sanctions were more lenient than conventional embargoes.

Enhanced united sanctions by the United States and Europe

After the IAEA Director General's report in November 2011 confirmed the continuation of Iranian nuclear development, the EU also decided to take action and imposed firm sanctions against Iran on its own. The EU banned the import of oil from Iran in January 2012, removed Iranian domestic banks from SWIFT in March, and strengthened sanctions on imports and transport of natural gas and several other products from Iran in October. These powerful EU sanctions went beyond smart sanctions and resulted in a significant damage to the Iranian economy and put enormous pressure on the livelihood of Iranians.

Meanwhile, the United States had added foreign companies to the list of sanctions targets through extraterritorial applicability under the Iran and Libya Sanctions Act of 1996 (Iran Sanctions Act (ISA) since 2004) while its own comprehensive sanctions included a ban on transactions and investments with Iran as well as financial sanctions, a ban on support for Iran, and anti-terrorist measures. The broad American sanctions on crude oil and natural gas were particularly damaging to the Iranian economy and in October 2010, the sanctions were imposed against the Iranian corporation Naftiran Intertrade Company for trying to evade the oil sanctions. In July 2010, President Obama signed CISADA, and added sales of gasoline, air fuel, and so on, amounting to over 1 million dollars or 5 million dollars over the course of a year to Iran, and sales of equipment and services that support gasoline manufacturing and import by Iran, to the list of bans. Obama continued to add sanction requirements to CISADA through executive orders and ordered Presidential Decree No. 13590 in November 2011 (ban on supply of oil-related products and services amounting to over 250,000 dollars or 1 million dollars annually) and Presidential Degree No. 13622 in July 2012 (imposing sanctions on actors and foreign financial institutions deemed to have purchased Iranian crude oil and oil products, and froze assets within US borders owned by individuals and companies that provided financial aid to the National Iranian Oil Company and the Central Bank of Iran or aided purchases of US dollars and precious metals by Iran). Additionally, American sanctions were re-strengthened in light of the aforementioned IAEA Director General's report in November 2011 that advocated for strengthening of EU sanctions by adding regulations on transport to Iran and participation in joint ventures and imposing sanctions on companies that promote purchase of bonds and issued by the Iranian government or conduct significant transactions related to the Islamic Revolutionary Guard Corps in 2012 (Iran Threat Reduction and Syria Human Rights Act), and expanded the authority on American sanctions against companies from third countries that support major sectors of Iranian economy other than oil and natural gas in 2013 (Iran Freedom and Counter-Proliferation Act, IFCA).

As a result, the Iranian crude oil production dropped sharply (4.37 million barrels a day in 2011 to 3.61 million barrels in 2014), but financial sanctions were one of the factors that led to policy shift by Iran while a change of government in the United States and Iran were also other factors. Oil-based barter transactions were also observed to some extent with China, India, and South Korea as a way of avoiding financial and economic sanctions. As recounted by Zarate, various approaches to avoiding sanctions were available and there were limits to independent sanctions by the United States based on LFW.

Joint comprehensive plan of action (JCPOA)

After a regime change in Iran (from conservative hardliner Mahmoud Ahmadinejad to the moderate conservative Hassan Rouhani) in August 2013, EU3 plus the United States, China, and Russia (EU+3), and Iran tentatively agreed to a Joint Plan of Action in November of the same year and the sanctions by the international community against Iran were partially withheld in exchange for halting uranium enrichment activities for concentrations exceeding 5% from 2014 onwards. This was followed by the conclusion of the JCPOA, the final agreement document, in July 2015, in which Iran committed to: (1) reduce the number of installed centrifuges used in uranium enrichment from 19,000 to 5,060 in 10 years, and (2) limit the degree of enrichment to 3.67% for the next 15 years and keep the uranium reserve below 300 kg. As a result, the breakout period Iran needed for nuclear armament was extended from two to three months at the time of the signing of the agreement to a year.

The JCPOA had some problems due to unclear points on conducting inspections (e.g. inspection of the Parchin military complex near Tehran was unclear). While some experts note with skepticism that Iran can resume nuclear development after 10 years, others consider the JCPOA a success for the fact that had it failed, and Iran would have gotten closer to the manufacturing of nuclear weapons.

UN Security Council resolutions

In July 2015, the UN Security Council passed Resolution 2231[18] and approved JCPOA, which came into effect in October. Following this, the UN and EU have successively lifted sanctions since January 2016. However, while the United States did lift the nuclear-related sanctions against Iran,[19] it nonetheless added new sanctions on missile development in Iran (discussed later). According to JCPOA, if Iran neglected to implement the agreement and cannot solve the problem within 35 days, a referral could be made to the UN Security Council and the UN sanctions re-applied if the Security Council does not decide to continue the halt on sanctions within 30 days (Article 36, i.e. snap-back clause).

Exit of the United States from JCPOA and resumption of sanctions

In November 2016, the US Congress approved an extension of ISA by 10 years. While the United States argues that it does not violate the JCPOA agreement, the Grand Ayatollah Ali Khamenei of Iran claimed that the extension of ISA violates JCPOA and warned that it would encourage retaliatory measures by Iran. On February 2017, the Trump administration imposed its first Iranian sanctions (transactions banned for 25 individuals and companies as well as US companies. Iran criticized the sanctions imposed by the United States as illegal and retaliated by imposing regulations on Americans who support local terrorist organizations) for the development of nuclear missiles and passed a law strengthening the Iranian sanctions (sanctions against the Islamic Revolutionary Guard Corps who support the development of ballistic missiles) in the US Senate in June, and added add-itional sanctions (added 18 organizations and individuals) while expressing a desire to reimpose the sanctions lifted by JCPOA on July 17. As a result, President Rouhani of Iran warned that Iran would withdraw from JCPOA if the American sanctions continued. However, the United States withdrew from JCPOA despite the opposition by the EU on May 8, 2018, and re-imposed Iranian sanctions. As a countermeasure, the EU enacted a blocking statute to nullify US sanctions in August 2018, and established the Instrument in Support of Trade Exchanges (INSTEX) for non-USD transactions with Iran in January 2019. However, Iran was not satisfied with such efforts by the EU and announced in July 2019 an increase in uranium enrichment beyond the agreed limit. The Trump Administration extended sanctions in September 2019, but the UN Security Council blocked its effort to re-impose snapback sanctions on Iran on August 25, 2020. On the next day, Iran agreed to allow IAEA inspections. As these series of events show, this problem is influenced not only by Iran, but also by foreign policies of the United States that can be interpreted as a violation of the agreements.

Legal issues regarding implementation of sanctions by a state

The case of Iranian sanctions shows that there are several legal issues that should be considered with regards to implementation of sanctions by a state, in this case the United States.[20]

Protection of human rights of sanctioned individuals

First, while the UN Security Council resolution aims for smart sanctions that reduce the burden on the citizens of the sanctioned country, the United States does not consider the burden on citizens and instead strengthens the conventional comprehensive embargoes. The EU also utilized a comprehensive embargo when it implemented its own sanctions, but it lifted the sanctions after JCPOA was implemented. Preventive measures and protection of human rights in sanctions are coordinated and partial rights related to criminal laws are not applied to those under financial sanctions, as demonstrated by the case of Kadi (see Chapter 8). Financial sanctions are interpreted as purely preventive in nature and do not include a punitive connotation. In the United States however, financial sanctions are positioned as a new kind of warfare based on its national strategy supported by both the public and private sectors and aims to maintain the American hegemony, and considerations for protection of human rights for foreign individuals targeted for sanctions are considered weak and civil sanctions, criminal punishment, and administrative penalties are all involved as if the sanctions were imposed by a single mobilized country. Additionally, when a regulatory authority in the United States (DOJ, OFAC, etc.) prosecutes within the US based on American laws, the sanctioned foreign individuals and companies are de facto deprived of opportunities to dispute the legitimacy of prosecution in a court. In other words, if the prosecution was reported by the media and they participate in a long-drawn out legal process, most companies or businesspeople cannot withstand the risk of damaged reputation. Normally, the US authorities offer reconciliation through either a non-prosecution agreement (NPA) or a deferred prosecution agreement (DPA), impose a heavy fine without any fact finding based on strict evidence or sufficient examination by the court and a severe penalty is imposed to settle the case. This approach is highly dangerous as someone who has not committed a crime is treated as though guilty of such a crime and violates due process and the human rights for the sanctioned individuals.

Extraterritorial application

Unlike in Europe and Japan, where grounds for extraterritorial application are carefully considered based on the nationality principle, conservatism, the universality principle, and the effect principle, the jurisdiction of domestic US laws is extended to the world under the assumption that international laws are undeveloped. For example, a US law is applicable if a transaction is conducted in US dollars, an internationally key currency, even if the settlement transaction is conducted outside of the United States (e.g. company X in Tokyo sends US dollars to company Y in Frankfurt via bank remittance). The territorial principle or some other unknown principle would apply, and could be interpreted thus if one focuses on the fact that remittances are made in US dollars to a corresponding US bank account in New York electronically as a cover (however, it would be more appropriate to recognize regulatory and judicial jurisdiction to the location of the party involved rather than the location of the correspondent account). The universality principle could apply if we assume that the aim is to protect common interests of the international community similar to counter-terrorism measures (however, this will not be applicable here since the action is based on a national strategy aiming to maintain the American hegemony), and protective principle could apply if the goal is to secure currency sovereignty of the US dollar and its acceptance (however, it should not be recognized as such unless it is for a strong protective objective such as preventing counterfeit currency). Other mechanisms for expanding the American jurisdiction include punishment of foreign corporations and individuals for mail and wire fraud under the accusation of conspiring with an American citizen.

Is there a way to suppress the effort by the United States to implement illegal sanctions or extraterritorial application or attempt to enforce sanctions that prioritize its own interests by using its own influence on the UN? Legally, countries other than the United States could enact a countering law that abates the effectiveness of the US laws, submit an amicus curiae brief that opposes extraterritorial application to an American court (European countries have taken this approach for a case of extraterritorial application of anti-trust laws) or file a suit in an international court. However, countering laws could easily escalate into serious international conflict. The impact of written opinions on the American decision making is up to the United States and filing a suit in the international court is hampered by undeveloped legal principles of international law, where even if a judgment is issued against the United States, the US federal governments are not bound by it. Therefore, economic countermeasures also need to be considered. In other words, non-American companies could avoid the use of US dollars and increase the use of alternate currencies, such as the euro, Japanese yen, and Chinese yuan, or expand the use of new products, such as cryptocurrencies, Facebook Libra and Digital Renminbi (with CIPS (RMB Cross-Border Interbank Payment System)), to counter the aggressive extraterritorial application and financial sanctions by the United States. As Zarate pointed out, this is also an element of concern for LFS, which could work as a deterrence principle in cases where the United States imposes illegitimate financial sanctions. As seen in the BNP Paribas Bank case, if an American financial sanctions authority (OFAC, etc.) damages a foreign bank that supports payments in US dollars, it would lead to a destabilization of the US dollar-based financial system and result in disharmony with the policy objectives set forth by the American financial policy authorities (FRB, etc.), meaning the need to adjust policies amongst authorities within the United States could also function as a control principle.

Conversely, the extraterritorial application of executive jurisdiction has also presented the problem of applicability of legislative jurisdiction. In recent years, the Federal Bureau of Investigation (FBI) has conducted criminal investigations by installing spyware overseas without permission (e.g. the case of Silk Road in which an illegal transactions website was exposed in 2013, etc.) in response to crimes in cyberspace. Extraterritorial application of legislative power has some room for extraterritorial applicability based on certain grounds, such as the nationality principle, but this is generally not recognized as it is an extraterritorial application of executive power, and installing spyware in foreign territories without permission is illegal due to violation of sovereignty. Nonetheless, espionage as defined by international law does not satisfy the local requirements in cyberspace (a widely accepted theory). No charges can be pressed against legal accountability,[21] which gives us an issue in terms of international law.[22] However, the United States and associated countries are reported to have conducted investigations by coordinating with each other in the case of the illegal website Alphabay that was exposed in 2017. Thus, the problem of violation of sovereignty did not occur.

Issues surrounding the effectiveness of financial sanctions

How does Japan look at the issue of securing effectiveness of financial sanctions? Common issues in financial sanctions by Japan, the United States, and Europe include: (1) difficulty in determining individuals and groups to be sanctioned, (2) sanctions are not very effective against countries that do not access the international financial system (e.g. North Korea), (3) there is a significant burden on the general public of the sanction country as well as the country imposing sanctions, (4). Sanctions inhibit normal financial transactions while encouraging risk-avoiding behaviors by financial institutions (for example, it may encourage de-risking by banks as a result of the growing burden of compliance by banks against strict AML/CFT regulations, increasing financial removal in which remittance services exit from African countries), and (5) remittance paths that do not pass through banks are developed (e.g. the danger of lowered filtering function of financial institutions as transactions become anonymous through the expansion of cryptocurrencies and blockchain, increased difficulty of conventional law enforcement, and the possibility of dysfunction of legal tenders in the future). While the United States may promote the concentration to US dollars that enables LFS as a national strategy, addressing adverse effects brought about by such a concentration (e.g. overload of compliance burden for domestic companies as a result of excessive extraterritorial application by the US government, destabilization of the international financial system) would be the top priority for Japan and Europe.

Next, let us consider cryptocurrencies which utilize blockchain technology and currently have the maximum number of transactions. Cryptocurrencies and blockchain cannot be managed by the government, but their scale of transactions are not large enough for them to be a major means of payment. However, the possibility of a rapid popularization of cryptocurrencies cannot be neglected, in which case it may even threaten the existence of bank payments and currencies (legal tender) in various countries. For this reason, BIS and central banks of countries around the world, including Japan, are working on research and development of digital legal tenders for the purpose of improving the convenience of legal tenders (e.g. China's Digital Renminbi). However, there would be various implications if this was to become a reality. For example, central banks can directly manipulate the amount of money and interest rate of currencies against individuals and companies in place of conventional monetary supply management via banks, while enforcement and tax collection would also become easier. Over-management by the state is a concern as information and authority are concentrated in the state, and payments by private banks could suffer. Competition among legal tenders and expulsion of digital legal tenders through issuance by information platforms, such as Facebook Libra can reveal monopoly issues, and so on, and the direction in which it may develop in the future is unknown.

While there are no international financial institutions that organize financial sanctions at the moment, existing international financial institutions, such as the IMF, BIS, and Basel Committee on Banking Supervision need to actively participate in discussions on financial sanctions at the UN Security Council, which is not a group of finance professionals.

Notes

1 For details, see Takashi Kubota, "Kinyu Kantoku Kisei ni kansuru Kokusai Seido no Tenkai" [Development of international policies on regulation of financial supervision] *Ronkyu Juristo* [*Quarterly Jurist*], Vol. 19, (2016), pp. 43–50.

2 For details, see Takashi Kubota, "Saishin no Jirei kara mita 'Ikigai Tekiyou' ron no saikenshou—Keizai seisai wo chuushin ni" [Reconsiderations of 'extraterritorial applicability' observed in latest cases—with a focus on economic sanctions], Kokusai Shoutorihiki Gakkai Nenpou [*Academy for International Business Transactions Annual Bulletin*], Vol. 17 (2015), pp. 33–47.

3 Juan C. Zarate, *Treasury's War: The Unleashing of a New Era of Financial Warfare* (Public Affairs, 2013).

4 Takashi Kubota, "Asia Kinyu Sistemu kaikaku ni okeru ABAC no yakuwari to kadai" [The Role of ABAC in Asian Financial System Reform and Its Challenges], *Kokusai Keizaiho Gakkai Nenpo* [*International Economic Law*], Vol. 20, (2011): pp. 137–153.

5 For example, see Takashi Kubota, "Saishin Jirei ni miru Beikoku keizaiho ihan no Ikigai teki eikyou to sono kadai – Piscotti Jiken to BNP Paribas Jiken" [Extraterritorial Impact of Violation of US Economic Laws in Latest Cases and Its Legal Challenges— Pisciotti and BNP Paribas Incidents], *Kokusai Shouji Houmu* [*International Business Law and Practices*], Vol. 42, No. 8 (2014): pp. 1242–1245.

6 Foreign Exchange and Foreign Trade Act Article 16 Item 1,

> The competent minister can impose a responsibility to obtain a permission on applicable payment or payments against a resident or non-resident who attempts to make a payment or a resident who attempts to make a payment between non-residents—omitted—when the competent minister recognizes the need to do so

in order to implement agreements our country has concluded and other international agreements in a honest manner, the need to do so particularly to contribute as a country to an international effort towards international peace, or when the cabinet approves Article 10 Item 1.

7 Shunichi Fukushima, "Current State of Economic Sanctions and Its Challenges—With a Focus on Financial Sanctions," paper presented at United Nations Financial Sanctions Research Group, at Kwansei Gakuin University Tokyo (Campus, January 29, 2017).

8 Foreign Exchange and Foreign Trade Act Article 5

This law applies to acts for assets or businesses in a foreign country owned by a corporation whose primary office is located in this country, and acted by the representative, agent, user, or other employees of the said corporation. The law is also applied for actions taken in a foreign country on assets or businesses of an individual whose address is within this country, and acted by that person, its agent, user, or its employees.

9 For the press release by the United States Department of Justice, see www.justice.gov/opa/pr/bnp-paribas-agrees-plead-guilty-and-pay-89-billion-illegally-processing-financial (last accessed: January 27, 2018).

10 For details, see Meredith Rathbone, Peter Jeydel, and Amy Lentz, "Sanctions, Sanctions Everywhere: Forging A Path Through Complex Transnational Sanctions Laws," *Georgetown Journal of International Law*, Vol. 44, Issue 3 (2013): 1055–1126, and Chiharu Yamazaki, Hitoshi Suzuki, and Daisuke Nakao eds., "Manee Roondaringu Kisei no Shintenkai" [New Developments in Regulations on Money Laundering] Kinzai (Institute for Financial Affairs, 2016): pp. 83–117.

11 For revised guidance on OFAC, see the United States Department of Treasury www.treasury.gov/resource-center/sanctions/OFAC-Enforcement/pages/20140813.aspx.

12 Ikuya Kozuka, "Kokusai Shakai no tai Iran Seisai: Sumaato Sankushon purasu arufa no Keizai Seisai no Jikkousei nit suite" [Iranian Sanctions by the International Community—On the Effectiveness of Economic Sanctions by Smart Sanctions + α], *Bouei Kenkyuujo Kiyou* [*NIDS Security Studies*], Vol. 19, No. 2 (March 2017): pp. 107–125.

13 S/RES/1696, July 31, 2006.

14 S/RES/1737, December 23, 2006.

15 S/RES/1747, March 24, 2007.

16 S/RES/1803, March 3, 2008.

17 S/RES/1929, June 9, 2010.

18 S/RES/2231, July 20, 2015.

19 Secondary sanctions were partially lifted (sanctions related to SDN remained), but primary sanctions were not lifted. For details, see Nakao Daisuke, "Houkatsuteki Kyoudou Sagyou Keikaku 'Rikou no Hi' ikou no tai Iran torihiki no chuui ten" [Cautionary Points on deals with Iran since the day of Implementation of the Joint Comprehensive Plan of Action], Kokusai Shouji Houmu [*International Business Law and Practices*], Vol. 44, No. 5 (2016): pp. 746–750.

20 Takashi Kubota (footnote 2) and Takashi Kubota, "Financial Stability Concern of the Extraterritorial Impacts Caused by the Recent US Financial Sanctions on Foreign Banks," *Japanese Yearbook of International Law*, Vol. 59 (2016): pp. 229–250.

21 Keiko Kohno "Saibaa Kuukan wo tsuujita kanshi katsudou no houteki hyouka: kanchou koui, syukenshingai to jinkenhou (puraibashii no shingai) no kanten kara" [Legal Assessment of Supervising Activities Through Cyberspace—from Perspectives of Espionage, Violation of Sovereignty, and Human Rights Laws (Violation of Privacy)], *Bouei Kennkyuusho Kiyou* [*NIDS Security Studies*], Vol. 19, No. 2 (March 2017): pp. 49–69.
22 Ahmed Ghappour, "Searching Places Unknown: Law Enforcement Jurisdiction on the Dark Web", *Stanford Law Review*, Vol. 69, Issue 4 (April 2017): pp. 1075–1136.

7 Financial sanctions implementation by the European Union—the jurisprudence of the CJEU on the balance between protections of fundamental rights and effectiveness of the restrictive measures implementing the UN Security Council Resolution 1373

Kazushige Yagyu

Introduction

This chapter examines how the Court of Justice of the European Union (CJEU) is attempting to balance the protection of human rights with the effectiveness of sanctions during EU's implementation of financial sanctions imposed by the UN Security Council, mainly against private persons (or entities). The more heavily protected the human rights of individuals are, especially the procedural rights, the less effective the sanctions will be. In particular, if the CJEU invalidates the enforcement of UN sanctions by the EU on the grounds of human rights violations, it may impede the implementation of globally standardized sanctions. There is also the possibility of the dissipation or the flight of assets subject to sanctions once the sanctions, such as the freezing of assets, are removed.

However, as pointed out by many international organizations, the human rights of private individuals should not be trampled upon in the name of the effectiveness of sanctions. This issue has been discussed in the CJEU mainly in relation to the *Kadi I* and *Kadi II* cases. The cases occurred during the process of the EU's implementation of UN Security Council sanctions resolutions[1] against al-Qaeda; this was one of the sanctions whose targets were specified by the Security Council. For some other financial sanctions, as stipulated by Security Council resolutions, the EU itself may determine targets, posing legal problems different from those in the sanctions whose targets are determined by the Security Council.

This chapter focuses on the process by which the EU implements UN Security Council Resolution 1373,[2] which allows UN Member States to determine targets of sanctions and analyzes two relevant judgments of the Grand Chamber rendered by the Court of Justice, the higher court of the CJEU, to discuss how the CJEU attempts to balance the protection of human rights with the effectiveness of sanctions. In the *LTTE* case[3] and the *Hamas* case,[4] which involved the financial sanctions imposed on terrorist organizations, the issue was whether to limit the scope of information on which to base the decision of the Council of the EU when imposing sanctions to decisions made by state organs guaranteeing human rights. The contrasting rulings on the cases issued by the two courts composing the CJEU namely, the General Court and the Court of Justice highlighted the issue of balance between the protection of human rights and the effectiveness of sanctions.

First, this chapter overviews the system of EU financial sanctions regimes. The next section analyzes the *LTTE* case. Drawing upon this analysis, this chapter finally identifies an elaborate approach by the CJEU to secure effectiveness of financial sanctions.

The EU financial sanctions regimes

Classification and legal bases of EU financial sanctions

Financial sanctions imposed by the EU are often theoretically categorized based on two criteria: geographical limitations and the decision-making entity of the target of sanctions.[5] First, they can be roughly categorized into sanctions against terrorism that are free from geographical restrictions and geographically limited sanctions against third countries. Sanctions against terrorism can then be divided into two categories: sanctions against al-Qaeda and autonomous sanctions giving effect to UN Security Council Resolution 1373 based on the decision-making entity of the target of sanctions; in the former, the target of sanctions is determined by the UN Security Council, while the Council of the EU specifies the target of the latter. Sanctions on third countries refer to the sanctions imposed on the government officials and relevant organizations, and so on, of third countries.[6] These include the implementation of (1) UN sanctions, (2) independent EU sanctions, and (3) combinations of the two.

Under the Treaties of the European Union (TEU) and the Treaty on the Functioning of the European Union (TFEU), however, there is no distinction between the three regimes. They are all referred to as restrictive measures and are based on the same legal grounds. For all sanctions, the Council adopts two types of documents: decisions (or common positions before the entering into force of the Lisbon Treaty) and regulations. With regard to financial sanctions, the provisions of decision and the provisions of regulations regarding the requirements to determine targets of sanctions are usually identical for all three regimes of sanctions. In particular, the form of the lists in the Annex of the EU instruments that detail the targets of sanctions is uniform in the decisions and regulations.

The procedure of listing a person in the case of autonomous sanctions

In the case of autonomous sanctions, if the Council, at its own discretion, determines a private individual to be subject to EU sanctions, it is mandatorily required that a domestic institution of at least one country recognize the individual's involvement in acts of terrorism before the Council specifies the person subject to EU sanctions. Article 1, paragraph 4 of Common Position 2001/931[7] stipulates this as follows:

> The list in the Annex shall be drawn up on the basis of precise information or material in the relevant file which indicates that a decision has been taken by a competent authority in respect of the persons, groups and entities concerned, irrespective of whether it concerns the instigation of investigations or prosecution for a terrorist act, an attempt to perpetrate, participate in or facilitate such an act based on serious and credible evidence or clues, or condemnation for such deeds. Persons, groups and entities identified by the Security Council of the United Nations as being related to terrorism and against whom it has ordered sanctions may be included in the list.

For the purposes of this paragraph "competent authority" shall mean a judicial authority, or, where judicial authorities have no competence in the area covered by this paragraph, an equivalent competent authority in that area.

In this case, the country determining the individual's involvement may be a member State of the EU. The question as to whether or not an authority of third countries is included within the meaning of "competent authority" will be discussed later. This procedure of autonomous sanctions is called the two-tier system. The Court of Justice explained the aim of this two-tier system as follows:

> [I]t is apparent from the references to a national decision, "precise information" and "serious and credible evidence or clues" that Article 1(4) of Common Position 2001/931 aims to protect the persons concerned by ensuring that they are included on the list at issue only on a sufficiently solid factual basis, and that the Common Position seeks to attain that objective by requiring a decision taken by a national authority.

In the absence of means on the part of the EU to carry out its own investigations regarding the involvement of a given person in terrorist acts, that requirement aims to establish that evidence or serious and credible clues exist of the involvement of the person concerned in terrorist activities, regarded as reliable by the national authorities and having led them, at the very least, to adopt measures of inquiry, without requiring the national decision to have been taken in a specific legal form or to have been published or notified.[8]

In this way, the Court interpreted the procedure established by Common Position as a system designed to protect targets of sanctions, that is, to guarantee human rights based on the Council's assumed lack of means to collect information by itself.

Two problems on the two-tier system

While accumulated court judgments clarify the content of the Common Position and regulations defining autonomous sanctions, two questions remain unanswered: (i) whether the first national competent authority to determine the involvement of a private individual in acts of terrorism in the two-tier system is limited to authorities under EU Member States that comply with human rights standards such as the European Convention on Human Rights and the Charter of Fundamental Rights of the EU; (ii) whether it is only the initial sanction that requires such a domestic decision in advance in terms of the protection of human rights. In other words, it is not clear if sources of information available to the Council when reviewing the list of targets of sanctions and maintaining the already-listed persons in the list is limited only to decisions by domestic authorities. These two questions affect the effectiveness of sanctions because they are related to the practical question of whether the scope of the information on which the Council can rely in preparing the list of persons subject to sanctions is limited.

The lack of explicit provisions on the above questions in the Common Position or the regulations regarding autonomous sanctions is a problem. As regards whether or not institutions of third countries are included in a "competent authority" that determines the involvement of private individuals in acts of terrorism, practical documents[9] issued by the Council stipulate only the treatment of proposals of sanctions on certain private individuals made by the authorities of third countries. The judicial branch of the EU, thus, needs to make a conclusive decision to resolve the problem through its interpretation in a decision.

There is no explicit provision in Common Position 2001/931 or regulations with regard to question (ii), that is, whether the Council needs to rely solely on domestic decisions when reviewing the list of targets of sanctions. No provision specifies whether, like the initial inclusion of targets in a list, the domestic decision should be the only resource on which the Council should rely to determine the involvement of targets in an act of terrorism when the list is reviewed to decide whether to maintain the already-listed individuals in the lists of new decisions and regulations. This leads to the more specific question of whether the Council can, upon reviewing the list, base its decisions on information that is not included in domestic decisions—information that is not subject to review by the relevant domestic authorities. If the resource on which the Council bases its decisions is limited to the information included in national decisions, persons will have the opportunity to dispute domestic decisions at their national courts and enhance the protection of their procedural rights, while the information used by the Council to impose sanctions will be limited. This will make it difficult to recognize the involvement of persons in acts of terrorism, which may in turn impede the continuation of sanctions.

Because question (ii) largely depends on the interpretation of Article 1(6) of Common Position 2001/931,[10] the conclusion regarding whether or not the information required to continue listing a target needs to involve a domestic decision is likely to depend on the importance which the courts attach to the human rights of private individuals in relation to the effectiveness of sanctions.

In the next session, we overview the *LTTE* judgments, in which the CJEU answered those two questions.

The *LTTE* case and the *Hamas* case

The judgment of the General Court

The two questions were examined as important issues by the CJEU in the *LTTE* case and the *Hamas* case. We mainly focus on the *LTTE* case here, because the facts and findings of the courts of those two cases are almost identical. The facts of the case are as follows:

The Council adopted Regulation 2580/2001 to implement the measures set out in Common Position 2001/931. By Decision 2006/379 implementing Article 2(3) of Regulation 2580/2001, the Council placed the LTTE on the list relating to frozen funds provided for in Article 2(3) of Regulation 2580/2001. Its name had remained on that list by successive implementing regulations ever since. The LTTE brought an action for annulment of the implementing regulations in so far as that measure concerned it.

The Council invoked the UK and Indian decisions as "a decision of a competent authority" within the meaning of Article 1(4) of Common Position 2001/931 in the grounds for the contested implementing regulations. However, no terrorist acts committed by the LTTE were examined in the national decisions invoked in the grounds for the contested regulations. The Council based the contested regulations not on assessments contained in the decisions of competent authorities, but on information from the press and the internet.

In regard to the question/issue (i), the General Court held as follows:[11] As a general rule, a national authority of a third State may have the status of a competent authority within the meaning of Common Position 2001/931, on condition that the activity of the authority is carried out with sufficient human rights safeguards to allow the Council to rely on a decision of the authority. That is, the Council must, before acting on the basis of a decision of an authority of a third State, carefully verify that the relevant legislation and its practical applications of that State ensures protection of the rights of defense and a right to effective judicial protection equivalent to that guaranteed at EU level. Unlike Member States, many third States are not bound by the Convention for the Protection of Human Rights and Fundamental Freedoms and none of them is subject to the provisions of the Charter of Fundamental Rights of the EU.

In the present case, the grounds for the contested regulations do not contain any evidence to suggest that the Council carried out such a thorough verification of the extent to which human rights were protected under the Indian legislation. Consequently, the Council was not entitled to classify the Indian authorities as competent authorities, which leads to also a violation of the Article 296 of the TFEU, which obliges the Council to state the reasons why it intended to maintain the LTTE on the list, including an existence of a decision of a competent authority.

The Court rejected the Council's argument that the failure to assess the protection levels resulted from the fact that the contested regulations concerned reviews and not the initial listing, which would have given rise to a more detailed initial assessment of the Indian legislation. The Court emphasized that fund-freezing measures, notwithstanding their preventive nature, are measures which may have a very substantial negative impact on the persons and that therefore, both the adoption and the extension of those measures must be based on a sufficiently sound and express statement of reasons.[12]

As regards the issue (ii), the CJEU had already held in the *Al-Aqsa* case that

> the essential question when reviewing whether to continue to include a person on the list at issue is whether, since that person was included in that list or since the last review, the factual situation has changed in such a way that it is no longer possible to draw the same conclusion in relation to the involvement of the person at issue in terrorist activities.[13]

The General Court, quoting this judgment and reaffirming the aim of Article 1(4) of Common Position 2001/931, noted that the factual basis of a decision of the EU to freeze funds concerning terrorism was based not on information that the Council derived from the press or the internet, but on information which has been specifically examined and upheld in decisions of competent national authorities.[14]

The General Court emphasized that even a review of the list relating to frozen funds, which therefore takes place after previous examinations, cannot justify that a priori classification of the LTTE as a terrorist. Accordingly, a review is by definition open to the possibility that the person is no longer terrorist at the time of the Council's decision.

The Council disputed the obligation to derive the factual basis of the fund-freezing regulations from decisions of competent authorities on the grounds that that could lead, in the absence of such decisions, to unjustified removals of persons from the list, referring to the fact that the timing of review in the Member States may differ from the review at EU level. The Court argued that in the two-tier system of that Common Position and for the purposes of ensuring the effectiveness of the fight against terrorism, it is for the Member States to regularly transmit to the Council, and for the Council to collect, the decisions of competent authorities. According to the Court, if a decision of a competent authority concerning a specific act capable of constituting a terrorist act is not available to the Council, the Council must ask a competent national authority to assess that act, with a view to a decision being taken by that authority. Therefore, "[H]aving regard both to the two-tier structure of the system" and to the mutual duties of sincere cooperation existing between the Member States and the EU, the Member States must respond without delay to the Council's requests to them for an assessment and a decision of a competent authority.

The General Court concluded that that the Council no longer relied on facts assessed by national authorities, but itself makes its own independent imputations of fact on the basis of the press or the internet contravened the two-tier system established by Common Position 2001/931, which led to also the violation of Article 296 TFEU. The Court annulled contested regulations, but maintains the effects of Implementing Regulation No. 790/2014 for three months following delivery of this judgment.

The Council appealed against the judgment of the General Court, submitting that the General Court erred in law on both issues. Especially, the Council insisted that the GC wrongly held that the Council must demonstrate in the statement of reasons that it has verified that the activity of the listing authority in the third State is carried out with sufficient safeguards.

However, the opinion of Advocate General Sharpston resulted in almost the same conclusion on both the first and second issues and consistently put the emphasis on the protection of fundamental rights.[15]

The judgment of the Court of Justice

The Court (Grand Chamber) dismissed the appeal, but took a different approach to the second issue from the original court and the Advocate General.

In regard to the first issue, The Court of Justice, like the General Court, interpreted the term "competent authority" within the meaning of Article 1(4) of Common Position 2001/931, in principle, including the authorities of third States.[16] This interpretation was justified, first, in the light of the wording of Common Position 2001/931, which does not limit the concept of "competent authorities" to the authorities of the Member States, and, second, in the light of the objective of that Common Position, which was adopted in order to implement UN Security Council Resolution 1373. According to the Court, the need for the verification by the Council arises from its general obligation, when adopting restrictive measures, to respect the fundamental rights and the purpose of the requirement laid down in Article 1(4) of Common Position 2001/931. That requirement is designed to protect the persons or entities concerned.

When the Council bases that listing on a decision by a third State, the guarantee that that decision has been taken in accordance with the human rights standards has decisive importance in the context of that listing and of subsequent fund-freezing decisions, although it is sufficient, for the purpose of the obligation to state reasons, that the Council briefly refer in the statement of reasons relating to a decision to freeze funds to the reasons why it considers the decision of the third State to have been adopted in accordance with human rights.

As regards the second issue, the Court of Justice concluded that Article 1(6) of Common Position 2001/931 does not require any new material on which the Council may rely in order to justify the retention of the person on the list to have been the subject of a national decision taken by a competent authority after the initial listing. The reasons given by the Court for this conclusion were threefold:[17]

In the first place, Article 1 of Common Position 2001/931 draws a distinction between the initial entry of a person or entity on the list, referred to in paragraph 4 thereof, and the retention on that list of a person or entity already listed, referred to in paragraph 6 thereof. Under Article 1(4) of Common Position 2001/931, the initial entry of a person or entity on the list presupposes the existence of a national decision by a competent authority. No such condition is laid down in Article 1(6) of Common Position 2001/931. That distinction is attributable to the fact that the retention of a person or entity on the list is, in essence, an extension of the original listing and presupposes, therefore, that there is an ongoing risk of the person or entity concerned being involved in terrorist activities, as initially established by the Council on the basis of the national decision on which that original listing was based.

By imposing the requirement of verification on the Council, the General Court transposed the condition concerning the existence of such a decision, which is laid down in Article 1(4) of Common Position 2001/931 solely in relation to the initial listing, to the reviews which the Council is required to carry out under Article 1(6) thereof. In so doing, the General Court failed to have regard to the distinction between the original decision placing a person on the list and the subsequent decision maintaining the person on that list.

Next, the General Court's interpretation of Article 1 of Common Position 2001/931 was based on the consideration that either the competent national authorities regularly adopt decisions on which the reviews under Article 1(6) thereof may be based, or the Council has the option of asking those authorities to adopt such decisions. However, that consideration has no basis in EU law. In the absence of any specific basis in the restrictive measures regime established by Common Position 2001/931, the principle of sincere cooperation enshrined in Article 4(3) TEU does not permit the Council to require the competent authorities of the Member States to adopt national decisions that may serve as the basis for the reviews by the Council. If that regime requires the Council to carry out those reviews entirely on the basis of national decisions, the means available to the Council for that purpose are restricted unduly.

Lastly, the General Court's interpretation of Article 1 of Common Position 2001/931 was also not justified by the need to protect the persons. In the case of subsequent fund-freezing decisions, the person is protected, inter alia, by the possibility of bringing an action against such decisions before the Courts of the EU. These are required to determine, in particular, first, whether the obligation to state reasons laid down in Article 296 TFEU has been complied with and, therefore, whether the reasons relied on are sufficiently detailed and specific, and, second, whether those reasons are substantiated.

It follows that the General Court erred in law when it ruled that the Council had infringed Article 1 of Common Position 2001/931 by relying, in the statements of reasons, on material from sources other than national decisions adopted by competent authorities as well as Article 296 TFEU. However, although the grounds of a decision of the General Court revealed an infringement of EU law, that infringement was not capable of leading to the annulment of that decision, because the operative part of its judgment can be seen to be well founded on other legal grounds.

An analysis of the case

The verification of compliance by the third countries with human rights standards

The balance between the protections of fundamental rights and the effectiveness of the sanctions

Based on some academic perspectives, let us discuss the problems of the two cases presented in relation to the above two questions/issues with regard to autonomous sanctions.

With regard to the question (i) concerning decisions by authorities of third countries, both the General Court and the Court of Justice have consistently prioritized the human rights of persons subject to sanctions. Some evaluate such decisions of the General Court positively, arguing that the reliance on the decisions of the authorities of third countries should not be a means to circumvent the standard of human rights protected under EU laws when listing the targets of autonomous sanctions imposed by the EU and that the ruling that third countries must provide "equivalent protection" to that offered by the EU is reasonable.[18] Those adhering to this viewpoint, however, hold that the Court itself should have determined in more detail whether or not third country India meet the standard of human rights protection. This assessment would also apply to the Court of Justice, which came to almost the same conclusion.

In this context, the position of the CJEU will also be evaluated positively from the perspective of understanding the risk of abuse of the EU sanctions list by the governments of third countries (and EU Member States sympathetic to them).[19] In other words, many of the initiatives that attempt to include persons on the autonomous sanctions list come from foreign governments. The targets of terrorism are not limited to democratic countries; nonetheless, dictators often tend to consider their opponents to be terrorists. Because dictatorships rarely guarantee human rights to a satisfactory level, the requirement for human rights protection could counter the decisions by the authorities of third countries conducive to proposals of unfair listing by foreign governments.

Further, even if the EU seeks human rights protection by third countries, it may not impede the effectiveness of financial sanctions. When one country's legal authorities violate human rights protections, "other national authorities often become reluctant to co-ordinate transnational investigations and enforcement efforts."[20] If this is the case, the demand for human rights protection will be a requirement to facilitate cooperation between countries in implementing financial sanctions.

In light of the above academic views, it can be said that the CJEU provides an appropriate balance between the protection of human rights and the effectiveness of sanctions. However, although the Court of Justice referred to the decision of the General Court, it did not use the term "equivalent" nor, unlike the Advocate General, specify the extent to which the Council should verify the compliance with human rights by third countries. This may be interpreted as a "margin" left by the Court of Justice to ensure the effectiveness of sanctions.

Remaining issues in relation to other sanctions regimes

The reference to third countries or international organizations in EU sanctions is not limited to the instrument of autonomous sanctions. Although it is not possible to go into details, this part lists five questions related to other sanctions. The principal issue is whether the protection of human rights demanded by the EU from third countries and international organizations is consistent across three sanctions regimes and within every sanctions regime. To be more specific, the important points are (a) whether it is necessary to verify the compliance with human rights when a private individual is included in the list of targets of autonomous sanctions based on the resolution of the UN Security Council as in the case of a decision by the authorities of a third country and (b) whether it is the same as the protection of human rights required for the procedures of the UN in rendering resolutions related to sanctions against al-Qaeda in which EU sanctions are imposed on private individuals specified by the Security Council. It is yet difficult to grasp a complete view of the Court's case-law on the differences between sanctions regimes.[21] Furthermore, this issue is also related to the reason why the Court of Justice allowed the reliance on information outside domestic decisions in relation to question (ii), relying on the significance of a full judicial review at the EU level, as well as to the discussion of its necessity.

The significance of the purpose of the two-tier system is also related to the above questions. The "a sufficiently solid factual basis" refers to the standard to be met by the agencies of the EU for the proof of facts in relation to the grounds for sanctions at the stage of judicial review of the other sanctions regimes. This poses question (c), that is, whether the judicial institutions of a third country are required to guarantee human rights when the country's judgment is provided for this proof and whether the level of protection is the same as in the case of autonomous sanctions. This is a part of question (d)[22] as to whether the same degree of human rights protection should be sought from the third country when the Council imposes sanctions based on the decision of a third country and when the decision of a third country is used as evidence to prove the ground for sanctions at a stage where the sanctions are contested at the CJEU.

In third countries sanctions, references to the authorities of third countries may be included in the requirements for the determination of targets of sanctions.[23] This poses another question (e) as to whether these authorities are required to provide human rights protection. This problem mainly arises in the context of independent EU sanctions, yet the risk of the abuse of EU sanctions lists by the governments of third countries is existent, like in the context of autonomous sanctions. The CJEU appears to seek a certain degree of human rights protection, but it does not straightforwardly require the Council to verify the guarantees of human rights by authorities of third countries.[24]

Although the willingness of the Court to seek human rights protection from third countries may be widely supported, given the extent to which the consideration of the effectiveness of sanctions is shaped and its consistency with the other sanctions regimes, there is room for future clarification in a judgment by the Court of Justice.

Need for a domestic decision on new information serving as a basis to continue the imposition of EU sanctions on their targets

Three main points of conflict in relation to question (ii) between the General Court, which values and affirms human rights, and the Court of Justice, which prioritizes the effectiveness of sanctions, are summarized as follows:

First, with regard to the nature of continued listing, the Court of Justice considers the continued listing of persons as an extension of their initial listing and that the risk of those persons' involvement in terrorist activities persists. In contrast, the General Court prohibits the a priori recognition of persons as terrorists even upon continued listing, thus expanding the possibility of the removal of their names from the list.

Second, in terms of the relationship between the Council and Member States to ensure decisions by the authorities of each country, unlike the General Court, which assumed the obligation of cooperation between the two, the Court of Justice denied the existence of its legal basis.

Third, in relation to the degree of need for judicial protection for persons, the General Court and the Advocate General considered the situation as problematic wherein the guarantee of effective judicial protection of rights is reduced if domestic decisions become unnecessary. This is because persons who are continuously listed based on domestic decisions are given the opportunity not only to oppose financial sanctions in the CJEU but also to challenge the validity of the domestic decision in a national court, whereas only judicial relief by the EU is secured for those whose continued listing is determined by the Council based on facts other than those in the decision of the authorities. The General Court underlined the importance of the guarantees provided by human rights in this context and the Advocate General insisted that procedures should be rigorous due to the serious impact of listing on persons who are subjected to freezing of assets.[25] The Court of Justice, however, decided that the need for protection of individuals did not justify the interpretation of the General Court on the grounds of existence of relief by the CJEU.

Although the interpretation of the General Court is preferable from the viewpoint of human rights protection, it may be problematic in terms of the effectiveness of sanctions. Pantaleo criticizes the judgment of the General Court in that its interpretation of the Common Position was too strict.[26] The Common Position does not exclude the independent citation by the Council of the events occurring after the decisions. He stresses that this kind of reinforcement of sanctions lists should be allowed and that unlike the context in which the right to defense in legal proceedings poses a problem, the use of publicly known information other than those in the decisions of the authorities should be allowed, given the preventive nature of sanctions. This seems to support the position taken in the decision by the Court of Justice.

Even though whether or not the balance between the protection of human rights and the effectiveness of sanctions maintained by the Court is appropriate is not a simple question to answer, the conclusion of the Court of Justice is appropriate in both the *LTTE* and the *Hamas* cases based on the arguments and appropriateness of the conclusion. In fact, the General Court, in its judgment, placed restrictions on the acquisition of information proving acts of terrorism in the process of imposing sanctions on organizations publicly claiming responsibility for acts of terrorism, hindering the Council in obtaining information other than decisions of domestic authorities. As stressed by the General Court, violations of the obligation to provide reasons for imposing sanctions are indeed procedural issues and are irrelevant to the substantive judgment of whether a litigant person is a terrorist (organization). Nonetheless, if the Council were not unable to impose financial sanctions on terrorist organization publicly claiming responsibility for acts of terrorism, this would suggest that the EU does not implement Security Council resolutions effectively and in good faith. As the Council claimed in the *Hamas* case, this kind of situation goes against the purpose of the Common Position to fight against terrorism. From this perspective, the Court of Justice seems to have maintained an appropriate balance between human rights protection and the effectiveness of sanctions. However, the difference between the judgment of the upper and lower courts demonstrates the difficulties faced in balancing the two values.

The significance of findings by the EU to Japanese courts

Are imputations by the EU of a risk of involvement in terrorism to persons or entities conducive to Japanese financial sanctions? In Japanese courts, judges do not frequently refer to fund-freezing cases in the EU, much to less decisions by the Council. So far, less than 10 judgments referred to sanctions by the EU on terrorists, but these findings, including one on the LTTE, seldom, if ever, played a decisive role in the Japanese cases, let alone bolster a financial sanction imposed by a Japanese authority on terrorists, because most of the cases concerned recognitions of refugees from Turkey entering Japan. Exceptionally, in *Aleph* case, a court cited a financial sanction imposed by the EU authority on Aleph as information proving a risk of that religious cult, when reviewing maintenance of surveillance action on that entity.[27]

Conclusion

With regard to EU autonomous sanctions, the initial listing of a person to be sanctioned by the Council is based solely on the judgment of national authorities finding the involvement of the person in an act of terrorism. The purpose of this two-tier system is to ensure the accuracy of the facts that form the basis of the reason for imposing sanctions through examinations by the national authorities that have determined the involvement of certain persons in acts of terrorism to protect their human rights.

This has resulted in the questions as to (i) whether the Council can rely on the decisions of the authorities of countries other than EU Member States and (ii) whether the information on which the Council depends is limited to domestic decisions as in the initial listing when reviewing the list and determining the continuation of sanctions to stick to the purpose of the two-tier system.

With regard to (i), the Court of Justice approved of reliance on such decisions, provided that the Council verifies the protection of human rights by the authorities of third countries and explains it as the reason provided in support of their decision to impose sanctions. However, while the General Court and the Advocate General demanded human rights protection in third countries to be equivalent to that of the EU, the Court of Justice did not mention the degree of the guarantee of human rights. It is possible to say that the Court of Justice left room to ensure the effectiveness of sanctions in the future.

As for (ii), the General Court prioritized the protection of human rights and limited the information used by the Council to determine the continuation of sanctions to domestic decisions, while the Court of Justice claimed that the means of the Council should not be restricted unduly and approved the finding of facts that would be the basis for a decision to continue imposition of sanctions based on information other than domestic decisions.

Thus, in the two cases related to autonomous sanctions, the Court of Justice was more cautious about emphasizing human rights protection than the General Court to ensure the effectiveness of sanctions. After the first instance, both cases were described as challenges that remain to be faced by the EU.[28] After writing her opinions on both cases, the Advocate General Sharpston described the case of listing and freezing of funds as a "awkward questions."[29] Given the nature of these cases, the ruling of the Court of Justice should not be described as a setback in the protection of human rights because it in fact represents the struggle of the Court to balance the effectiveness of sanctions with human rights protection even after 15 years since the beginning of autonomous sanctions.

It is important to observe whether and how the balance between the guarantee of human rights and the effectiveness of sanctions indicated by the two rulings of General Chamber on the autonomous sanctions of the EU is reflected in other issues related to sanctions. The consistency and systematicity of CJEU cases including autonomous sanctions and sanctions against al-Qaeda and third countries are not clear. The European Commission observed that in the LTTE case, the regulations were annulled for "procedural reasons," which is different from the *Kadi II* case.[30] The accumulation of future court decisions in relation to the repercussion of the two rulings of the Grand Chamber on EU autonomous sanctions on the other sanctions regimes enforced by the EU, as well as their impacts on the implementation of financial sanctions by the UN, must be observed.

Notes

1 For example, S/Res/1267, 15 October 1999.
2 S/Res/1373, 28 September 2001.
3 Case C-599/14 P *Council v Liberation Tigers of Tamil Eelam (LTTE)* (ECLI:EU:C:2017:583).
4 Case C-79/15 P *Council v Hamas* (ECLI:EU:C:2017:584).
5 See, e.g., Christina Eckes, "EU restrictive measures against natural and legal persons: From counterterrorist to third country sanctions," *Common Market Law Review* 51, Issue 3 (2014), pp. 869–874.
6 See further, Charlotte Beaucillon, "Opening up the Horizon: the ECJ'S New Take on Country Sanctions," *Common Market Law Review* 55, Issue 2 (2018), pp. 387–416.
7 Council Common Position 2001/931/CFSP of 27 December 2001 on the application of specific measures to combat terrorism [2001] OJ L 344/93.
8 Joined Cases C-539/10 P & C-550/10 P *Stichting Al-Aqsa v Council* (ECLI:EU:C:2012:711) paras. 68–72.
9 Council of the European Union, Annex II Working methods of the Working Party on implementation of Common Position 2001/931/CFSP on the application of specific measures to combat terrorism, 10826/1/07 REV 1 [2007].
10 "The names of persons and entities on the list in the Annex shall be reviewed at regular intervals and at least once every six months to ensure that there are grounds for keeping them on the list."
11 Joined Cases T-208/11 & T-508/11 *LTTE v Council* (ECLI:EU:T:2014:885), paras. 127–149.
12 Ibid., paras. 143–144.
13 *Al-Aqsa, supra* note 8, para. 82.
14 *LTTE, supra* note 11, paras. 158–229.
15 AG Sharpston in Case C-599/14 P *Council v LTTE* (ECLI:EU:C:2016:723). As far as the issue (i) is concerned, the AG, unlike the General Court, "see no need for the Council to verify systematically whether the third State in practice fails to apply its legislation protecting the rights of the defense and guaranteeing effective judicial protection." The AG slightly alleviate a burden on the Council which is imposed by the GC.
16 *LTTE, supra* note 3, paras. 25–33.
17 Ibid., paras. 58–71.
18 Luca Pantaleo, "Of Terrorists and Combatants: The Application of EU Anti-Terrorist Measures to Situations of Armed Conflict in the General Court's Ruling Concerning the Liberation Tigers of Tamil Eelam," *European Law Review* 40, (2015), p. 609.
19 Iain Cameron, "Introduction," in *EU Sanctions: Law and Policy Issues Concerning Restrictive Measures*, ed. Iain Cameron (Intersentia, 2013), 25.
20 Kern Alexander, *Economic Sanctions Law and Public Policy* (Palgrave Macmillan, 2009), 316.
21 Compare *Al-Aqsa, supra* note 8, para. 72 and Case T-348/07 *Stichting Al-Aqsa v Council* (ECLI:EU:T:2010:373), para. 98 with Case T-85/09 *Kadi v Commission* (ECLI:EU:T:2010:418), paras. 186–187.
22 *Cf.* Case T-248/13 *Al-Ghabra v Commission* (ECLI:EU:T:2016:721), para. 144.
23 For example, Article 1 (1) of Council Decision (CFSP) 2015/143 of 29 January 2015 amending Decision 2014/119/CFSP concerning restrictive measures directed against certain persons, entities and bodies in view of the situation in Ukraine [2015] OJ L 24/16.

24 See Case C-599/16 P *Yanukovych v Council* (ECLI:EU:C:2017:785), paras. 58–78 and Case T-348/14 *Yanukovych v Council* (ECLI:EU:T:2016:508), paras. 111–116.
25 *LTTE, supra* note 11, para. 224 and A.G. Sharpston, *supra* note 15, paras. 100–102.
26 Pantaleo, *supra* note 18, pp. 610–611.
27 *Aleph (Aum Shinrikyo) v. State* (Tokyo District Ct., Dec. 8, 2011).
28 Ricardo Gosalbo-Bono and Frederik Naert, "The Reluctant (Lisbon) Treaty and Its Implementation in the Practice of the Council," in Piet Eeckhout and Manuel Lopez-Escudero eds. *The European Union's External Action in Times of Crisis* (Hart Publishing, 2016), pp. 67–68.
29 Eleanor Sharpston, "Of the State of the (European) Union and of Trade Deals," *IEL Working Paper* (University of Birmingham, 2017), p. 5.
30 European Commission, "Report from the Commission to the European Parliament, the Council, the European Economic and Social Committee and the Committee of the Regions 2014 Report on the Application of the EU Charter of Fundamental Rights," COM (2015) 191 final, p. 6.

8 Implementation and enforcement of UN sanctions—the private sector's key role and evolving standards

Alexander Dmitrenko[1]

Introduction

This chapter will focus on the role of the private sector, and primarily financial institutions, in implementing and enforcing the UN sanctions.

The effectiveness of a sanctions regime largely depends on its implementation and enforcement by both public and private entities. The UN sanctions regime lacks its own enforcement apparatus and, therefore, must rely on individual UN member states to adopt and implement UN sanctions measures into domestic legal systems. Broadly, there are two modes of implementing UN sanctions in domestic law: (i) by making UN sanctions directly part of the domestic legal system; or (ii) by passing new legislation that specifically deals with sanctions.[2] Many jurisdictions, particularly those which have not yet developed their own sanctions legislation, choose to adopt UN sanctions directly into their legal systems.[3] However, such adoption does not necessarily translate into successful implementation of UN sanctions (mainly due to countries lacking enforcement capabilities and/or leaving the pragmatic implementation to the corporate sector to self-regulate).[4]

UN member states' governments have the primary responsibility for implementation of UN sanctions; however, the role and actions of the private sector have become a critical vehicle for the sanctions implementation. Stephen Tully goes as far as arguing that "[c]orporations are in effect conduits through which governments unilaterally implement economic sanctions. National legislation contemplating rights of actions against other private parties for their extraterritorial behavior shifts the execution of foreign policy onto non-state actors."[5] Corporate entities increasingly: (i) implement internal steps to ensure compliance with UN sanctions; and (ii) require compliance with UN sanctions from their contractual counterparties. This effort is primarily led by financial institutions.

This chapter focuses on various internal and external measures adopted by the corporate sector to effectively implement UN sanctions. After setting out the continuously evolving legal framework for sanctions compliance this chapter will identify the "gold standard" of sanctions compliance followed by the detailed analysis of its two key elements—due diligence and contractual protections. The discussion will rely on recent practical examples from domestic and international corporations from across Asia, while identifying best practices and providing recommendations for common definitions and contractual clauses to ensure sanctions compliance and implementation by the corporate sector according to regulatory requirements and industry standards (ideally aiming for the "gold standard" set out by the financial industry).

Legal framework for sanctions compliance

Corporate sanctions compliance must be based on internal policies and procedures aimed to ensure ongoing sanctions compliance while taking into account the ever-changing sanctions risks, regimes and enforcement practices. However, there is no specific guidance on what elements would constitute an adequate UN sanctions compliance system. Thus, governments have taken it upon themselves to fill this regulatory void. For instance, in March 2019, the US Department of Treasury's Office of Foreign Assets Control (OFAC), the primary sanctions regulator in the United States and undeniably the most active sanctions enforcer, published "A Framework for OFAC Compliance Commitments."[6]

The framework is aimed to ensure "that the private sector implements strong and effective compliance programs" and "to strengthen sanctions compliance practices across the board."[7] It outlines the five "essential components" of a compliance program. These include: (1) the commitment of senior management; (2) risk assessments which "consist of a holistic review of the organization from top-to-bottom and assess its touchpoints to the outside world"; (3) internal controls to clarify expectations, define procedures and processes, and minimize the risks identified; (4) comprehensive testing and auditing; and (5) a training program provided on a periodic basis. This framework provides "OFAC's perspective on the essential components of a sanctions compliance program"[8] for sanctions compliance programs, which applies not only to US companies, but also to non-US companies that may be subject to US sanctions laws through a US nexus (such as conducting business in or with the United States, dealing with US persons, or using US goods or services). Although the framework primarily focuses on the US sanctions, it, arguably, is also meant to offer guidance on and ensure compliance with the UN sanctions, which have been historically aligned with the US sanctions.

OFAC's hope is that the above guidance does not fall on deaf ears. In fact, most major US corporations and major financial institutions have been implementing strict sanctions compliance systems in response to OFAC's enforcement actions. However, it is no secret that many Asia-based companies, even those in riskier industries (such as energy, construction, and telecommunications) or with significant cross-border operations and US nexus, have not established systematic sanctions compliance. Such insufficient sanctions compliance is primarily due to the lack of: (i) corporates' appreciation that they and their operations are subject to certain sanctions imposed by the UN and the United States (which, in the case of US secondary sanctions, could apply to any entity in the world);

(ii) enforcement against Asia-based corporates (which, in my opinion and experience, is bound to change); (iii) sanctions professionals with expertise in UN sanctions (which is partly due to insufficient sanctions compliance education); and (iv) peer pressure (which, as this chapter will illustrate, is mounting, particularly from the financial sector).

One possible exception is the export controls compliance at major trading houses, which has been thoroughly implemented, but typically focused only on relevant domestic export control laws, thus, leaving international sanctions compliance susceptible to potential non-compliance. Therefore, the global private sector would be expected to enhance its sanctions compliance based on this regulatory guidance, and precedents (primarily from the financial industry).

"Gold standard" of sanctions compliance promulgated by the financial sector

In the last decade, major financial institutions have been the primary target of sanctions enforcement in the United States,[9] the European Union, and most recently in the United Kingdom,[10] resulting in significant monetary penalties for sanctions violations. In response to such strict enforcement measures and to mitigate the significant risks they present, financial institutions are making efforts to adopt or enhance robust internal sanctions compliance programs, and have begun requiring sanctions compliance from clients and counterparties.

A typical compliance function at a major international financial institution has a wide reach both vertically (running from the headquarters down to global subsidiaries) and horizontally (covering all business units and all relevant sanctions regimes, including UN sanctions). It is important that sanctions compliance functions as an intrinsic part of the financial institution's regulatory compliance system and is administered by those with expertise in sanctions and export controls.

In essence, financial institutions are often regarded as important enforcers of various sanctions regimes, playing a "gate-keeper" role against sanctions violators, but at the same time, they are private actors and often become sanctions enforcees by the respective governments. Therefore, financial institutions must preempt any dubious actions that might be regarded as sanctions-busting. In doing so, the financial industry has over time established a comprehensive "gold standard" for sanctions compliance policies and procedures, which are clearly and strongly communicated from the top management and enshrined in each corporation's Code of Conduct, which outlines fundamental rules, principles, responsibilities, and proper practices by which the corporation and all its directors, officers, and employees should be bound.[11]

Based on recent examples and practices, an effective compliance system should therefore include the following elements:[12]

(i) compliance culture instilled by management with the right tone from the top,[13] including robust management oversight and support as well as financial resources;

(ii)   a compliance function independent of business functions in terms of deci-sion making, but coordinated with respect to information and data sharing;

(iii)   interdependence between various compliance sub-divisions which could assist spotting issues, making compliance a cost-effective and efficient function;

(iv)   a sanctions administrative team with expertise in relevant sanctions and export controls, which for any cross-border business should include US and UN sanctions;

(v)   a compliance pyramid to encompass all subsidiaries, or at least key regions;

(vi)   risk mapping and risk mitigation assessed on a periodic, and ideally annual, basis;

(vii)   access to legal and other external counsel with expertise in specific areas of compliance, including jurisdictional expertise; and

(viii) company-wide periodic training and alerts to any relevant changes in applic-able sanctions regimes.

This list is not exhaustive and will likely continue to expand due to a persistent market tendency towards broader and more rigid compliance as sanctions regimes grow increasingly more complex and continue to be rigorously enforced.

The key purpose of a robust compliance system is to prevent sanctions violations. Financial institutions are particularly exposed to potential violations due to the nature of their operations; from financing to money transfers. Entities targeted by sanctions need funds and are constantly looking for innovative ways to evade sanctions. Therefore, financial institutions and other businesses that aim to prevent sanctions violations must: (i) conduct careful due diligence to identify potential connections to sanctioned parties or countries; and (ii) ensure their counterparties continually comply with sanctions regimes, which is typic-ally achieved through contractual protections in relevant agreements. The critical concepts of due diligence and contractual protections are discussed in more detail in the sections that follow.

Due diligence

Corporate due diligence typically means an investigation or exercise of care that a reasonable business is expected to take during its business operations, particularly before entering into a contractual relationship with another party.[14] This type of investigation is meant to enhance and systematize relevant information to prop-erly inform the decision makers about potential costs, benefits, and risks. Due diligence is therefore expected, or in some cases required, to be conducted (e.g., anti-bribery and anti-money laundering regulations).

There is no set standard for what constitutes "reasonable" sanctions due dili-gence. Instead, due diligence is risk-based and is determined on a case-by-case basis. Due diligence is also a continuing obligation that does not end once a new counterparty has been screened, as regulations and sanctions lists change over time. Therefore, in order to ensure effective sanctions compliance, a business must conduct periodic due diligence reflecting the latest information related to developments in economic sanctions.

The difficulty of effectively complying with sanctions is combining business expertise with legal and regulatory oversight over every field of operations. Businesses use decentralized compliance setups in order to account for the particularities of different departments and branches. The nature of associated risks and activities may vary within each department; compliance teams should be in close contact with operational teams. Institutions with international branches have dedicated staff to monitor and enforce regulatory requirements for each jurisdiction.

Banks and businesses use multiple methods to comply with UN sanctions. Typically, due diligence involves preparing in advance for a transaction that may be subject to sanctions. In order to conduct due diligence, entities and institutions will typically use contingency planning to help react to events. Understanding new sanctions is also essential as sanctions rules can be complex. Entities protect themselves by engaging with contractual counterparties, speaking with regulators and updating internal policies. Consulting with local counsel to prevent breaching local law is important, and often essential. Most businesses and institutions will assess the risk in the context of their products, services and location of transactions.

Institutions will take various steps when concerned about whether a transaction may breach sanctions laws and regulations. In order to ensure compliance with sanctions laws, many companies empower a central team to coordinate investigation and PR messaging (as it is important to build a central response team to coordinate the investigation); instruct PR contacts to work with legal counsel for public statements to preserve reputation; and employ individuals who are not line managers to ensure there are independent parties supporting investigations. Due diligence includes considering who should receive legal representation; assessing whether employee discipline is appropriate; working out how to preserve evidence and manage data efficiently; assessing how to preserve legal privilege and comply with data protection laws; and considering issues relating to self-reporting. Institutions also keep track of sanctions being imposed during contractual negotiations in order to remain compliant with sanctions laws.

Contractual protections

While due diligence aims to identify and prevent potential sanctions risks, it alone may not be sufficient, particularly when sanctions-related risks arise due to a contractual counterparty's conduct or an unexpected change in sanctions regimes. Therefore, a contractual relationship should ensure sanctions compliance by counterparties, which is typically achieved through sanctions compliance clauses in the core agreements. These clauses serve as a key safeguard, particularly against counterparties who lack satisfactory internal sanctions compliance.

Sanctions compliance clauses are generally designed to protect parties from entering into transactions with counterparties that are or could become sanctioned; protect parties from potential historical and ongoing liability due to non-compliance; and protect against reputational harm. Sanctions clauses typically include assurances that the contractual counterparty is not sanctioned; does not and will not have unlawful dealings with sanctioned persons or in a manner that could result in becoming sanctioned; has compliance policies and procedures in place; and will not use proceeds of the transaction in a manner that is restricted. Although not every agreement will contain sanctions-related clauses, major financial institutions expect and require thorough sanctions clauses for financing agreements.

The primary place in which UN sanctions-related representations are incorporated into financing agreements is through definitions. Typical sanctions-related definitions in a financing agreement include the following:

(i)   "Sanctions" [or "Economic Sanctions Law"] means any economic or financial sanctions administered by the US Treasury Department's Office of Foreign Assets Control (OFAC), the US State Department, or any other governmental agency of the US government, the United Nations, the European Union or any member state thereof, the United Kingdom [list any others that might be relevant, such as Canada, Australia, Japan, or Switzerland].

(ii) "Sanctioned Person" means any person, organization, or vessel: (a) designated on the OFAC Specially Designated Nationals and Blocked Persons List, the EU Consolidated List, the list of Financial Sanctions Targets maintained by Her Majesty's Treasury, or on any list of targeted persons issued under Sanctions; (b) that is, or is part of, a government of a Sanctioned Country; (c) owned or controlled by, or acting on behalf of, any of the foregoing; (d) operating from a Sanctioned Country; or (e) otherwise targeted under any Sanctions.

(iii) "Sanctioned Country" [or "Sanctioned Territory"] means any country or other territory targeted by a general export, import, financial or investment embargo under Sanctions, which countries and territories, as of the date of this [Agreement], include the Crimea region, Cuba, Iran, North Korea and Syria.

The example definitions above incorporate UN sanctions into their scope by referring to UN sanctions explicitly in the definition of "Sanctions." Further, any person or entity designated under UN sanctions is also incorporated into the defined term "Sanctioned Person" as the definition includes "any person ... designated on ... any list of targeted persons issued under Sanctions." Because "Sanctions" include UN sanctions by definition, UN sanctions are also captured by "Sanctioned Person." UN sanctions are similarly incorporated into the defined term "Sanctioned Country" through reference to the defined term "Sanctions."

In a typical contract, these definitions set the framework and should be closely relied upon in various representations and undertakings. A typical financing agreement, for example, could contain some or all of the following sanctions-related provisions:

(i) Non-Sanctioned Status

None of the [Obligor/Seller/Buyer/etc.] and its Subsidiaries is, or is owned or controlled by, a Sanctioned Person, and no officer or director [nor, to the knowledge of the [Obligor/Seller/Buyer/etc.], any employee, agent, representative or Affiliate] of any such person is a Sanctioned Person.

(ii) No Dealings with Sanctioned Persons

None of the [Obligor/Seller/Buyer/etc.] and its Subsidiaries has, during the past five years, [knowingly] entered into any agreement, transaction, or dealing with or for the benefit of any Sanctioned Person (or involving any property thereof) or involving any Sanctioned Territory[, in breach of, or in a manner that could expose such person to penalties under, any applicable sanctions].

(iii) Sanctions Compliance, Policies and Procedures

The [Obligor/Seller/Buyer/etc.], its Subsidiaries, and their respective directors and officers and, to the knowledge of the [Obligor/Seller/Buyer/etc.], their respective employees and agents, are in [material] compliance with applicable Sanctions and have instituted and maintain policies and procedures reasonably designed to promote and achieve compliance with applicable Sanctions.

(iv) Sanctions Compliance

No [Obligor/Seller/Buyer/etc.] shall breach applicable Sanctions in any material respect.

(v) Sanctions Use of Proceeds

[Each Obligor/Seller/Buyer/etc.] will ensure that none of the proceeds of the [transaction] will, directly or knowingly indirectly, be used or paid: (i) to any person that is a Sanctioned Person[, in a manner that would be in breach of applicable Sanctions]; or (ii) in any other manner that would reasonably be expected to result in [Obligor/Seller/Buyer/etc.] or, to the best of its knowledge, any other party, being in breach of applicable Sanctions.

As evidenced by the above sample provisions, each sanctions representation and warranty incorporates at least one of the three definitions referenced above, which all include UN sanctions within their scope. Such inclusion of a reference to UN sanctions therefore requires compliance with such sanctions and illustrates the practical implementation of UN sanctions, to the extent those who offer such representations and warranties are actually doing so while relying on the compliance system or specific transactional due diligence that ensures their compliance with UN sanctions.

Conclusion

The corporate sector, led by financial institutions, has proven to be an essential implementation vehicle for UN sanctions both internally (through a comprehensive set of internal sanctions compliance policies and procedures) and externally (through due diligence of counterparties and contractual clauses aimed at addressing sanctions risks). Recent enforcement trends and practical experience indicate that compliance with UN sanctions by corporations will continue to strengthen across various industries due to expanding internal compliance functions and requirements to ensure UN sanctions compliance imposed by counterparties (particularly from the financial sector). Therefore, compliance with UN sanctions would ultimately become a norm of the international business operations, thus increasing effectiveness and global outreach of UN sanctions, which would be a desired outcome.

Notes

1 Alexander Dmitrenko is Head of Asia Sanctions in the Tokyo office of Freshfields Bruckhaus Deringer, a leading international law firm. His practice focuses on advising Asian and other clients on sanctions, export controls, anti-bribery, anti-money laundering and other regulatory as well as compliance-related issues. The author would like to convey gratitude to his colleagues Weronika Bukowski and Shini Pattni for providing generous assistance with this chapter. This chapter is written in my personal capacity and does not represent the views or opinions of Freshfields Bruckhaus Deringer.
2 For example, the EU enacts both "derived sanctions," which implement UN sanctions, and "autonomous sanctions" where the EU decides to go further than the UN sanctions (or where there are no UN sanctions). The European Council has stated that

> [i]f necessary, the Council will impose autonomous EU sanctions in support of efforts to fight terrorism and the proliferation of weapons of mass destruction and as a restrictive measure to uphold respect for human rights, democracy, the rule of law and good governance [...] in accordance with our common foreign and security policy, as set out in Article 11 TEU, and in full conformity with our obligations under international law.
>
> Council of the EU, "Basic Principles on the Use of Restrictive Measures (Sanctions)," CFSP 450, 7 June 2004, paragraph 3.

3 Some of the most notable examples include Hong Kong, India, and Singapore.
4 In the aftermath of the 2015 1MDB scandal (when a former Malaysian Prime Minister and his aides were accused for syphoning nearly 700 million dollars of state funds, including through the Singaporean financial system), Singapore boosted domestic regulatory compliance systems, including money laundering and sanctions program, which still implements the UN sanctions into domestic law.
5 Stephen Tully, *Corporations and International Lawmaking* (Brill, 2007), p. 282.
6 See full text of OFAC's *A Framework for OFAC Compliance Commitments* at www.treasury.gov/resource-center/sanctions/Documents/framework_ofac_cc.pdf   (last accessed 28 April 2020).
7 See Press Release by the OFAC, announcing the issuance of *A Framework for OFAC Compliance Commitments* at https://home.treasury.gov/index.php/news/press-releases/sm680 (last accessed 29 April 2020).
8 Ibid.
9 For example, in 2015 BNP Paribas SA settled for USD 9 billion with the US Department of the Treasury's Office of Foreign Assets Control ("OFAC") for sanctions violations. The settlement resolved OFAC's investigation into BNP Paribas'

systemic practice of concealing, removing, omitting, or obscuring references to information about US-sanctioned parties in 3,897 financial and trade transactions routed to or through banks in the United States between 2005 and 2012 in apparent violation of the Sudanese Sanctions Regulations, 31 C.F.R. part 538; the Iranian Transactions and Sanctions Regulations, 31 C.F.R. part 560; the Cuban Assets Control Regulations, 31 C.F.R. part 515; and the Burmese Sanctions Regulations, 31 C.F.R. part 537.

www.treasury.gov/press-center/press-releases/Pages/jl2447.aspx
(last accessed 28 April 2020).

10 See e.g. Freshfields Risk and Compliance Blog Posts, *Regulatory ramp-up: UK's OFSI imposes landmark £20m fine* https://riskandcompliance.freshfields.com/post/102g3uf/regulatory-ramp-up-uks-ofsi-imposes-landmark-20m-fine (last accessed 28 April 2020).

11 See e.g. Morgan Stanley's 2020 Code of Conduct available from www.morganstanley.com/about-us-governance/code-of-conduct (last accessed 28 April 2020).

12 See e.g. J.P. Morgan's list of five key sanctions compliance elements at www.jpmorgan.com/jpmpdf/1320747764044.pdf (last accessed 28 April 2020).

13 See e.g. Morgan Stanley's 2020 Code of Conduct is premised by the message from the Chairman and CEO www.morganstanley.com/about-us-governance/code-of-conduct (last accessed 28 April 2020).

14 *Black's Law Dictionary* defines due diligence as "[T]he diligence reasonably expected from, and ordinarily exercised by, a person who seeks to satisfy a legal requirement or discharge an obligation." For a practical definition of "due diligence" related to commonplace business transactions, see Jeffrey Berkman, *Due Diligence and Business Transaction* (Apress, 2013), pp. 9–11. To learn more about "due diligence" process, see Craig E. Chapman, *Conducting Due Diligence* (Practicing Law Institute, 2006). Interestingly, with respect to the United Nations Guiding Principles on Business and Human Rights, which should form part of the "gold standard" compliance process, some authors have argued that such Guiding Principles invoked two different concepts of due diligence—first, a process to manage business risks and, second, standard of conduct required to discharge an obligation. See e.g. J. Bonnitcha and M. McCorquodale, *UN Guiding Principles on Business and Human Rights*, available at https://academic.oup.com/ejil/article/28/3/899/4616670 (last accessed 20 May 2020). This chapter only deals with the former concept, particularly as it relates to the contractual relationships involving the financial sector.

9 Judicial challenges against UN financial sanctions

Akira Kato

Introduction

The United Nations Security Council (UNSC) has the powers to adopt sanctions under the Chapter VII of the UN Charter, which impose legally binding obligations on UN Member States.[1] The measures include financial sanctions, such as asset freezing in accordance with Article 41 of the UN Charter.[2] Notably, Article 103 provides that:

> In the event of a conflict between the obligations of the Members of the United Nations under the present Charter and their obligations under any other international agreement, their obligations under the present Charter shall prevail.

By virtue of this Article, legally binding obligations of UN Member States arising from UNSC decisions prevail over their obligations under other international treaties.[3] This is the interpretation firmly established in literatures and case law.[4] In the *Lockerbie* case, the International Court of Justice admitted the prevalence of UNSC Resolution 748 over the parties' obligations under the 1971 Montreal Convention for the Suppression of Unlawful Acts against the Safety of Civil Aviation.[5] This effect is quite remarkable in a decentralized international society.

In the post-Cold War period in which security threats are becoming more and more multifaceted, the UNSC has triggered a series of sanctions, which required UN Member States to direct a travel ban or asset freeze against individuals or groups designated in the UN sanctions lists. These "targeted sanctions," coupled with the extraordinary effect of UNSC decisions, have caused a serious dilemma—on the one hand, UN Member States are obliged to implement financial sanctions without a sufficient procedure for human rights protections at the UN level while, on the other hand, they are also required to comply with human rights obligations under other international treaties.

In order to discuss the way to reconcile the requirements of UN financial sanctions and those of human rights protections, this chapter analyzes and compares the legal approaches employed by the European Court of Human

Rights (ECtHR) and the Court of Justice of the European Union (CJEU) with a particular focus on the *Kadi* judgments and the *Al-Dulimi* judgment.[6]

The judicial cases involving the UNSC financial Sanctions

The cases before the CJEU: the autonomy of the EU legal order

The first Kadi judgment by the CJEU

The UNSC Al-Qaida sanctions regime, established by UNSC Resolution 1269 (1998) and strengthened by the subsequent resolutions,[7] provides asset freeze, travel ban, and arms embargo against an individual or group who "is associated with ISIL or Al-Qaida."[8] The UNSC Sanctions Committee receives information from Member States and updates the sanctions list.[9]

In 2001, Kadi, a national of Saudi Arabia, was designated as a sanctions target by the Sanctions Committee and subsequently by the relevant EU regulations intending to implement the UNSC resolutions. He lodged applications at the Court of First Instance of EU (CFI), claiming that the EU regulations, which set out the asset freeze against him, should be annulled because his fundamental rights, particularly the right to respect for property, the right to be heard, and the right to effective judicial review, were breached.[10]

The September 2005 judgment of the CFI put emphasis on the primacy of the UN Charter, rejecting Kadi's argument. The Court found that reviewing the internal lawfulness of the relevant regulations in the light of fundamental rights would mean "that the Court is to consider, indirectly, the lawfulness of those resolutions," and that this would be incompatible with the obligations arising from Articles 25, 48, and 103 of the UN Charter.[11] It was also established that, although the Court could indirectly review the lawfulness of the UNSC resolutions with regard to *jus cogens*, the relevant regulations did not infringe Kadi's fundamental rights covered by *jus cogens*.[12]

However, the CJEU took a completely different approach, setting aside the CFI's judgment.[13] According to CIEU, the EC treaty "established a complete system" for the review of the legality of the EC institutions, and international treaties cannot affect the allocation of powers fixed by the treaties as well as "the autonomy of the Community legal system."[14] It followed that, respect of human rights being a condition of legality of the Community acts, the review by the Community judicature applied even to the Community act giving effect to the UN Charter and the relevant UNSC resolutions in this case. The CJEU cautiously pointed out that this kind of review would not mean a challenge to the primacy of the UNSC resolutions in international law.[15] In the Court's view, any judicial review of the internal lawfulness of the contested regulation is not excluded by the principles of the international legal order under the UN even when that regulation intends to implement the UNSC resolution, because the UN Charter gives Member States leeway in terms of how they transpose UNSC resolutions into their domestic order.[16] It claimed that the Community judicature must "ensure the review, in principle the full review, of the lawfulness of the all Community acts," even if those acts intend to implement UNSC resolutions.[17]

Based on this theoretical position, the Court then considered whether Kadi's fundamental rights were breached. It found that the contested regulation did not provide for a procedure for communicating the evidence for the listing of Kadi, that Kadi could not defend his rights with regard to such evidence before the Community judicature,[18] and that the contested regulations did not furnish any guarantee allowing him to put his case to the authorities.[19] Consequently, the CJEU concluded that the right to be heard, the right to an effective legal remedy and the rights to respect for property had been infringed, thereby annulling the contested regulations.[20]

The crux of CJEU's argument is that the autonomous character of the EU legal order precludes, at least within the EU legal order, the prevalent effect of the UNSC resolutions based on Article 103 of the UN Charter with regard to EU fundamental rights.[21] This is regarded as "dualist approach."[22]

The actual impact of the CJEU's Kadi *judgment: the establishment of the UNSC Ombudsperson*

The CJEU's judgment seemed to be taken seriously within the UNSC, as a report of the Analytical Support and Sanctions Monitoring Team regarded the judgment as "arguably the most significant legal development" to affect the Al-Qaida sanctions regime.[23] Even though CJEU did not directly review the legality of the UNSC resolutions, it is obvious that the finding of annulation of the relevant EU regulations intending to implement those resolutions could practically hinder the carrying out of the UNSC sanctions regime. Before the first *Kadi* judgment, the UNSC resolution 1730 had already set up the focal point within the Secretariat to receive a de-listing request directly from individuals or groups, not via their governments.[24] This procedure, however, still lacks a review organ that is independent of the Sanctions Committee and the UNSC members, so the CJEU argued that the procedure of the Sanctions Committee remains "in essence diplomatic and intergovernmental," ever after the introduction of the focal point.[25]

It is against this background that the UNSC established an Office of the Ombudsperson by UNSC Resolution 1904 so as to ensure that the Sanctions Committee procedures "are fair and clear."[26] According to the resolution and its Annex II, the Ombudsperson, who is appointed by the Secretary General, performs its tasks "in an independent and impartial manner." After receiving a delisting request from an individual or group, the Ombudsperson seeks relevant information from states and UN bodies, it has a dialogue with the petitioner, and finally lays out the principal arguments on the delisting request. UNSC Resolution 1989 (2011) further strengthens this procedure.[27] The Ombudsperson, after the dialogue with the individual, presents to the Sanctions Committee a recommendation on the delisting of the individual. If the Ombudsperson recommends the delisting of the individual, the sanction measures, including asset freezing, shall terminate in relation to that individual. Somewhat surprisingly, the delisting recommendation could be overturned only by consensus in the Sanctions Committee.[28] This procedure, known as a "reverse consensus,"[29] means that any single vote of a Sanctions Committee member could sustain the recommendation for delisting. The achievement of the Ombudsperson process has so far been impressive. According to the Ombudsperson's report of 23 January 2017, the total number of delisting requests that had been submitted was 78, and 46 individual and 28 entities had been delisted through the Ombudsperson process.[30]

Opinions are divided on Ombudsperson procedure. The Watson Report claims that, although it is not a formal judicial review, it offers "what arguably are equivalent elements to address due process concerns, in essence, *de facto* judicial review."[31] On the contrary, Ben Emmerson, the UN Special Rapporteur, strongly criticized this procedure as not meeting the human rights standard because of many defects, including a lack of legally binding effect of the Ombudsperson's recommendations.[32]

However, the establishment and improvements of the Office of the Ombudsperson could not satisfy the CJEU. After the adoption of the EU regulation of November 2008 imposing asset freeze on Kadi again, he submitted an application on February 2009. The CJEU delivered the judgment on July 2013 (the second *Kadi* judgment), which found the annulment of that regulation.[33] Confirming the holdings in the first *Kadi* judgment, the second *Kadi* judgment claimed that the delisting procedures at the UN level do not provide to the listed person "the guarantee of the effective judicial protection," surprisingly without explicit reference to the UNSC Ombudsperson.[34] The Court then scrutinized the summary of reasons for listing Kadi provided by the UNSC Sanctions Committee, and found that the reasons provided were insufficient and information or evidence enough for substantiating the reasons were not furnished.[35] As a result, the CJEU confirmed the annulment of the contested regulation in spite of the establishment of the Office of the Ombudsperson,[36] the decisive response on the part of the UNSC to the first *Kadi* judgment.

The cases before the ECtHR: the harmonious approach

The Al-Jedda case and the Nada case

Before proceeding to the *Al-Dulimi* case, it is necessary to review the *Al-Jedda* case and the *Nada* case as an important precedent of the *Al-Dulimi* case. UNSC Resolution 1546, adopted on 8 June 2004, provides the security framework of the Iraq situation in the aftermath of the Iraq War. Paragraph 10 of the resolution stipulates that the multinational force has "the authority to take all necessary measures to contribute to the maintenance of security and stability in Iraq."[37] Al-Jedda was held in internment in the detention center in Iraq run by British forces for his alleged involvement in terrorist activities. He then lodged an application to the ECtHR, stating that his detention by the UK was in breach of Article 5 (1) of the European Convention on Human Rights (ECHR).[38] As is the case in the *Kadi* cases, the central issue here is whether the UK's obligations or authorities under the UNSC resolution could prevail over the UK's obligations under the ECHR in accordance with Article 103 of the UN Charter.

The Court's July 2011 judgment, in order to clarify the relationship between the UN Charter and the ECHR, refers to the principle that the principles of the ECHR cannot be interpreted in a vacuum and "the Court must take into account relevant rules of international law," including the UN Charter.[39] Considering the fact that Article 1 (3) of the UN Charter lay downs "promoting and encouraging respect for human rights and fundamental freedoms" as one of the purposes of the UN and Article 24 (2) requires the UNSC to act in accordance with the purposes and principles of the UN, the Court submitted that "there must be presumption that the Security Council does not intend to impose any obligation on Member States to breach fundamental principles of human rights."[40]

The Court could not find, in the relevant UNSC resolution, "clear and explicit language," which is necessary for rebutting that presumption.[41] This means that the UK's detention of Al-Jedda could not be based on the authorization under resolution 1546. Therefore, the Court concluded that the detention violated Article 5 (1) of the ECHR, because Article 103 of the UN Charter could not operate without a conflict between obligations.[42]

The *Nada* judgment of September 2012 of the ECtHR followed a similar path.[43] Nada, an Italian and Egyptian national, lived in Campione d'Italia which is an Italian enclave in the Province of Como surrounded by the Swiss territory. In accordance with UNSC resolution 1390,[44] Switzerland adopted national measures that imposed a travel ban on Nada. He challenged the Swiss measures, claiming that those restrictions on his freedom of movement caused serious difficulties, such as preventing him from participating in family events, thus constituting a violation of Article 8 of the ECHR, which provides the right to respect for his private and family life.

The ECtHR first reiterated the principle that the ECHR "cannot be interpreted in vacuum but must be interpreted in harmony with the general principles of international law."[45] What distinguishes the *Nada* case from the *Al-Jedda* case is that the UNSC resolution set out the travel ban with "the clear and explicit language, imposing an obligation to take measures capable of breaching human rights," which has the effect of rebutting the presumption developed in the *Al-Jedda* judgment that "the Security Council does not intend to impose any obligation on Member States to breach fundamental principles of human rights."[46]

That being said, the Court still stuck to a harmonization of the allegedly conflicting norms. Paragraph 8 of UNSC resolution 1390 urges

> all States to take immediate steps to enforce and strengthen through legislative enactments or administrative measures, where appropriate, the measures imposed under domestic laws or regulations against their nationals and other individuals or entities operating on their territory [...].[47]

According to the ECtHR, the terms "where appropriate" mean a certain flexibility for the government in the mode of implementation of the resolution.[48] The Court held that, taking into account the ECHR's special character for the collective enforcement of human rights, the respondent state must take all possible measures to harmonize the allegedly conflicting obligations. Because the respondent state failed to persuade the Court that it did so in the present case, the ECtHR concluded that there was a violation of Article 8 of the ECHR.[49]

Moreover, the ECtHR claimed that the Swiss authorities did not carry out the review of the conformity of the Swiss national implementing measures with the ECHR, by referring to the *Kadi* formula that any judicial review of the internal lawfulness of the regulation is not excluded even when the regulation intends to implement the UNSC resolutions. Therefore, the ECtHR also found a violation of Article 13 of UCHR, which guarantees an effective remedy in the domestic legal order.[50]

The Al-Dulimi *case*

After Iraq's invasion of Kuwait in 1990, the UNSC triggered a general embargo by resolutions 661 and 670. The assets of Al-Dulimi and Montana Management Inc., the applicants in this case, had been frozen since the Swiss authority adopted national measures to implement the UN sanctions.[51] UNSC Resolution 1483, adopted after the Iraq War, set out asset freezing relating to the Saddam Hussein regime.[52] In accordance with the Swiss domestic measures to implement the relevant UNSC resolutions, the applicants' assets were confiscated in 2006. The applicants submitted an application, claiming that their assets were confiscated without a procedure complying with Article 6 (1) of the ECHR.[53]

The Court again found a violation of the rights under the ECtHR. According to the Court, Article 6 (1) requires a court or tribunal to have "full jurisdiction" to examine questions relating to a dispute, scrutinize the litigant's grounds and give clear reasons for its rejection.[54] In the present case, the Swiss Federal Court's judgments of January 2008 refused to examine the compatibility of the procedure for the confiscation with the procedural safeguards enshrined in Article 6 (1), mainly based on the primacy of the obligations stemming from the UNSC resolution by virtue of Article 103. Therefore, the key question was whether this restriction to the applicants' rights of access to a court under Article 6 of the ECHR could be justified or not.[55]

Before arguing a possible restriction, the Court reiterated the principles of interpretation as already explained in the *Al-Jedda* judgment; the ECtHR is to be interpreted in accordance with the relevant rules of international law,[56] and "there must be a presumption that the Security Council does not intend to impose any obligation on member States to breach fundamental principles of human rights."[57]

The Court found that UNSC Resolution 1483 and Resolution 1518 did not contain any provisions preventing the Swiss courts from reviewing the Swiss national measures to implement the UN sanctions.[58] According to the ECtHR, the ECHR is "a constitutional instrument of European public order" and one of the fundamental components of this order is the principle of the rule of law. Thus, the national authorities are, even when applying domestic law, subjected to a prohibition of arbitrariness.[59] Taking into consideration the seriousness of consequences for the applicants' rights and a lack of any clear or explicit wording in the UNSC resolutions excluding the judicial supervision of the national measures, the resolution must be interpreted to allow the Swiss courts to carry out sufficient scrutiny for the avoidance of arbitrariness.[60] Here, the *Al-Jedda* formula of presumption resurfaced again.[61]

In the view of the ECtHR, the Swiss courts were unable to access sufficiently precise information to securitize the allegation presented by listed persons. This fact, coupled with the prolonged lack of access, constituted the indication that the Swiss national measure was arbitrary. The ECtHR confirmed the formula in the first *Kadi* judgment that the principles of international law do not exclude any judicial review of the internal lawfulness of the contested regulations.[62] From the above considerations, the Court held there was not a conflict of obligations, by which the prevalent effect under Article 103 of the UN Charter would kick in.[63]

The ECtHR was of the opinion that, without a genuine opportunity for sufficient scrutiny before a court, the very essence of the applicants' rights under Article 6 (1) of the ECHR was impaired. In addition, the focal point, which was available for the applicants at the UN level, could not compensate for that deficiency. Therefore, the Court concluded that there has been a violation of Article 6 (1).[64]

Following the two precedents, the *Al-Dulimi* judgment of the ECtHR clearly shows its harmonious approach toward conflicts between the financial sanctions obligations and the human rights obligations. This sharply contrasts with the dualist approach adopted by the CJEU, which separates the EU legal order from the international legal order.

The legal approaches taken by the two courts

Common characteristics of the legal approaches

The judgments of the CJEU and the ECtHR both reviewed the relevant measures intending to implement the UN financial sanctions in the light of their own rules for individual rights protection, which resulted in the findings of the breaches of individual rights.

First, the way the two courts reviewed the implementing measures is indeed "indirect" in relation to the UN Charter and the UNSC resolutions. In the first *Kadi* judgment, the CJEU did not forget attaching to its own finding the caution that the CIEU's review of the EU regulations would not mean any challenge to the primacy of the UNSC resolution in terms of international law.[65] In the same manner, the *Al-Jedda* judgment and the *Al-Dulimi* judgment of the ECtHR made it crystal clear that it is not the Court's role to decide authoritatively the meaning and the legality of the UNSC resolutions,[66] though the ECtHR did not hesitate to look into deeply what the UNSC resolutions said about the legal positions of the parties to each case. This is a judicial strategy where the two courts wanted to submit an objection to the UN sanction regimes and protect their own rules, at the same time avoiding the direct review, which could lead to a very destructive situation for the international legal order and possibly also for the EU legal order and the ECHR themselves.

These courts' holdings that the implementing measures violated individual rights could motivate actions on the part of states to modify their national implementing measures or perhaps trigger their unwillingness to carry out the UN sanctions. This *de facto* pressure on the UNSC could pave the way for improvements in the political and opaque procedures of the UN financial sanctions. This was actually the case with the establishment of the UNSC Ombudsperson.[67]

Second, the two courts are referring to each other's findings in their own judgments. The formula established by the first *Kadi* judgment—any judicial review of the internal lawfulness of the relevant regulations implementing UNSC resolutions is not excluded by the principles of the international legal order under the UN—was cited by the *Nada* and *Al-Dulimi* judgments of the ECtHR in order to justify the national authorities' review of the national implementing measures.[68] Moreover, the second *Kadi* judgment rejected the procedure for delisting at the UN level as the guarantee of effective judicial protection, referring to the ECtHR's holding in the *Nada* judgment.[69] This cross-referencing between the courts' judgments enhances the legitimacy and persuasiveness of the two courts' findings.

Third, the courts both have a very critical attitude toward the UN financial sanctions, particularly in respect of the procedures for listing and delisting of individuals. The first *Kadi* judgment reproached the delisting procedure of the UNSC including the focal point, because an applicant submitting a delisting request to the Sanctions Committee could not be given real opportunity to assert applicants' cases or to receive the reasons and evidence for the listing.[70] The *Al-Dulimi* judgment joined this criticism by holding that the procedure at the UN level did not provide "satisfactory protection" that was able to "replace appropriate judicial scrutiny" at the national level.[71] Their evaluation is perfectly understandable and certainly one of the main reasons for the courts' *de facto* pressure strategy. Nevertheless, the second *Kadi* judgment might be too critical toward the UNSC financial sanctions procedure, which was clearly improved by the establishment of the UNSC Ombudsperson. Therefore, it can be said to be "counterproductive."[72]

Differences between the legal approaches

The ultimate purpose of the two courts' strategy is the same, i.e. the protection of individual rights, but there are distinct differences in the way they construct their legal arguments. For the CJEU, the autonomous character of the EU legal order is the key to its reasoning. Owing to this autonomy, the obligations imposed by an international agreement, such as the UN Charter, cannot change the Community's fundamental principle that all Community acts must respect fundamental rights regardless of rules of international law, including the UNSC resolutions. In other words, the legal character of the EU legal system as a whole excludes the application of the prevalent effect of Article 103 of the UN Charter in the EU legal order.

On the other hand, the ECtHR underscored a harmonious relationship between the ECHR and the UN Charter. According to the report of the Study Group of the International Law Commission, which the ECtHR referred to in the *Al-Dulimi* judgment, "a strong presumption against normative conflict" exists in international law.[73] Following this principle, the ECtHR interpreted the ECHR and the UNSC resolutions in a way that excluded the alleged norm conflict, or a conflict of obligations, which could trigger the operation of Article 103 of the UN Charter. This is rather how to interpret the relevant rules than how to situate the legal order at issue.[74]

There are of course pros and cons in each approach. The ECtHR's approach presupposes a common legal framework between the ECHR and the UN Charter, in which such harmonization is possible. It has been argued that the ECtHR approach could avoid an open challenge against the UN system and work as a "counter-force against fragmentation of international law."[75] However, there is a serious problem with this approach that could not be overlooked. The *Al-Jedda* judgment has been strongly criticized by the opinion of judge Poalelungi; the ECtHR placed the UK's detention outside the scope of the authorization given by UNSC Resolution 1546, although the letter of the Secretary of State attached to that resolution clearly and expressly indicated the possible use of interment by the multilateral force.[76] In addition, although the *Al-Dulimi* judgment interpreted the UNSC resolution as not ruling out sufficient judicial supervision by the Swiss courts of the national implementing measures, it is argued that the resolution, in fact, did not leave room for such supervision.[77] The ECtHR's interpretation has even been referred to as "fake harmonious interpretation."[78] To sum up, the ECtHR's judgments attempted to harmonize the rules, that could not be harmonized.

This kind of problem does not exist in the CJEU's approach. Apart from whether one accepts the CJEU's theoretical preposition, namely the dualist approach between EU law and international law, the CJEU's approach did not rely on an unpersuasive interpretation of UNSC resolutions. The CJEU's assertion that the prevalent effect of Article 103 cannot intrude the EU legal order because of the autonomy of that order seems to be more straightforward than the ECtHR's arguments. The first *Kadi* judgment resulted in the establishment of the Office of the Ombudsperson in Security Council procedure, which showed the effectiveness of the *de facto* pressure by the CJEU. Whether the difference in the way the two courts construct their arguments affected the practical consequences with the financial sanctions regimes is a very interesting point, but requires further careful consideration.

Nevertheless, the CJEU's approach has also encountered criticism. It has been opined that the CJEU should have taken "an internationally-engaged approach" by relying on the principles of international law, such as customary international law on due process protection, rather than stressing the particularism of the EU fundamental rights. By failing to do so, the Court is said to have lost the opportunity to establish a meaningful relationship between the EU legal order and the UN.[79]

Conclusion

The targeted financial sanctions are said to set a huge adversely effect in terms not only of legal consequences but also of *de facto* consequences with listed individuals, what is called "ripple effect"; UN sanctions lists are informally duplicated by many other actors, such as banks or immigration authorities, which could cause serious ramifications beyond formal effects.[80] The judgments analyzed in this chapter attempt to realize human rights improvement in the UNSC sanctions procedures.

The *Kadi* judgments, based on the dualist approach between international law and EU law, rejected the primacy of the UN financial sanctions obligations over the fundamental rights at least as a matter of EU law. On the other hand, the ECtHR, through harmonious interpretations between the ECHR and the UNSC resolutions, avoided a finding of a conflict of obligations, which could activate Article 103 of the UN Charter. While these two kinds of approach both exert *de facto* pressure on the UN for improvement in its sanction procedures, they are criticized for the different reasons; the CJEU created remoteness between international law and EU law, and the ECtHR distorted the meanings of the UNSC resolutions.

Satisfactory resolutions for both sides—the UN financial sanctions regimes on the one hand and the EU legal order and the ECHR on the other—are yet to be found. As the *Al-Dulimi* judgment pointed out, the focal point of the UNSC certainly has deficiencies for individual protection. The CJEU remains still critical of the UNSC Ombudsperson, despite the considerable number of delistings through that process.

If this trend in case law continues, it is likely to hurt the legitimacy of the UNSC, thereby seriously hampering the effective implementation of the UN financial sanctions.

Notes

1 This chapter is an edited version of my paper published in Japanese. Akira Kato, "Kokuren no Kinyu Seisai to Kokusai Hanrei" [United Nations Financial Sanctions and Judicial Precedents], Sachiko Yoshimura (ed.), *Kokuren no Kinyu Seisai* [United Nations Financial Sanctions] (Toshindo Publishing, 2017), pp. 192–213.
2 Nico Krisch, "Article 41," in Bruno Simma, Daniel-Erasmus Khan, Georg Nolte and Andreas Paulus (eds.), *The Charter of the United Nations: A Commentary*, Vol.2 (3rd ed., Oxford University Press, 2012), pp. 1312–1313.
3 On comprehensive surveys of this article, see Alix Toublanc, "L'article 103 et la valeur juridique de la charte des Nations unies," *Revue générale de droit international public*, Vol. 108 (2004), pp. 439–462.

4 Jean-Marc Thouvenin, "Article 103," in Jean-Pierre Cot and Alain Pellet, *La charte des Nations unies: commentaire article par article*, Vol. 2 (3rd ed., Economica, 2005), p. 2135.

5 Case Concerning Questions of Interpretation and Application of the 1971 Montreal Convention Arising from the Aerial Incident at Lockerbie (*Libyan Arab Jamahiriya v. United States of America*), Order of the International Court of Justice, 14 April 1992, paras. 41–42. This was only a *prima facie* finding, but the other judicial precedents to be analyzed in this chapter cast no doubt on this interpretation.

6 The European Court of Justice (ECJ) was transformed into the Court of Justice of the European Union by the Lisbon Treaty, but only "CJEU" will be used in this chapter for simplicity.

7 For example, Resolutions 1333 (2000), 1455 (2003), 1730 (2006), 1904 (2009), 2083 (2012), and 2341 (2017).

8 S/RES/2368, 20 July 2017, op. para. 1–2.

9 On the procedure of listing in the UN, see Guidelines of the Committee for the Conduct of its Work, 23 December 2016, at www.un.org/sc/suborg/en/sanctions/1267 (as of 5 January 2018).

10 *Yassin Abdullah Kadi v. Council of the European Union and Commission of the European Communities*, Case T-315/01, Judgment of the Court of First Instance (Second Chamber), 21 September 2005.

11 Ibid., paras. 209–225.

12 Ibid., paras. 233–292.

13 *Yassin Abdullah Kadi and Al Barakaat International Foundation v. Council of the European Union and Commission of the European Communities*, Joint Cases C-402/05 P and C-415/05P, Judgment of the Court of Justice (Grand Chamber), 3 September 2008.

14 Ibid., paras. 281–282.

15 Ibid., paras. 284–288.

16 Ibid., paras. 298–299.

17 Ibid., para. 326.

18 Ibid., paras. 345–353.

19 Ibid., para. 369.

20 Ibid., para. 372.

21 Akira Kato, "Kokuren Kensyo Dai 103 jyo to Kokusai Jinken Ho: Osyu Jinken Saibansyo ni Okeru Kinjino Tenkai" [Article 103 of the UN Charter and International Human Rights Law: Recent Development before the European Court of Justice], *Kokusai Kokyo Seisaku Kenkyu* [International Public Policy Studies], Vol. 18 (2013), p. 166.

22 Erika de Wet, "From *Kadi* to *Nada*: Judicial Techniques Favouring Human Rights over United Nations Security Council Sanctions," *Chinese Journal of International Law*, Vol.12 (2013), p. 791.

23 Ninth Report of the Analytical Support and Sanctions Monitoring Team, S/2009/245, 13 May 2009, p. 10, para. 19.

24 S/RES/1730, 19 December 2006, De-listing Procedure.

25 The first *Kadi* judgment, *supra* note 13, para. 323.

26 S/RES/1904, 17 December 2009, pre.para. 9 and op. para. 20. On the details of the Ombudsperson's procedure, See Jared Genser and Kate Barth, "Targeted Sanctions and Due Process of Law," in Jared Genser and Bruno Stagno Ugarte (eds.), *The United Nations Security Council in the Age of Human Rights* (Cambridge University

Press, 2014), pp. 195–246; Dire Tladi and Gillian Taylor, "On the Al Qaida/Taliban Sanctions Regime: Due Process and Sunsetting," *Chinese Journal of International Law*, Vol. 10 (2011), paras. 1–44.

27 S/RES/1989, 17 June 2011, Annex II.

28 If consensus does not exist, the Chair of the Sanctions Committee shall, on the request of a Committee member, submit the case to the Security Council itself. Ibid., Annex II, para. 12.

29 Remarks by Kimberly Prost, Ombudsperson, Security Council Al-Qaida Sanctions Committee, to the 49th meeting of the Committee of Legal Advisors on Public International Law (CAHDI) of the Council of Europe, 20 March 2015, p. 3.

30 Thirteenth Report of the Office of the Ombudsperson, S/2017/60, 23 January 2017, pp. 2–3 and 19.

31 Sue E. Eckert and Thomas J. Biersteker, *Due Process and Targeted Sanctions: An Update of the "Watson Report,"* (Watson Institute, 2012), pp. 24 and 37.

32 Report of the Special Rapporteur on the Promotion and Protection of Human Rights and Fundamental Freedoms while Countering Terrorism (Ben Emmerson), A/67/396, 26 September 2012, para. 59.

33 *European Commission and Others v. Yassin Abdullah Kadi*, Joined cases C-584/10 P, C-593/10 P and C-595/10 P, Judgment of the Court of Justice (Grand Chamber), 18 July 2013. The September 2010 judgment of General Court found the infringement of the fundamental rights, annulling the contested regulation. *Yassin Abdullah Kadi v. European Commission*, Case T-85/09, Judgment of the General Court (Seventh Chamber), 30 September 2010.

34 Ibid., para. 133.

35 Ibid., paras. 135–163.

36 Ibid., paras. 164–165.

37 S/RES/1546, 8 June 2004, op. para. 10.

38 *Al-Jedda v. The United Kingdom* (Application no. 27021/08), Judgment of the European Court of Human Rights (Grand Chamber), 7 July 2011.

39 Ibid., para. 76.

40 Ibid., paras. 101–102.

41 Ibid., paras. 105.

42 Ibid., para. 109

43 *Nada v. Switzerland* (Application no. 10593/08), Judgment of the European Court of Human Rights (Grand Chamber), 12 September 2012.

44 S/RES/1390, 28 January 2002, op. para. 2. Switzerland became a UN member state in 2002.

45 The *Nada* Judgment, *supra* note 43, para. 169.

46 Ibid., paras. 171–172.

47 S/RES/1390, *supra* note 44, op. para. 8.

48 The *Nada* Judgment, *supra* note 43, para. 178.

49 Ibid., paras. 196–199.

50 Ibid., paras. 207–214.

51 *Al-Dulimi and Montana Management Inc. v. Switzerland* (Application no. 5809/08), Judgment of the European Court of Human Rights (Grand Chamber), 21 June 2016. The Second Chamber of the ECtHR delivered the judgment on this case, which applied the equivalent protection doctrine and found a violation of Article 6 of the ECHR. Al-Dulimi et Monatana Management Inc. c. Suisse (Requête no 5809/08), Arrêt de la Cour européenne des droits de l'homme (Deuxième section), le 26

novembre 2013. On the analysis of this judgment, Akira Kato, "Kokuren Kensyo Gimu no Yusen to Osyu Jinken Saibansyo ni Okeru 'Doto no Hogo' Riron" [The Prevalence of Obligations under the UN Charter and the Doctrine of "Equivalent Protection" before the European Court of Human Rights], *Kokusai Kokyo Seisaku Kenkyu* [International Public Policy Studies], Vol. 19 (2014), pp. 147–164.

52 S/RES/1483, 22 May 2003, op. para. 23.

53 The *Al-Dulimi* judgment, *supra* note 51, para. 81.

54 Ibid., para. 128.

55 Ibid., para. 131.

56 Ibid., para. 134.

57 Ibid., para. 140.

58 Ibid., para. 143.

59 Ibid., para. 145.

60 Ibid., para. 146.

61 Anne Peters, "The New Arbitrariness and Competing Constitutionalisms: Remarks on ECtHR Grand Chamber Al-Dulimi," *EJIL: Talk!*, 30 June 2016.

62 The first *Kadi* judgment, *supra* note 13, para. 299.

63 The *Al-Dulimi* judgment, *supra* note 51, paras. 148–149.

64 Ibid., paras. 151–155.

65 The first *Kadi* judgment, *supra* note 13, para. 288.

66 The *Al-Jedda* judgment, *supra* note 38, para.76; the *Al-Dulimi* judgment, *supra* note 51, para. 139.

67 Akira Kato, "Kokuren Ho to EU Ho no Soukoku: Radical Tagensyugi no Riron Kozo to Sono Jissenteki Igi" [Struggle between UN Law and EU Law: the Theoretical Structure and Practical Significance of Radical Pluralism], *Kokusaiho Gaiko Zasshi* [*Journal of International Law and Diplomacy*], Vol. 116 (2018), pp. 480–508.

68 The *Nada* Judgment, *supra* note 43, para. 212; the Al-Dulimi judgment, *supra* note 51, para. 148.

69 The second *Kadi* judgment, *supra* note 33, para. 133.

70 The first *Kadi* judgment, *supra* note 13, paras. 322–325.

71 The *Al-Dulimi* judgment, *supra* note 51, para. 153.

72 Antonios Tzanakopoulos, "The *Solange* argument as a Justification for Disobeying the Security Council in the *Kadi* judgments," in Matej Avbelj, Filippo Fontanelli and Giuseppe Martinico (eds.), *Kadi on Trial: A Multifaceted Analysis of the Kadi Trial* (Routledge, 2014), p. 134.

73 Fragmentation of International Law: Difficulties Arising from the Diversification and Expansion of International Law (Report of the Study Group of the International Law Commission), A/CN.4/L.682, 13 April 2006, paras. 37–39; The Al-*Dulimi* judgment, *supra* note 51, para. 138.

74 On the comparison between the *Nada* case and the *Kadi* cases, de Wet, *supra* note 22, pp. 806–807; Akira Kato, "Kokuren Kensyo Dai 103 jyo to Kokusai Jinken Ho: Osyu Jinken Saibansyo niokeru Kinji no Doko" [Article 103 of the UN Charter and International Human Rights Law: Recent Development before the European Court of Human Rights], *Kokusai Kokyo Seisaku Kenkyu* [*International Public Policy Studies*], Vol. 18 (2013), pp. 171–178.

75 de Wet, *supra* note 22, p. 806.

76 Partially Dissenting Opinion of Judge Poalelungi (The *Al-Jedda* judgment, *supra* note 38).

77 Marko Milanovic, "Grand Chamber Judgment in Al-Dulimi v. Switzerland," *EJIL: Talk!*, 23 June 2016.
78 Dessenting Opinion of Judge Nussberger (The *Al-Dulimi* judgment, *supra* note 51).
79 Gráinne de Búrca, "The European Court of Justice and the International Legal Order after *Kadi*," *Harvard International Law Journal*, Vol. 51 (2010), pp. 41–42.
80 Larrisa J. van den Herik, "Peripheral Hegemony in the Quest to Ensure Security Council Accountability for its Individualized UN Sanctions Regimes," *Journal of Conflict & Security Law*, Vol. 19 (2014), p. 449.

10 UN financial sanctions against the Democratic People's Republic of Korea

Challenges and proposal for efficient implementation

Maiko Takeuchi

Introduction

To counter the nuclear tests and ballistic missile programs of the DPRK, the United Nations Security Council has adopted ten resolutions under Article 41 of Charter of the United Nations, to impose sanctions against the DPRK.

Sanctions imposed by the UN Security Council resolutions on the DPRK cover a wide range of aspects to urge the regime to abandon nuclear and ballistic missile programs. In addition to directly prohibiting the transfer of items used for its nuclear, ballistic missiles and other weapons of mass destruction (WMD) related programs, the sanctions put restrictions on the country's acquisition of energy and income to be used for the programs. However, UN Panel of Experts monitoring the implementation of the UN sanctions points out that the DPRK is continuing its nuclear and ballistic missile programs and procurement. This situation suggests insufficient implementation of the sanctions which is taken advantage of by the DPRK. This chapter discusses the UN Security Council's practice on sanctions against the DPRK and analyzes the challenge in the implementation of UN financial sanctions, based on the actual cases of the DPRK's sanction evasion. Furthermore, based on this analysis, this chapter also proposes how both the Member States and the UN Security Council can make improvements for efficient implementation.

UN Security Council's practice on the sanctions against the DPRK

The DPRK's nuclear and ballistic missile program and the diplomatic effort until 2006

On May 29, 1993, the DPRK conducted a test launch of a midrange ballistic missile, Nodong-1, following the March 12 announcement of its withdrawal from the Treaty on the Non-Proliferation of Nuclear Weapons (NPT) .[1] Only two weeks after, on June 11, 1993, the United States and the DPRK reached an agreement to pursue denuclearization of the Korean peninsula and to continue dialogue. The DPRK also announced its suspension of the withdrawal from NPT.[2]

On June 13, 1994, the DPRK withdrew its membership of the International Atomic Energy Agency (IAEA),[3] followed by the establishment of the Agreed Framework between the United States and the DPRK on October 21 of the same year.[4] Based on this framework, the DPRK froze several nuclear projects including the 5MW (e) experimental graphite-moderated reactor and pluto-nium reprocessing facility, and instead, construction of light water reactors were planned, and until they were constructed 500,000 metric tons of crude oil were to be provided to the DPRK. To support these actions the Korean Peninsula Energy Development Organization (KEDO) was established. However, the agreement was not fully implemented. Construction of the light water reactor has been delayed, and the United States also reported that the DPRK was engaged in a uranium enrichment project in 2002, which resulted in the suspension of the supply of crude oil in December 2002. KEDO announced that the con-struction of the light water reactor was suspended in 2003 as the DPRK did not meet the conditions of the relevant agreement, and the light water project was officially terminated on May 31, 2006. Meanwhile, in January 2003, the DPRK also announced its withdrawal from the NPT and resumed operation of the nuclear facilities in Yongbyon. To address this issue, United States-China-DPRK three-party talks in April 2003 and multiple sessions of six-party talks (the United States, China, the DRPK and Japan, the Republic of Korea and Russian Federation) have taken place.

Despite the diplomatic efforts, on July 5, 2006, the DPRK had resumed launch tests for the first time since 1998, with seven test launches of ballistic missiles. In condemnation of this test, UN Security Council Resolution 1695 (2006) was adopted on July 15.[5] However, this resolution does not impose sanctions by calling upon actions under Chapter VII of Charter of the United Nations. This resolution urges the DPRK to return to the six-party talks, and return to the NPT and the IAEA safeguards. To achieve this goal, this resolution requires Member States to prevent procurement for this country's missile development and transfer of financial resources related to its missile or WMD programs.[6]

Development of UN sanctions against the DPRK

Despite the international message expressed by the Resolution 1695(2006), the DPRK conducted the first nuclear test on October 9, 2006.[7] The UN Security Council swiftly adopted Resolution 1718 (2006) on October 14, 2006.[8] This is the first resolution to address this country's nuclear and missile development based on Article 41 of the Charter of the United Nations, determining existence of a clear threat to international peace and security.

This resolution imposed a ban on the DPRK of importing and exporting important military equipment, including tanks, armored vehicles, combat air-craft, and missiles, as well as items, materials, equipment, goods, and technology that could contribute to the DPRK's nuclear, ballistic missiles, and other WMD programs.[9] Furthermore, it imposed a ban on the import of luxury goods by the DPRK.[10] It also established the Sanctions Committee of the Security Council (hereafter 1718 Committee) consisting of all members of the Security Council to monitor and oversee the sanctions program.[11]

As a financial measure, this resolution obliges Member States to freeze assets of entities and individuals that are designated as being engaged in or supporting the missile and WMD programs of the DPRK.[12] However, essentially the article has not been in effect until April 24, 2009, when the 1718 Committee designated three entities including the Tanchon Commercial Bank, the main financial entity the DPRK used for transactions related to conventional arms and ballistic missiles.[13]

Resolution 1874(2009) was adopted on June 12, 2009, after the second nuclear test conducted by the DPRK on May 25, 2009.[14] This resolution expands the arms embargo to all arms, related materiel, relevant services, as well as financial transactions.[15] It also calls upon Member States to inspect vessels, as well as authorizing the Member States to dispose of the seized items found during the inspection.[16]

As for financial measures, it calls upon Member States to take action to prevent the provision of financial services or the transfer of finances or other assets which could contribute to the DPRK's nuclear, ballistic missiles and other WMD programs.[17] In addition, paragraph 24 of this resolution decides to adjust the measures imposed by paragraph 8 of Resolution 1718 (2006) and pursuant to this paragraph, the Committee designated five entities including Hong Kong Electronics which had transferred proliferation-related funds on behalf of the Tanchon Commercial Bank, and five individuals to be subject to the measures imposed in paragraph 8 of Resolution 1718 (2006).[18] This resolution for the first time calls upon all Member States and international financial and credit institutions not to enter into new commitments for grants, financial assistance, or concessional loans to the DPRK as well as calls upon exercising enhanced vigilance with current commitments.[19] It also calls upon Member States to not provide public financial support for trade with the DPRK where such financial support could contribute to the WMD and ballistic missile-related programs or activities of the DPRK.[20] This resolution also established a Panel of Experts (hereafter "1874 Panel of Experts") consisting of a maximum of seven experts, which carry out tasks to support the Committee.

Resolution 2087(2013) was adopted on January 22, 2013, to respond to the DPRK's test launch using ballistic missile technology conducted on December 12, 2012.[21] This resolution directs the 1718 Committee to issue implementation assistance notices regarding vessel inspection and clarifies the methods of disposal of seized material.[22] It also expands the list of restricted items.[23]

Concerning financial measures, this resolution expands the individuals designated for asset freeze and travel ban and entities designated for asset freeze.[24] It should be noted that among those newly added four individuals, two were officials of the Tanchon Commercial Bank. Furthermore, the Bank of East Land which facilities weapon-related transactions was designated. Furthermore, it calls upon Member States for enhanced vigilance in monitoring individuals under the States' jurisdiction and entities including financial institutions acting with or for the financial institutions of the DPRK.[25]

Resolution 2094(2013) was adopted on March 7, 2013, in response to the third nuclear test conducted by the DPRK on February 12, 2013.[26]

This resolution added wider aspects of financial measures to this sanctions regime. First, in the preamble, it welcomes Recommendation 7 of the Financial Action Task Force (FATF) and urges Member States to apply the Interpretative Note to Recommendation 7 for effective targeted financial sanction implementation. FATF Recommendation 7 requires implementation of targeted financial sanctions to fulfill financial measures of WMD-proliferation related UN Security Council resolutions.[27] This recommendation was newly adopted in the FATF Recommendation renewed in 2012.

Furthermore, this resolution was decided upon to prevent the provision of financial service, transfer of assets, or the provision of financial services for trade that could contribute to programs prohibited by the relevant resolutions.[28] It further calls upon Member States to prohibit opening branches, subsidiaries, or representative offices of the banks of the DPRK in their territories, as well as to prohibit opening Member States' financial institutions from opening branches, subsidiaries, or banking accounts in the DPRK if they have information that provides reasonable grounds to believe such financial services could contribute the DPRK's prohibited programs.[29] This resolution also expands the criteria of the individuals and entities subject to the asset freeze and travel bans[30] to the individuals or entities acting on behalf or at the direction of the designated individuals and entities, as well as entities owned and controlled by the designated individuals and entities.[31]

Furthermore, it aims to prevent evasion of measures imposed by the relevant resolutions. This resolution calls upon enhanced vigilance on the country's diplomatic personnel's proliferation-related activities. Also, a non-exhaustive list of prohibited luxury goods and a list of additional items, materials, equipment, goods, and technology that could contribute to the DPRK's WMD and missile programs were annexed.[32]

Resolution 2270 (2016) was adopted on March 2, 2016 after the fourth nuclear test conducted on January 6 and ballistic missile test on February 7, 2016.[33] It drastically expands measures imposed by previous resolutions. One of the most significant measures was a ban on the export of coal, iron, and iron ore (with limited exceptions), gold, titanium ore, vanadium ore, and rare earth minerals.[34] This resolution also requires Member States to prevent the sale of aviation fuel to the DPRK.[35] Small arms and light weapons, which had been exempt from earlier bans, were made subject to the arms embargo.[36] WMD and conventional weapons "catch-all" provision are adopted.[37]

This resolution also requires Member States to expel DPRK diplomats and foreign nationals if they are involved in prohibited activities of the DPRK.[38] Furthermore, there is a mandatory inspection of cargo to/from the DPRK, and various services, such as leasing or chartering the service of vessels and aircraft and provision of crews for the DPRK are prohibited. This resolution enforces new cargo inspections and maritime procedures, including mandatory inspection of cargo destined for and originating from the DPRK.

Financial measures are also expanded. The resolution prohibits overseas branches and offices of DPRK banks including existing ones, establishment of new joint ventures, ownership interest in or correspondent relationship with DPRK banks.[39] It also prohibits Member States' banks from opening new branches and bank accounts in the DPRK.[40] It further decides the closure of existing representative offices and subsidiaries in the DPRK if such financial services could contribute to prohibited programs or violation of the relevant sanctions.[41] The resolution also recalls FATF Recommendation 7, which was first stated in the preamble to Resolution 2094(2013) and calls upon Member States to apply this recommendation.[42]

Resolution 2321(2016) was adopted on November 30, 2016 after the fifth nuclear test on September 9, 2016.[43] It placed an annual cap on the export of coal by the DPRK and established a system on reporting and monitoring the export of coal.[44] The DPRK's supply, sale, or transfer of copper, nickel, silver, and zinc were newly banned.[45]

Furthermore, it clarifies multiple obligations imposed in Resolution 2270(2016). It prohibited the provision of insurance or re-insurance services to vessels owned, controlled, or operated by the DPRK.[46] Moreover, the resolution introduced procedures to designate vessels that were or had been related to prohibited programs or activities, and requires the Flag State to de-flag such vessels and subject them to the asset freeze.[47]

The resolution strengthened the financial measures, including the prohibition of public and private financial support of trade with the DPRK,[48] and required States to expel individuals believed to be working on behalf of or under the direction of a DPRK bank or financial institutions.[49]

Out of eleven designated individuals, only one is related to financial institutions, but two individuals served as ambassador and provided support to the Korea Mining Development Trading Corporation were included. This designation of diplomats corresponds to the concern of the commercial activities of diplomats stated in this resolution. Out of ten designated entities, four entities are financial institutions and front companies.

Resolution 2356(2017), adopted on June 2, 2017 to address repeated missile launches, additionally designated fourteen individuals including the Tanchon Commercial Bank representative in Vietnam and four entities including Koryo Bank, which is associated with Office 38 and Office 39 of the Korean Workers' Party.[50]

Resolution 2371(2017) was adopted on August 5, 2017, after the DPRK's missile launches on July 4 and 28, which the country stated were intercontinental ballistic missile tests.[51] The resolution imposed a full ban on the export of coal, iron, and iron ore;[52] added lead and lead ore to the export ban;[53] and banned the export of seafood.[54] New authority was given to the 1718 Committee to designate vessels related to prohibited activities and requires States to prohibit the entry of designated vessels into their ports.[55] The resolution restricts the total number of work authorizations to DPRK nationals.[56]

In regard to finances, this resolution clarifies that companies performing financial services equivalent to banks are considered "financial institutions" in this sanctions regime and further clarifies that the clearing of funds is also prohibited by paragraph 11 of resolution 2094(2013).[57] It further prohibits new or expanded joint ventures and cooperative entities with the DPRK.[58]

In this resolution, nine new individuals and four entities are designated. In relation to the financial sanctions, it should be noted that all the individuals are representatives of either financial institutions or entities for military related acquisition. Furthermore, among these four designated entities, three of them are financial institutions, and one entity is generating revenue and conducting business overseas.[59]

Resolution 2375(2017) was adopted on September 11, 2017, after the sixth nuclear test on September 2, 2017.[60] It prohibited DPRK's import of all condensates and natural gas liquids.[61] It restricted the annual supply, sale, or transfer of all refined petroleum products to the DPRK to two million barrels and requires the 1718 Committee and the Committee Secretary to monitor and periodically report the amount of refined petroleum products provided to the DPRK.[62] The resolution also limits the annual amount of crude oil supplied, sold, or transferred to the DPRK by a State to that amount supplied, sold, or transferred in the twelve months preceding the resolution's adoption.[63] It also introduced a ban on the export of textile products[64] and banned new overseas work authorizations for DPRK nationals.[65] It prohibits all joint ventures or cooperative entities with entities or individuals of the DPRK.[66] Newly designated were an individual and three entities, all related to the Workers Party of Korea.

The final resolutions in the series, Resolution 2397(2017) was adopted on December 22, 2017, after the ballistic missile launch of November 28.[67] This resolution reduced the annual cap on refined petroleum products transferred to the DPRK from two million to five hundred thousand barrels.[68] It also set a cap on crude oil transfers of four million barrels or 525,000 tons.[69] Sectoral sanctions were expanded through a ban on the DPRK export of food and agricultural products, machinery, electrical equipment, earth and stone (including magnesite and magnesia), wood, and vessels.[70] The resolution prohibits the export of all industrial machinery, transportation vehicles, iron, steel, and other metals to the DPRK.[71] It strengthened the prohibition on the overseas work of DPRK nationals by requiring States to repatriate all DPRK nationals earning income within the State and all DPRK government attachés monitoring the workers within twenty-four months from the date of adoption of the resolution.[72] It also strengthened the vessel-related measures by obligating States to prohibit the provision of insurance or re-insurance services by its nationals, and persons and entities subject to its jurisdiction of vessels believed to be involved in activities or the transport of items prohibited by Security Council resolutions.[73] Further, the resolution requires States to de-register vessels involved in prohibited activities.[74]

Out of sixteen newly designated individuals, fourteen individuals are oversea representatives of the DPRK banks.[75]

Characteristics of the UN DPRK Sanctions: comparison with UN Iran sanction

In more than fourteen years and the adoption of a total of ten sanction resolutions, there is a wide range of restrictions concerning the transfer of goods, financial transactions, and individuals. Furthermore, the details of each area of restrictions are also significant. This comprehensive characteristic of UN sanctions against DPRK can be seen when compared with the UN sanctions concerning the nuclear program of the Islamic Republic of Iran, another example of WMD non-proliferation, targeted sanctions. Both sanctions regimes were established in 2006.

However, sanction measures imposed on Iran are limited compared to those on the DPRK. First, the restriction imposed on Iran under the UN sanctions only affected non-proliferation sensitive nuclear activities, whereas the DPRK is required to abandon by the relevant resolutions all nuclear-related programs. Second, sanction measures are also limited in Iran. As shown in the previous section, in the sanctions against the DPRK, in addition to the transfer of the items that contribute to the country's WMD programs, there are restrictions on a wide range of sources of revenue. Furthermore, in the case of the DPRK, restrictions on overseas diplomatic mission are imposed. In contrast, the sanctions against Iran do not prohibit non-military exports such as crude oil and other national resources.

Under financial sanctions, both sanctions against the DPRK and Iran did not allow the provision of financial services which could contribute to the programs prohibited by the relevant sanctions. Both sanctions imposed the freezing of the assets of designated entities and individuals. However, the sanctions differ when it comes to other aspects of financial and commercial activities. Whereas Iran was restricted from opening representative offices overseas and foreign banks from opening representative offices in Iran, the DPRK sanctions prohibited the establishment of both new and existing representative offices. The prohibition of existing bank representative offices affected the already established financial network and activities in the DPRK, and was therefore a much stricter measure compared to the restriction on opening new representative offices.

Challenges in implementation of the financial sanctions

As described in the last section, financial measures under the sanctions against the DPRK are broadened along with the development of the sanction regime. However, the 1874 Panel of Experts and other monitoring groups still bring to attention continuing sanction evasions. This suggests shortcomings in implementing the sanctions, in both legal and technical aspects.

Case study: the DPRK's sanction evasion techniques

Use of cyber space

The 1874 Panel of Experts pointed out the DPRK's financial activities using virtual assets, including money laundering and cryptocurrency mining.[76] The DPRK also uses cyber-attacks against financial institutes including cryptocurrency exchanges to acquire money.[77] FATF defines virtual assets as "a digital representation of value that can be digitally traded or transferred and can be used for payment or investment purposes"[78] and defines cryptocurrency as "a math-based, decentralized convertible virtual currency that is protected by cryptography."[79]

The DPRK has a highly developed capability of cyber-attacks and cyber espionage. In December 2017, Japan, the United States, the United Kingdom, Canada, Australia and New Zealand blamed the DPRK for the WannaCry cyber-attack.[80] Furthermore, in the criminal complaint of the *United States of America vs Park Jin Hyok*,[81] the United States accused Park of being a computer programmer working on behalf of the government of DPRK. According to this criminal complaint, he was involved in several cyber-attacks including cyber-attacks on Sony Pictures Entertainment in November 2014, and cyber-attacks on computers in more than 150 countries using ransomware "WannaCry 2.0" in May 2017, and the fraudulent transfer of eighty-one million dollars from the Bangladesh Bank. In September 13, 2019, the US Department of the Treasury's Office of Foreign Assets Control announced sanctions targeting three State-sponsored cyber groups of the DPRK "Lazarus Group," "Bluenoroff," and "Andariel," for their malicious activities, and for acquiring money by cyber-attacks on financial institutions.[82] These Member States' actions raise awareness of the DPRK's cyber-attacks and promote capacity building in targeted countries.

DPRK's bank representatives

The 1874 Panel of Experts points out that more than thirty representatives of DPRK financial institutions are still operating abroad. These financial institutions include the Tanchon Commercial Bank, the Korea Kumgang Bank, the Foreign Trade Bank, the Cheil Credit Bank, the Daesong Bank, the Ilsim International Bank, the Bank of East Land, the Daedong Credit Bank, the Unification Development Bank and the Ryugyong Commercial Bank. Those banks are operating through representatives in China, Indonesia, Libya, the Russian Federation, the Syrian Arab Republic and the United Arab Emirates.[83] These overseas representatives are still playing active roles in facilitating illicit transactions.[84]

Use of overseas financial networks

Currency is a tool, not the objective of the procurement. Therefore, currency does not have to be transferred to the DPRK, as money can be kept in a third country, in bank accounts opened by individuals, sometimes local, in a third country, and used as payment for procurement through local bank accounts.

Furthermore, sometimes deals are made at different times, or even with different parties to avoid monitoring by authorities. For example, in a recent seizure of vodka allegedly exported to the DPRK via China, a payment for the vodka purchased by the Chinese buyer was made by a Singaporean human resources company. The owner of the Singaporean company claimed this payment was only made to his Chinese friend, denying his involvement in exporting vodka to the DPRK. However, considering this owner has been committed in trade with the DPRK, it is not unlikely that this was payment for vodka to be smuggled to the DPRK in exchange for another deal. However, when transfer of item and payment are conducted at different times or not even by direct transaction between the buyer and seller, it is very difficult to monitor the transaction and detect the connection to the DPRK.

Use of diplomatic status

DPRK diplomats and international organizations' staff also figure in the DPRK's procurement network. The 1874 Panel of Experts reports several representatives of UN designated entities remaining in the Islamic Republic of Iran under diplomatic cover.[85] Furthermore, DPRK attachés in the DPRK embassy in Tehran are believed to be involved in cash and gold smuggling between the Tehran airport and the Dubai airport through diplomatic channels.[86] The Panel also reported a procurement attempt by DPRK diplomats stationed in Europe, as well as a case of DPRK international organization staff who were working on behalf of the DPRK's designated entity, Reconnaissance General Bureau.[87]

Use of high-value goods to acquire money

Furthermore, items not specifically listed as prohibited items by the resolutions can be transferred to be sold or exchanged for goods or services in a third country. For example, diplomats of the DPRK can carry high-value goods to procure prohibited items in exchange, or by selling them for hard currency. According to the report issued by Global Initiative Against Transnational Organized Crime, DPRK diplomats have committed at least eighteen instances of rhino horn and ivory smuggling in Africa since 1986.[88] Furthermore, a defector stated this country's diplomats stationed in Africa often smuggle rhino horn, ivory, and gold to Beijing to sell for cash.[89] To address the fact that the transfer of gold is used to evade the sanction, paragraph 37 of Resolution 2270 (2016) clarifies that gold should also be covered by financial service restrictions. However, other high-value goods which could be also used to as funds are not specified in the resolution. These items are mostly sold outside of the DPRK, and this type of transaction has the same role as a money transfer when sold for cash in a third country. They are not just carrying bulk cash all the way to the final destination.

Limitations of resolutions

The measures, and consequently, the terminology used in UN Security Council resolutions demonstrate an increased level of complexity and political sensitivity. Resolutions leave certain elements undefined so that interpretation of the provisions are left for each Member State. However, often ambiguities in the resolutions and delay of adoption of new elements are the result of negotiations in the UN Security Council; thus such ambiguities may have been created to weaken the effect of the provisions.

Slow adoption of new elements in the resolutions

The need to prohibit financial transactions used for procurement by the DPRK was recognized from the beginning of the sanctions regime, but the actions decided in the resolutions were delayed. Several obligations are first reflected in the resolution in weaker language, such as "call upon," or put in preamble and await the following new resolution becoming an obligation or a prohibition. For example, in Resolution 1874 (2009), the Security Council calls upon the restriction of financial services, grants and financial assistance, but these measures were not prohibited until Resolution 2094(2013). FATF Recommendation 7 concerning implementation of target financial sanction was first stated in the preamble to Resolution 2094(2013) and then stated in the operative paragraph in Resolution 2270(2016).

Moreover, elements to strengthen the effect of the sanctions are not always adopted swiftly. For example, cyber activity by the DPRK is not directly prohibited. Furthermore, the elements to address emerging virtual assets are not sufficiently incorporated into the resolutions. The DPRK is enjoying the lack of measures that specifically prohibit cyber activity. One example in 2019 was when the DPRK hosted an international "cryptocurrency conference" in Pyongyang. The website advertised that the conference was for international experts in the blockchain and crypto industry to share knowledge. However, according to an individual who participated in the conference as a presenter, the host requested him to make a presentation focusing on money laundering and sanction evasion techniques using virtual currency.[90]

Furthermore, delay of designation by the Security Council gave a good "warning" to the DPRK. For example, the Mansudae Overseas Project Group of Companies (hereafter "Mansudae") was designated by the United States in December 2, 2016.[91] However, designation by the Security Council had not been done until August 5, 2017, in Resolution 2371(2017). It should be noted that the designation was not made in Resolution 2356 (2017) adopted in June 2017. In Namibia where one of the largest Mansudae subsidiaries was located, the authority tried to freeze the asset after the designation by the Security Council, but found that the Mansudae subsidiary had already sold its mobile assets at an auction in July 2017.[92]

Lack of definition

Paragraph 18 of Resolution 2375(2017) prohibits the opening, maintaining, and operating joint ventures and cooperative entities. Member States are obliged to close existing joint ventures and cooperative entities. However, in the resolution, there is no definition of a joint venture or a cooperative entity. On the one hand, a specific definition of prohibited joint ventures and cooperative entities could create loopholes by modifying organizational structure or ownership of the entity. But on the other hand, a lack of definition leaves room for Member States' legislatures to make their own definitions. For example, the Russian Federation informed the 1874 Panel of Experts that Russian companies whose sole founder was a citizen of the DPRK were registered strictly as Russian limited liability companies, and these companies were not subject to the restriction of joint ventures or cooperative entities imposed by the resolution.[93]

Challenges of Member States' implementation

Financial systems and customs in this industry make the implementation of financial sanctions more complex compared to conventional strategic trade control, which is another core aspect of this sanctions regime. It is worth discussing three challenges in countries' administrative and legal systems to the implementation of these financial sanctions.

Financial transfer in the third country

To address the DPRK's sanction evasion, Resolution 2094(2013) prohibits financial transactions by nationals of a third country which could contribute to the prohibited activities. However, there are limited resources for monitoring such transactions, especially when the transactions are not directly to/from the DPRK. Moreover, proving that the transaction is for the DPRK's illicit programs is very difficult. Intelligence information is needed for monitoring the whole transaction network which is difficult even for government authorities. Paragraph 16 of Resolution 2321(2016) limits the number of bank accounts of diplomats and diplomatic missions to one each. However, a bank cannot tell if the diplomat's account is the only bank account the diplomat has, unless the competent authority facilitates the disclosure of information on account holders. Furthermore, nationals of the DPRK often use several alphabetical spellings of their names overseas, which makes tracing and monitoring difficult. In the financial industry, confidentiality of the account holder is vital and this is the most difficult piece of information to collect, even for authorities. The sanctions also do not limit the number of bank account held by DPRK citizens living overseas who are not diplomats.

Insufficient inter-agency information exchange

In most countries, government agencies in charge of financial control are not the same as the agency in charge of strategic export control. Furthermore, none of them is an intelligence agency, although usually these agencies have intelligence sections. As a result, information sharing among finance agencies and intelligence agencies is not always sufficient. On the other hand, if the government actions are controlled by the foreign ministry or cabinet, then the lead ministry is not the most experienced organization in these particular areas. However, since financial activities are closely related to the activities of individuals and procurement of items, information sharing among competent agencies is vital for efficient implementation of sanctions.

Lack of legal systems to cover non-registered financial service provider

Another aspect of the difficulty in implementing financial sanctions is a lack of a legal systems to control entities which are not officially registered as banks or financial institutions. Paragraph 14 of Resolution 2371(2017) expands the scope of the entities controlled as financial institutions. It clarifies companies performing financial services as essentially the same as those provided by banks and are considered financial institutions by the relevant resolutions. However, in common practice, financial institutions and banks are legally registered. Therefore, the regulation to control financial institutions covers those registered institutions only. As a result, domestic laws do not meet the requirements of the relevant paragraph.

Monitoring of DPRK's cyber space activities

Owing to the anonymity of virtual currency, detecting involvement of the DPRK in these attempts would be difficult, especially with apparently legal activities such as use or collection of virtual currency and mining. As recommended by the Panel of Experts, since virtual currency is used by the DPRK as a new tool to avoid financial sanctions, it is necessary to raise awareness of this problem and establish systems to monitor virtual currency.

Concerning cyber-attacks, attribution is a challenge. David E. Graham explains that the difficulty of attribution of cyber-attacks is due to the anonymity built into the technology. Even if a State could detect the source of the attack, the "attacker" might be a hijacked system. Moreover, a State could claim that the attackers are solely private individuals, negating the State's involvement.[94] However, in the case of the DPRK, as access to the internet is only limited to select nationals, DPRK hackers are selected and trained by the country. Likewise, cyber-attacks against oversea targets need access to the internet which is tightly restricted by the government, and it is likely that large-scale cyber-attacks were conducted by State-sponsored actors.

Conclusion

This chapter analyzed the challenges in the implementation of UN sanctions focusing on the financial sanctions, and proposed how the Member States and the

UN Security Council make implementation more efficient. Sanctions imposed by the UN Security Council resolutions on the DPRK adopt a wide range of measures to urge the regime to abandon nuclear and ballistic missile programs. In addition to directly prohibiting the transfer of items used for its nuclear, ballistic missiles and other WMD related programs, the sanctions restricted the country's acquisition of income to be used for the programs. To counter the DPRK's proliferation financing, financial measures were imposed by this UN sanctions regime. These measures include asset freezes, prohibitions on providing financial services, prohibitions on operating financial institutions, prohibitions on joint ventures, and limitations on the number of bank accounts belonging to diplomatic missions.

However, the DPRK has continued to violate and evade the sanctions using various techniques, taking advantage of the shortcomings of sanctions implementation. To evade sanctions, the DPRK utilizes overseas networks, diplomatic missions, and cyber space as routes, while using high-value items, virtual currency, gold, and bulk cash as tools. The loopholes in the sanctions are not only caused by the shortcomings of UN Member States in their implementation, but also were created as a result of negotiation within the UN Security Council.

For efficient implementation, Member States should be more active in sharing information. On the other hand, the UN Security Council has to swiftly adopt new elements to leave the DPRK no time to prepare for the change. Furthermore, the use of clear language and definitions in the resolutions will facilitate implementation by Member States.

Since 2018, no sanctions resolution was adopted by the UN Security Council, and in these two years, Kim Jong Un held an unprecedented amount of bilateral talks including three United States-DPRK summit meetings. However, the DPRK is still continuing its nuclear and ballistic missile programs, as well as procurement of resources for these programs. The Security Council and Member States must do more to improve the effectiveness of the sanctions regime to urge the DPRK to discontinue these prohibited programs, or it will remain a threat to international peace and security.

Notes

1 "IAEA and DPRK: Chronology of Key Events," IAEA, accessed on November 15, 2019, www.iaea.org/newscenter/focus/dprk/chronology-of-key-events. The dates of the events in this article are local times at the locations of the events.
2 "A joint statement of the Democratic People's Republic of Korea and the United States of America," New York, June 11, 1993.
3 IAEA, *supra* note 1.
4 "Agreed Framework Between the United States of America and the Democratic People's Republic of Korea," Geneva, October 21, 1994.
5 S/RES/1695 (2006), July 15, 2006.
6 The descriptions of the resolutions in this article are summaries. For the exact provisions, refer to the original resolutions available at the 1718 Committee website, www.un.org/securitycouncil/sanctions/1718/resolutions.

7 "9 October 2006—First DPRK Nuclear Test," Comprehensive Nuclear-Test-Ban Treaty Organization (CTBTO), accessed December 5, 2019, www.ctbto.org/specials/testing-times/9-october-2006-first-dprk-nuclear-test.

8 S/RES/1718 (2006), October 14, 2006.

9 Ibid., paras. 8(a) (i)–(ii), 8(b).

10 Ibid., para. 8(a)(iii).

11 Ibid., para. 12.

12 Ibid., para. 8 (d).The resolution also banned the travel of the individuals identified as participating in the program. See Ibid., para. 8(e).

13 The other two entities are Korea Mining Development Trading Corporation and Korea Ryonbong General Corporation. See UN Security Council, "Security Council Committee Determines Items, Designated Entities subject to Measures Imposed in Resolution 1718(2006)" SC/9642, April 24, 2009.

14 "On 25 May 2009, The DPRK Announced It [*sic*] Second Nuclear Test," CTBTO, accessed on November 17, 2019, www.ctbto.org/specials/testing-times/25-may-2009-dprk-ii.

15 S/RES/1874, June 12, 2009, paras. 9, 10.

16 Ibid., paras 11- 14.

17 Ibid., para. 18.

18 UN Security Council, "Security Council Committee Determines Entities, Goods, Individuals Subject to Measures Imposed in Resolution 1718(2006)," SC/9708, July 16, 2009.

19 Ibid., para. 19.

20 Ibid., para. 20.

21 S/RES/2087, January 22, 2013.

22 Ibid., paras. 7,8.

23 Ibid., para. 5 (b).

24 Ibid., para. 5 (a).

25 Ibid., para. 6.

26 S/RES/2094 (2013), March 7, 2013.

27 FATF, *The FATF Recommendations 2012*, adopted February 16, 2012 and updated regularly since, last updated June 2019, www.fatf-gafi.org/media/fatf/documents/recommendations/pdfs/FATF%20Recommendations%202012.pdf.

28 S/RES/2094 (2013), supra note 26, para. 11.

29 Ibid., paras. 12, 13.

30 Travel bans are only imposed on individuals.

31 Ibid., para. 10.

32 Ibid., Annexes III, IV.

33 S/RES/2270 (2016), March 2, 2016.

34 Ibid., paras. 29, 30.

35 Ibid., para. 31.

36 Ibid., para. 6.

37 Ibid., paras. 8, 27.

38 Ibid., para. 13.

39 Ibid., para. 33.

40 Ibid., para. 34

41 Ibid., para. 35.

42 Ibid., para. 38.

43 S/RES/2321 (2016), November 30, 2016.

44 Ibid., para. 26(b).
45 Ibid., para. 28.
46 Ibid., para. 22.
47 Ibid., para. 12.
48 Ibid., para. 32.
49 Ibid., para. 33.
50 On November 18, 2010, US Department of the Treasury designated Office 39 for its illicit economic activities, management of slush funds, and generating revenues for the regime leadership. US Department of the Treasury, "Treasury Designates Key Nodes of the Illicit Financing Network of North Korea's Office 39," November 18, 2010, www.treasury.gov/press-center/press-releases/Pages/tg962.aspx. The UN Security Council designated Office 39 in March 2, 2016.
51 S/RES/2371(2017), August 5, 2017.
52 Ibid., para. 8.
53 Ibid., para. 10.
54 Ibid., para. 9.
55 Ibid., para. 6.
56 Ibid., para. 11.
57 Ibid., para. 13.
58 Ibid., para. 12.
59 Ibid., Annexes I and II. The designated individuals working for financial institutes are Choe Chun Yong (Representative of Ilsim International Bank), Han Jang Su (Chief Representative of Foreign Trade Bank), and Jo Chol Song (Deputy Representative for the Korea Kwangson Banking Corporation). The designated entities are Foreign Trade Bank (FTB), Korean National Insurance Company (KNIC), Koryo Credit Development Bank and Mansudae Overseas Project Group of Companies.
60 S/RES/2375(2017), September 11, 2017.
61 Ibid., para. 13.
62 Ibid., para. 14.
63 Ibid., para. 15.
64 Ibid., para. 16.
65 Ibid., para. 17.
66 Ibid., para. 18.
67 S/RES/2397 (2017), December 22, 2017.
68 Ibid., para. 5.
69 Ibid., para. 4.
70 Ibid., para. 6.
71 Ibid., para. 7.
72 Ibid., para. 8.
73 Ibid., para. 11.
74 Ibid., para. 12.
75 Ibid., Annex I.
76 1874 Panel of Experts, *Midterm report of the Panel of Experts submitted pursuant to resolution 2464 (2019)*, S/2019/691, 30 August 2019, paras. 57–66.
77 Ibid., para. 58.
78 FATF, *Guidance for a Risk-Based Approach to Virtual Assets and Virtual Asset Service Providers*, Paris, www.fatf-gafi.org/publications/fatfrecommendations/documents/Guidance-RBA-virtual-assets.html.

79 FATF, *Guidance for a Risk-based Approach to Virtual Currencies*, June 2015, www. fatf-gafi.org/media/fatf/documents/reports/Guidance-RBA-Virtual-Currencies. pdf.

80 White House, "Press Briefing on the Attribution of the WannaCry Malware Attack to North Korea," White House press briefing, December 19, 2017, www.whitehouse. gov/briefings-statements/press-briefing-on-the-attribution-of-the-wannacry-malware-attack-to-north-korea-121917/.

81 United States of America vs PARK JIN HYOK, aka "Jin Hyok Park," aka "Pak Jin Hek," MJ18-1479, 2018, United States District Court for the Central District of California.

82 US Department of the Treasury, "Treasury Sanctions North Korean State-Sponsored Malicious Cyber Groups," September 12, 2019. https://home.treasury.gov/news/ press-releases/sm774.

83 1874 Panel of Experts, supra note 76, para. 50.

84 Ibid., para. 51.

85 Ibid., para. 34.

86 1874 Panel of Experts, *Final Report of the Panel of Experts Submitted Pursuant to Resolution 2464 (2019)*, S/2020/151, March 2, 2020, para. 108.

87 Ibid., paras. 54–56.

88 Julian Rademeyer, "Diplomats and Deceit: North Korea's Criminal Activities in Africa." Global Initiative against Transnational Organized Crime, September 2017, https://globalinitiative.net/diplomats-and-deceit-north-koreas-criminal-activities-in-africa/.

89 Ibid.

90 1874 Panel of Experts, supra note 86, para. 180.

91 US Department of the Treasury, "Treasury Sanctions Individuals and Entities Supporting the North Korean Government and its Nuclear and Weapons Proliferation Efforts, December 2, 2016," www.treasury.gov/press-center/press-releases/Pages/ jl0677.aspx.

92 1874 Panel of Experts, *Final Report of the Panel of Experts Submitted Pursuant to Resolution 2407 (2018)*, S/2019/171, March 5, 2019, para. 79.

93 Ibid., para. 150.

94 David E. Graham, "Cyber Threats and the Law of War," *Journal of National Security Law & Policy*, Vol. 4, No.1 (August 13, 2010): 87–102.

11 UN sanctions on Iran and their financial elements

Kazuto Suzuki

Introduction

The JCPOA was agreed in July 2015 which ended the crisis caused by nuclear development in Iran since it was revealed in 2002. The JCPOA also terminated the sanctions set by a series of the United Nations Security Council Resolutions (UNSCR). The objectives of UN sanctions were to change the behavior of target countries, bring them to the negotiating table, and as a result, remove the source of threats to international peace and security. It can be said if these objectives were met, the sanctions would be effective and successful. In this sense, the UN sanctions on Iran were undoubtingly successful and could be a model for the future of sanctions.

However, it was not UN sanctions alone which brought Iran to the negotiating table and ushered in the JCPOA. The unilateral sanctions imposed by the United States, the European Union and many other countries were also very effective and contributed to the successful outcome. Particularly, both the sanctions by the US which included "secondary sanctions" (imposing sanctions on non-US entities and individuals if they break US unilateral sanctions) and the sanctions by the EU which included financial sanctions through cutting off Iranian banks from SWIFT (Society for Worldwide Interbank Financial Telecommunication) and insurance services were extremely effective and caused serious damage to the Iranian economy.

This chapter, therefore, discusses not only the financial sanctions imposed by the UN such as freezing funds and economic resources, but also financial sanction measures by the US and the EU. It aims to explain why and how sanctions by the UN, the US and the EU were able to lead the successful negotiation and conclusion of the JCPOA. In doing so, the author draws on his experience of serving as a member of the Panel of Experts pursuant of UNSCR 1929 (Panel of Experts on Iran) without violating the confidentiality agreement.

Financial measures in UN sanctions on Iran

The UN Security Council adopted UNSCR 1696 (2006)[1] following the report from IAEA in 2006 which stated Iran's non-compliance with the IAEA's request for inspections. This resolution is based on the Article 40 of the UN Charter for issuing a request to halt Iran's nuclear activities. However, Iran has not responded to the request stated in UNSCR 1696 (2006), and therefore, the Security Council has adopted UNSCR 1737 (2006)[2] followed by UNSCR 1747 (2007),[3] 1803 (2008)[4] and 1929 (2010).[5] These four resolutions are all based on Chapter VII of the Charter of the United Nations which means that they are legally binding on all Member States of the UN. They were effective until they were terminated as a result of the agreement of JCPOA and adoption of UNSCR 2231 (2015).

These UNSCRs demanded that Iran halt nuclear activities including the enrichment activities in the facilities in Fordow and Natanz, the construction of a heavy water nuclear reactor in Arak, and the activity related to ballistic missiles capable of delivering nuclear weapons, including satellite launches. The resolutions for sanctioning Iran are based on the concept of "targeted sanctions" which developed as a reflection of the "comprehensive sanctions" that led to humanitarian disaster in Iraq during the 1990s. The "targeted sanctions" on Iran focus on the trade ban on the items related to nuclear and missile activities, a travel ban on those who are involved in these activities, asset freezes on the individuals and entities involved in these activities, and an arms embargo which is considered to be the source of financing these activities.

At the same time, the Member States are called upon to inspect all cargo to and from Iran in their territory if the State has information that provides reasonable grounds to believe that the cargo consists of items related to prohibited activities. Furthermore, Member States may request inspection of vessels if there are reasonable grounds to believe that the vessel is carrying prohibited items, with the consent of the State where the vessel is registered.[6]

The UN sanctions on Iran are targeted on the nuclear and missile activities, and therefore, the sanctions focus on "items" rather than financial aspects. The only explicit financial aspect of UN sanctions is the asset freeze on designated individuals and entities. Member States are called upon to prevent the provision of financial services, including insurance or re-insurance, that could contribute to Iran's nuclear activities or missile development if they have information that gives reasonable grounds to believe. Furthermore, they are called upon to take appropriate measures that prohibit the opening of new branches, subsidiaries, or representative office of Iranian banks as well as establishing new joint ventures, showing interest in ownership or in establishing correspondent relationships within their jurisdiction if they have information with reasonable ground to believe that these financial activities are contributing to prohibited activities.[7] However, these provisions are only "called upon" by the Security Council, and they are not legally binding on Member States. They only provide legal grounds for and encourage Member States to take their own actions to establish domestic legislation. Therefore, these provisions that are called upon Member States are not considered as part of UN sanctions but the legal bases that justify Member States to establish and implement unilateral sanctions.

Asset freeze

The most effective financial measure of the UN sanctions is the asset freeze. Usually, when the UN Security Council decides to implement an asset freeze, Member States are obliged to freeze accounts of designated individuals and entities, or their aliases and subsidiaries, in banks and other financial institutions. If Member States implement these measures appropriately—proper identification, double-checking documents, red-flagging of all aliases and so on—it would have immediate effect. Also Member States exercise their financial intelligence capabilities and share intelligence sharing to root out bank accounts of front companies or individuals with fake IDs.

These assets are "frozen" by UNSCRs, which means that ownership is not transferred to Member States but remains with the original owner. When the sanctions are lifted, these assets will be able to be used by designated individuals and entities. In case of US sanctions which froze the assets owned by Iranian entities in the 1980s, the payment for Iranian oil and other services was entirely frozen in banks in the United States. These assets were "de-frozen" by the JCPOA in 2015, but the JCPOA did not lift the primary sanctions, which prohibited US banks from trading directly with Iranian banks, and thus, the Obama administration decided to transfer the funds in cash which was airlifted to Iran. President Trump saw the transaction of the cash transfer on TV (it was widely televised as historical moment of reconciliation between the United States and Iran) and blamed the Obama administration for "giving" the cash as a "gift,"[8] which of course is not an accurate understanding. Nevertheless, it is worth noting that the "de-freeze" of the assets may be misunderstood in certain political circumstances.

The assets which are frozen by UNSCRs are not limited to funds in bank accounts. UNSCR 1737 (2007) defines assets as "funds, other financial assets and economic resources."[9] Among these "assets," the most difficult to freeze is "economic resources." These include aircraft of designated airlines or vessels owned by designated shipping companies (in case of UN sanctions on Iran, Yas Air and the Irano-Hind shipping company, respectively, owned by the Islamic Republic Guard Corps, IRGC) and other resources such as mines owned by mining companies. The difficulties lie with movable assets such as aircraft and vessels.

These movable assets often move from Iranian jurisdiction and enter into other jurisdictions. In these cases, relevant Member States are obliged to seize those assets and freeze them. However, seizing aircraft or vessels provokes a lot of difficult questions with regard to the services they provide. If a Member State seizes these assets, it would also have to take care of how to transfer the cargo or passengers in those assets. The cost for transferring cargo and passengers would inevitably be the responsibility of Member States, which of course discourages Member States from taking action. Additionally, Member States also have to pay for the cost of holding those assets in their airports or ports. If they are financial assets, the cost of storage may not be a big issue, but in the case of physical assets such as aircraft or vessels, there is the inevitable cost to be borne by Member States.

Although this was not the case with UN sanctions, there was an incident when an Iranian ship was frozen for other reasons. When the *Sahand* owned by the Islamic Republic of Iran Shipping Lines (IRISL) called at the port of Singapore, French and German banks requested Singaporean authority to seize the vessel as collateral for debt owed by IRISL.[10] The Singaporean authority asked the court whether it should respond to the request or not. Although IRISL and its subsidiaries paid the debt and there was no necessity for the Singaporean authority to seize the vessel, the court held the view that IRISL was not designated by UNSCRs, and thus Singapore did not have legal responsibility to seize it, but at the same time, IRISL was designated by the EU and the United States, so if the vessel was seized, French and German bank could not use it as collateral since the value of asset would be frozen.

This ruling did not recognize active engagement with the seizure of vessels which was not designated by Singapore or the UN, and obviously the Singapore authority had no legal obligation to seize the vessel in favor of foreign banks. However, this case also demonstrates that Member States have little incentives to freeze on movable assets. Although IRISL is not designated by UNSCRs, UNSCR 1929 (2010) paragraph 22 states that all Member States shall

> exercise vigilance when doing business with entities incorporated in Iran or subject to Iran's jurisdiction, including those of the IRGC and IRISL, and any individuals or entities acting on their behalf or at their direction, and entities owned or controlled by them, including through illicit means.[11]

This paragraph only requires Member States to be vigilant and there is no legally binding obligation, but under this paragraph, the Singaporean authority may exercise its power to seize the vessel if there is reason to believe that it is necessary. However, as far as the court judgment is concerned, it seems that there was no reference to this paragraph because the court found it unnecessary to seize the vessel for banks and pay the cost for harboring vessel during the period of settlement negotiation.

In the case of UN sanctions on the DPRK (Democratic People's Republic of Korea), there was a seizure of a vessel in violation of the UNSCR. Indonesia seized MV *Wise Honest* one of North Korea's largest bulk carriers in 2018 as it recognized that the vessel had turned off its AIS (Automatic Identification System) and then the found out that the vessel was carrying coal shipped from North Korea. This vessel was operated by Korea Songi Shipping Co., which is a subordinate of Korean People's Army, which is designated by the UN.[12] Thus, the Indonesian action was legitimate and appropriate as an implementation of the UNSCRs, but Indonesia did not want to bear the cost of holding the vessel. The Indonesian authority asked for international help, and the United States responded to the request and identified that the DPRK was not only violating UN sanctions but also US sanctions. Thus, the US government decided to take control of the vessel and transferred it from Indonesian territorial water to a port on American Samoa.[13]

These incidents also demonstrate that it is a heavy burden for Member States to seize and keep the vessel in their territory, which may have an impact on the incentives for implementing UNSCRs. Even if an aircraft or vessel was landing in an airport or calling at port in a Member State's territory, Member States might not take any action even though there was reason to believe that the aircraft or vessel may carry prohibited goods. The implementation of asset freeze on "economic resources" has a lot of difficult problem to solve.

Ownership and control of assets

In the process of implementing sanctions, it is not only the definition of "economic resources" that troubles Member States' authorities to make judgments whether to freeze the asset or not, but also which assets need to be frozen. Paragraph 12 of UNSCR 1737 defines that all Member States shall freeze the funds, other financial assets and economic resources "that are owned or controlled by the persons or entities designated" or " by persons or entities acting on their behalf or at their direction, or by entities owned or controlled by them, including through illicit means."[14] This means that the Member States shall freeze assets which are owned and controlled by subsidiaries, agents, shell companies or someone under the direction of designated individuals or entities (such as family members).

The question here is what constitutes "owned or controlled." Usually, owners of entities are identified as shareholders, but how many shares does it take to show that the entity is "owned" by designated individuals or entities. Also, when the company is "controlled," it is assumed that the company is managed by designated individuals or entities, but it is not clear what percentage of shares is required to meet the criterion.

While the author was working as a member of the Panel of Experts on Iran Established Pursuant to Resolution 1929 (2010), the criterion for "owned" was 50% of shares based on the understanding of the Office of Foreign Asset Control (OFAC) of the US Treasury. There was consensus among Member States that 50% of shares is the acceptable criterion, but not the definitive one.

A more difficult problem emerged on the "controlled" part. There was a case that some designated individuals were appointed as members of the managerial board of foundations owned by the IRGC. Although the IRGC itself is not designated by the UN, the individuals who were commanders of the IRGC are designated as individuals involved in the arms trade which was prohibited by UNSCR 1747 (2008). Those commanders were appointed to manage the financial bodies of the IRGC after their retirement. Morteza Rezaie, former Deputy Commander of the IRGC and designated by UNSCR 1747 (2008), was appointed to the IRGC Cooperative Foundation (Bonyad-e Taavon-e Sepah) which provides pension funds and financial aid for economic activities or the IRGC. Morteza Bahmanyar, former Head of the Finance and Budget Department of Iran's Aerospace Industries Organization (AIO) and designated by UNSCR 1737 (2007), worked as a board member of the Mostazafan Foundation (Bonyad-e Mostazafan) which invests in a variety of industrial activities from agriculture to service industries. These foundations own 43 entities listed on the Teheran Stock Exchange and participate in a managerial board of 218 corporate entities with 1,073 individuals belonging to those boards.[15]

The IRGC was established after the Islamic Revolution of 1979 and the following Iran–Iraq War to defend the revolutionary regime instead of the regular armed forces. During the Iran–Iraq War, the IRGC was in charge of the construction of infrastructure and the production of armaments and equipment, which led the IRGC to penetrate deeply into Iranian economy and it maintained the economic role after the war.[16] Its foundations own many non-military companies as described above, so if the participation of IRGC personnel on managerial board is the criterion of asset freeze, Member States are obliged to freeze the assets of large number of companies.

This issue was raised in the Panel of Experts report in 2015, a few months before the conclusion of the Iran nuclear negotiation. Eventually all UNSCRs were terminated, so that the UN could not engage to find a solution to this issue, but there still remained unilateral sanctions by the United States that could possibly be a problem for other sanctions regimes.

Changing names of designated individuals and entities

Another issue with regard to asset freeze is that often designated individuals and entities change their names and attribution so that it would be difficult for national authorities and private companies to ascertain whether the person or company that they are dealing with is designated or not. The designated individuals and entities are listed in the Annex of UNSCRs or decided by the Sanctions Committee under the Security Council when significant non-compliance cases are identified. However, the list contains very limited information—often just names and affiliations—about these individuals and entities, so it would be difficult to trace the activities of these designated individuals and entities if they change names.

These names and affiliations are listed in the Consolidated United Nations Security Council Sanctions List,[17] together with other designations by other sanctions regimes. However, each sanctions regime has its own ways of listing information on the list, so that the UN Secretariat decided to use the format of the Al-Qaida/Taliban (currently ISIL/Al-Qaida) Monitoring Team. This format contains, in individual cases, the names, aliases, affiliations at the time of designation, date of birth, place of birth, quality of information (whether the listed information is reliable or not), nationality, passport number, other ID numbers, residential address and other information. In case of entities, the format consists of the name and other names of the entity (names in different languages), address and other information (telephone number, email address etc.). In case of sanctions on Iran, most of designations lacked detailed information on the Annex of UNSCRs, so the Panel of Experts was commissioned to research further information and additional information is listed after the approval of Sanctions Committee under the Security Council. However, there is a limitation for intelligence collection by the Panel alone, and therefore, the information is not often sufficiently complete.

The consolidated list is made available to the public so that private industry or banks will be able to integrate the list into their system for identifying suspicious trade and immigration authorities in Member States will be able to reject designated individuals when they arrive at the port of entry. However, those designated individuals often use forged passports or aliases, and designated entities often use front companies that are not linked to the names on the list. Thus, consolidated list alone will not be sufficient for implementing UNSCRs.[18]

Even if the change of names was evident, it is still difficult to freeze assets of designated individuals or entities. For example, UNSCR 1747 (2008) designated Pars Air, which was owned by Pars Aviation Service Company, a subsidiary of IRGC. However, as soon as Pars Air was designated, it established a new company, Yas Air, and transferred all the assets of Pars Air. Both Pars Aviation Service Company and Pars Air were dissolved, so it was not possible to identify Yas Air as an entity "owned or controlled" by Pars Air, and it was difficult to apply the provisions of the UNSCRs, even though it was clear that Yas Air was a successor company of Pars Air. The Panel of Experts did investigate the activities of Yas Air and established that Yas Air was involved in the transfer of arms from Iran. The Sanctions Committee the re-designated Yas Air in 2012. However, when the Sanctions Committee decided to designate Yas Air, it established a new company, Pouya Air, but maintained Yas Air as the holder of some retired aircraft. The Panel of Experts conducted an additional investigation and reported to the Sanctions Committee that there was a transfer of assets from Yas Air to Pouya Air. The Sanctions Committee recognized the report and identified that Pouya Air was an alias of Yas Air, so that there was no necessity to add Pouya Air as a designated entity.

In cases of US unilateral sanctions, the US Treasury designates not only the entities which are involved nuclear or missile development activities, but also assets such as vessels and aircrafts that are owned by the entities. In this case, US designation includes information which identifies those assets, such as the IMO (International Maritime Organization) number for vessels and the registration number for aircraft, so that even when the ownership of those assets is changed, there is no need to change or add a new designation. However, in the case of UN sanctions, the Security Council can only designate individuals and entities, and there is no tool to designate particular assets, except the case of DPRK sanctions. Thus, it is difficult to implement UNSCRs and to seize these assets if they change names.

Proliferation financing

Although it is not the measurement of implementing UN financial sanctions, proliferation financing has a lot of implications for UN sanctions. The definition of proliferation financing is

the act of providing funds or financial services which are used, in whole or in part, for the manufacture, acquisition, possession, development, export, trans-shipment, brokering, transport, transfer, stockpiling or use of nuclear, chemical or biological weapons and their means of delivery and related materials (including both technologies and dual use goods used for non-legitimate purposes), in contravention of national laws or, where applicable, international obligations.[19]

Proliferation financing attracted attention when Financial Action Task Force (FATF) issued a set of recommendations for combating money laundering and financing terrorist and proliferation activities in 2012.[20] Among all the recommendations, Recommendation 7 focused on the financing proliferation of weapons of mass destruction (WMD). The objective of this recommendation was to analyze with typologies of financing networks for the proliferation of WMD, to observe trading patterns of designated individuals and entities, to monitor the business activities of them and to prevent nuclear and missile development activities through their financial activities. FATF has developed expertise through its activities for monitoring money laundering and other global financial activities and developing its financial intelligence capability. Proliferation financing makes use of those capabilities and expertise applying to proliferation activities.

The recommendations of FATF are not sanctions *per se*, but it conducts a peer review of individual Member States whether they are following the recommendations. It certainly has strong implications for strengthening the implementation process of UNSCRs. For non-proliferation, UNSCR 1540 (2004) has provisions for preventing the proliferation of WMD, but it only aims to prevent to non-state actors. The FATF recommendation for combating proliferation financing may have greater impact on the implementation of Iran-related UNSCRs, but it was published in 2012 after the last Iran-related sanctions, UNSCR 1929 (2010), were adopted, so it was not possible to include provisions related to FATF recommendation in the series of UNSCRs on Iran. In this regard, the current FATF recommendation only monitors financial transactions with regard to the implementation of JCPOA.

Monitoring financial transactions based on UNSCR 1929 (2010)

UNSCR 1929 (2010) includes provision that calls upon Member States to "prevent the provision of financial services, including insurance or re-insurance" or transfer "of any financial or other assets or resources ... by freezing any financial or other assets or resources on their territories."[21] Although it is only a "called upon" provision, it provided legal grounds for the Panel of Experts to monitor financial transactions and to report cases which may infringe this provision. In its report in 2014, the Panel of Experts encouraged Member States to stay vigilant with regard to financial activities involving shell companies, payment through non-designated small and medium sized banks which do not have records of international transactions, and bank transactions via foreign branches of the Central Bank of Iran (CBI).[22] Since the CBI is designated by the US unilateral sanctions, but not by the UN, the EU or Japan, the accounts in branches of the CBI are not frozen in those countries, and it was possible for Iranian entities to set up businesses through these accounts. In fact, there were several incidents reported that deals made with forged document using the accounts of foreign branches of the CBI. Also, it was reported that an exchange student created a front company and traded through accounts in a foreign branch of the CBI.

The 2014 Panel of Experts report describes a unique financial transaction in Islamic culture called Hawala which bypasses ordinary financial channels. Hawala is the transfer of information from a contact point in Iran to another contact point in another state. A person who wants to send money to another country deposits money in an Iranian contact point and the agent makes a phone call to a foreign contact point. The agent of the foreign contact point pays the recipient from the pool of funds at the agent's disposal. If a person wants to send money to Iran, the reverse of this process took place. The point of using Hawala is that there is no actual exchange of funds, and the communication only takes place via telephone. In this way, the financial transaction can avoid the ordinary banking system so that it would be extremely difficult for the authority to prevent such a transaction. If the transfer of funds is large, some of the payment is done through the ordinary banking system and Hawala is used for the rest, but there are no instances of Hawala being used for proliferation financing.[23]

The other mode of transaction was barter. In order to avoid using the banking networks which are constantly monitored internationally, Iranians used barter as alternative to gain prohibited or below-threshold goods. The Panel of Experts report of 2014 stated that there was extensive barter trade in aluminum. A foreign private company exported alumina, which is the material for aluminum, and in return, this company received processed aluminum which was much less than the amount of alumina. In other words, the Iranian company received excess alumina as a reward for processing and manufacturing aluminum. This type of trade is not strange in material business and alumina is not prohibited, so it will not constitute suspicious trade or violation of UN sanctions, but some types of aluminum are on the list of prohibited dual-use items. The Panel of Experts expressed concern that this type of barter trade could be used for other prohibited transactions.[24]

The Panel of Experts report of 2015 investigated another method of circumventing UN sanctions and avoiding the international banking system. The Panel observed that there were some cases when Iranian private companies, which are designated by national sanctions, provided services to foreign companies but were not able to receive payment for the services. The Iranian company asked the company to pay the amount to the manufacturer in the same country which provided parts to the Iranian company (see Chart 11.1). In this way, the Iranian company does not have to be involved in the financial settlement in this triangular trade, so that it can avoid the monitoring by the international community.[25]

Although the Panel of Experts were actively engaged in investigating suspicious financial transactions which may be related to circumvention of UN sanctions or could be used as a model for violation of UNSCR provisions, these transactions remained as provisions which "call upon" Member States to implement through

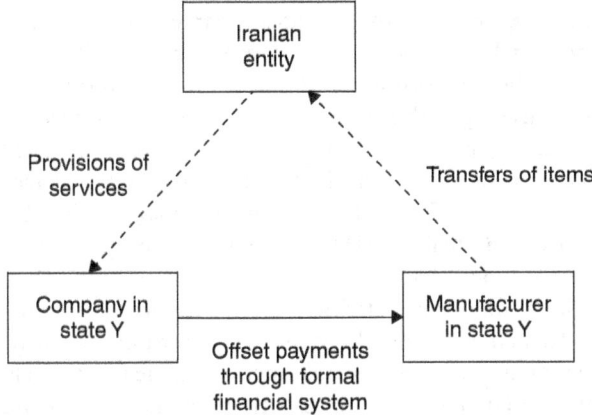

Chart 11.1 Circumventing financial system
(Source: Final Report of the Panel of Experts, 2015)

their national legal systems. Since Member States were not obliged to report these financial transactions, the Sanction Committee and the Security Council were not as well informed, and it was difficult to monitor the implementation of these provisions by Member States.

National sanctions

As discussed above, financial measures in UN sanctions are centered around asset freeze and the rest are based on the commitment of Member States to implement UNSCRs. Even in asset freeze, UN sanctions struggled to freeze movable assets. However, the sanctions on Iran are considered to be "successful" among other sanctions regimes, and especially the financial aspect of sanctions was important for their "success." National financial sanctions are lauded rather than UN sanctions.

US sanctions

It is not our objective to analyze and assess individual national sanctions, but there is no doubt that national sanctions played a huge role for leading sanctions to JCPOA. We especially need to pay attention to US financial sanctions, which have a power tool of so-called "secondary sanctions" where non-US individuals and entities are subject to sanctions if they make transactions with Iranian individuals or entities that are designated by US Treasury. If US authorities have sufficient reasons to believe that those transactions are involved in nuclear and missile development activities, they can impose penalties on non-US individuals or entities. Often, this is seen as an extraterritorial application of US national law, but it is different. The US authorities have the power to make judgments on whether to allow such non-US entities to trade on the American market. So, if US authorities recognized that the non-US entities are not complying with US sanctions, then these entities will lose their opportunity to trade in the US. In other words, they face a choice between trading with Iran or losing US market. In many cases, they choose the US market by paying a huge sum of money as a levy.[26] The legal justification of such enforcement mechanism is defined in the National Defense Authorization Act (NDAA) of 2012. Under this Act, many banks including French BNP Paribas, British HSBC and Japanese MUFG have paid heavy penalties.

Such unilateral sanctions would have a significant impact on non-US banks which conduct international monetary activities. They have acute awareness of the risk of trading with Iranian entities and try to refrain from dealing with any entities—even non-designated ones. US national sanctions made it extremely difficult for Iranian entities to enter into the international market. Even though some items such as food and medicine were exempt from US sanctions, many banks were afraid of making a deal with Iranian entities on these items.

Further, US financial sanctions are extremely effective because of the US dollar. The US dollar is the key currency for international trade. More than 60% of national foreign reserves are in US dollars and oil, a major source of foreign currency for Iran, is also traded in US dollars. When an international transaction take place in US dollars, it is highly likely that this transaction is conducted through a correspondent bank in the United States. The US authorities have power to intervene while the transaction going through US banks because they are physically in US jurisdiction. In short, as long as the Iranian entity needs to trade in US dollars for settling payments for oil exchange, it is always vulnerable to intervention by US authorities.

In addition to Congressional Statutes, such as NDAA, the International Emergency Economic Powers Act (IEEPA), the Iran Freedom and Counter-Proliferation Act of 2012 (IFCA), the Comprehensive Iran Sanctions, Accountability, and Divestment Act of 2010, the Iran Sanctions Act of 1996, and many others, there are two dozen Executive Orders and other legal instruments applied to sanctions imposed on Iran.[27] This complex labyrinth of legal texts would discourage exporters from engaging with Iranian counterparts because

Table 11.1 Non-US financial institutions levied for violating sanctions

Year	Banks	Levy
2012	HSBC Bank Financial Services	$1,256,000,000
2012	Standard Chartered Bank Financial Services	$667,000,000
2012	ING Bank N.V. Financial Services	$619,000,000
2013	Bank of Tokyo-Mitsubishi UFJ Financial Services	$259,000,000
2014	BNP Paribas S.A. Financial Services	$8,960,000,000
2015	Commerzbank AG Financial Services	$258,000,000

(Source: Various OFAC information sources)

they may unknowingly infringe upon some elements of these legal instruments. Although the OFAC provides various guidelines to navigate through these documents, there is always room for interpretation and ambiguity.

EU sanctions

The effect of financial sanctions on Iran was not achieved by US national sanctions alone but also ones imposed by the EU. The EU has jurisdiction over Brussels-based Society for Worldwide Interbank Financial Telecommunication (SWIFT) and EU Regulations to prohibit financial transactions with Iran had an effect on the activities of SWIFT.[28] SWIFT provides services for facilitating interbank transfer with electronic messaging, which is essential for global financial transactions. Cutting off Iranian banks from the SWIFT network under EU Regulations would isolate Iran from the web of interbank transactions.

Additionally, the EU has imposed oil embargoes on Iran, but the EU Regulation of 2012 further prohibited the provision of insurance and re-insurance for maritime traffic to strengthen the oil embargo.[29] The ban on providing insurance would not only impact the oil trade between Europe and Iran but also for other parties which trade with Iran. This is because most of the major maritime insurance companies such as Lloyd's, Concirrus and RSA Luxembourg, are based in Europe. They provide internationally competitive services, so non-EU shipping companies would find it difficult to insure their transactions with Iran. The EU Regulation does not apply for non-EU insurance companies or P&I (Protection and Indemnity Insurance) Union, but this EU Regulation made it difficult for Iran to export oil and to earn foreign currency for procuring prohibited goods.

Impact on Iran's economy

The national sanctions by the US and the EU had a significant impact on Iranian economy by isolating it from global market and especially cutting off its oil exports. As a result of tightening national and UN sanctions, people in Iran recognized that the blame for economic hardship lay in the policy of the conservative and anti-American Ahmadinejad government which escalated the development of nuclear capabilities. In addition, those who believed that President Mahmoud Ahmadinejad and his conservative allies were rigging the vote in the 2009 presidential election launched a massive popular movement called the "Green Movement." The conservatives used a militia force called "Basij" which took command from the IRGC to suppress the Green Movement and disqualify major political figures such as Mir Hossein Mousavi, a former Prime Minister, and Mehdi Karroubi, a former Speaker of the Majlis (Parliament). The Ahmadinejad government put them under house arrest and banned national media from reporting on them. These measures added fuel to the fire for those who criticized the president, which led to the landslide victory of Hassan Rouhani, the leading moderate candidate, in the 2013 presidential election.

During his campaign, Rouhani promised the nation that he would negotiate with major international powers—three European states (the UK, France and Germany) and three members of Security Council (the United States, Russia and China)—and lift sanctions for improving Iran's economy. The three European states (E3) engaged in the negotiation with Iran from 2002 which concluded in 2005 but the agreement was never realized due to the intervention of the United States. After the collapse of 2005 agreement, the negotiations took place with a framework of the E3 and the United States, Russia and China (E3+3 or P5+1). So when Rouhani claimed that he was going to negotiate with major powers, it was assumed that it should be E3+3 including the United States which Iran calls "Great Satan." Rouhani is a skillful politician who used to be the Commander of Air Defense Force during Iran–Iraq War, and was a long-time relationship with the Supreme Leader Ayatollah Khamenei. He had an agreement with Khamenei before he launched his campaign for negotiating with United States and he also convinced other conservative politicians at the center of national power. In other words, even the conservatives were not able to stop Rouhani from negotiating with the United States under dire economic circumstances.

As soon as Rouhani won the election in August 2013, he immediately engaged in the negotiation with E3+3 and concluded the Joint Plan of Action (JPOA), or First Interim Agreement. The JPOA allowed partial sanctions lifting and Iran began to sell a limited amount of oil. The negotiations continued after the conclusion of JPOA with Foreign Minister Javad Zarif as the chief negotiator and reached an agreement with E3+3 in July 2015.

Superficially, the agreement, the Joint Comprehensive Plan of Action (JCPOA), was a product of national sanctions by the United States and the EU, but it is important to note that the UN sanctions provided the foundation of these national sanctions. It was UN Security Council which identified that Iran's nuclear and missile development activities were a threat to international peace and security. National sanctions are based on the legitimacy of the UN Charter and its implementation of legally binding UNSCRs under Article 41 of Chapter VII of the Charter of the United Nations. The legal binding power of Chapter VII assures that not only United States or EU unilaterally enforce their national sanctions, but also all Member States are obliged to impose sanctions on Iran. Such legal foundation was fully used by EU sanctions, so when JCPOA was agreed and UN sanctions were lifted, EU sanctions were also lifted because they were based on UNSCRs and they were functioning as supplementary to UN sanctions. (US national sanctions as discussed above were based on their national laws but the secondary sanctions were lifted.)

UNSCR 2231 (2015) and financial sanctions

All UNSCRs are terminated in accordance with JCPOA and there are no effective UN sanctions on Iran. Since JCPOA was agreed between E3+3 and Iran, it should be endorsed by another resolution. UNSCR 2231[30] was adopted unanimously to make JCPOA legally binding under Chapter VII of the UN Charter to be effective on all Member States. Some individual Member States, such as Canada, Australia and Japan, which had a national sanctions regime based on UNSCRs but not being parties of JCPOA were supposed to disengage from their national sanctions after the adoption of UNSCR 2231.

Although JCPOA decided to terminate all sanctions regimes, which would include lifting sanctions related to missile development and the arms embargo, the JCPOA was only focused on nuclear affairs. In other words, there was no agreement on missile development and arms embargo, so that the sanctions on these activities were supposed continue under the UN sanctions regime. Annex B of UNSCR 2231 defined that the arms embargo should continue for five years after the implementation day (the day the resolution enters into force) and restrictions on missile development should continue for eight years.

The language used in this resolution is "restriction" rather than "sanctions" because Iran wanted to give the impression that it was no longer a subject of sanctions; however these "restrictions" are a *de facto* continuation of sanctions with so-called "sunset clauses." As long as these "restrictions" are effective, the designated individuals and entities related to missile development and arms embargo remain on the Consolidated United Nations Security Council Sanctions List. Thus, the asset freeze of these designated individuals and entities remained in place.

Conclusion

The decision by President Donald Trump in May 2018 changed the dynamics of sanctions on Iran. He unilaterally withdrew from JCPOA (though not from UNSCR 2231) and re-imposed national sanctions without coordinating with other E3+3 partners. E3 countries tried to convince the US administration to return to JCPOA, but President and the Secretary of State Mike Pompeo stubbornly resisted those solicitations based on the suspicion that Iran continues to provide armaments to conflict zones in Syria and Yemen, to threaten US allies such as Israel and Saudi Arabia, and to develop missile capabilities. All of them are legitimate concerns for Iranian activities in the region and could be regarded as violations of UNSCR 2231. But instead of imposing an internationally coordinated response to such Iranian activities, the United States unilaterally decided to withdraw from JCPOA since its primary intention is to put "maximum pressure" on Iran to change its behavior.

The re-imposition of US national sanctions includes reinstatement of secondary sanctions which prevents non-US companies from trading with Iran. There is an assumption among the major political figures in the Trump administration that financial sanctions were effective in changing the behavior of Iran and will bring Iran to the negotiating table. Probably, President Trump is expecting to strike a deal with Iran and draw up a better agreement than JCPOA.

However, this strategy has not been working. Iran has not ceased its missile development, although the number of missile launchers is dramatically reduced. Iran is reportedly continuing arms export to conflict zones in the Middle East.

Furthermore, Iran declared that it would halt complying with JCPOA and restarted enrichment activities (though the IAEA inspection team remained monitoring those enrichment activities).

The reason why unilateral sanctions by the Trump administration is not working is because they lack international legitimacy and failed to coordinate with other countries. The effect of secondary sanctions shrunk the business of non-US companies to trade with Iran, but there are number of clandestine economic activities by companies which do not have any business with the US market. Since there is little legitimacy in US sanctions, the enforcement of the sanctions is enormously difficult. It tells us that no matter how powerful the national sanctions are, they would not be sufficiently effective if there was no legitimacy, and the legitimacy provided by UN sanctions is extremely valuable to successfully achieve the goals of sanctions.

Notes

1 S/RES/1696 (2006), 31 July 2006.
2 S/RES/1737 (2006), 27 December 2006.
3 S/RES/1747 (2007), 24 March 2007.
4 S/RES/1803 (2008), 3 March 2008.
5 S/RES/1929 (2010), 9 June 2010.
6 UNSCR 1929 (2010) paras. 14 and 15.
7 UNSCR 1929 (2010) paras. 21 and 23.
8 For example, remarks by President Trump on Iran strategy, 13 October 2017, at www.whitehouse.gov/briefings-statements/remarks-president-trump-iran-strategy/ (accessed on 9 April 2020).
9 S/RES/1737 (2006) para. 12.
10 The Sahand and other applications [2011] 2 *SLR* 1093.
11 S/RES/1929 (2010) para. 22.
12 Report of the Panel of Experts established pursuant to resolution 1874 (2009), 1 February 2018, S/2019/171.
13 Department of Justice, "North Korean Cargo Vessel Connected to Sanctions Violations Seized by U.S. Government," Press Release, 9 May 2019.
14 S/RES/1737 (2006) para. 12.
15 Final report of the Panel of Experts established pursuant to resolution 1929 (2010), S/2015/401, 2 June 2015.
16 Steven O'Hern, *Iran's Revolutionary Guard: The Threat That Grows While America Sleeps* (Potomac Books, 2012), esp. Chapter 6; Frederic Wehrey *et al.*, *The Rise of the Pasdaran: Assessing the Domestic Roles of Iran's Islamic Revolutionary Guards Corps* (RAND Corporation, 2009), esp. Chapter 5.
17 Consolidated United Nations Security Council Sanctions List, at www.un.org/sc/suborg/en/sanctions/un-sc-consolidated-list (accessed on 9 April 2020).
18 Emanuele Ottolenghi, "In Latest Sanctions, U.S. Again, Targets Iranians Holding Caribbean Passports," *Foundation for Defense of Democracies*, 30 December 2014, at www.defenddemocracy.org/media-hit/emanuele-ottolenghi-in-latest-sanctions-us-again-targets-iranians-holding-caribbean-passports/ (accessed on 9 April 2020).
19 Financial Action Task Force (FATF) Report, *Combating Proliferation Financing: A Status Report on Policy Development and Consultation* (FATF, February 2010),

p.5 at www.fatf-gafi.org/media/fatf/documents/reports/Status-report-proliferation-financing.pdf (accessed on 9 April 2020).

20 FATF Recommendations, "International Standards on Combating Money Laundering and the Financing of Terrorism and Proliferation" (FATF, February 2012), at www.fatf-gafi.org/media/fatf/documents/recommendations/pdfs/FATF%20 Recommendations%202012.pdf (accessed on 9 April 2020).

21 S/RES/1929 (2010) para. 21.

22 Final report of the Panel of Experts established pursuant to Resolution 1929 (2010), S/2014/394, 11 June 2014.

23 Ibid.

24 Ibid.

25 Final report of the Panel of Experts established pursuant to Resolution 1929 (2010), S/2015/401, 2 June 2015.

26 Richard Nephew, *The Art of Sanctions: A View from the Field* (Columbia University Press, 2017).

27 US Treasury Department, "Iran Sanctions," at www.treasury.gov/resource-center/ sanctions/Programs/Pages/iran.aspx

28 Council Regulation (EU) No. 267/2012, 23 March 2012, *OJ* L 88, 24.3.2012

29 Ibid.

30 S/RES/2231 (2015), 20 July 2015.

12 The UN Security Council Resolution 1540 and counter proliferation financing

Kiwako Tanaka

Introduction

The purpose of this chapter is to understand the challenges that states face in implementing measures to counter proliferation financing, through analyzing trends in how states currently control proliferation financing, as stipulated under the United Nations Security Council Resolution 1540 (hereafter "UNSCR 1540"). The main conclusion of this chapter is that establishment of an effective mechanism for sharing information between exporters and financial institutions is critical for countering proliferation financing.

UNSCR 1540 was unanimously adopted on April 28, 2004, under the auspices of Chapter VII of the United Nations Charter.[1] The objective of this resolution is to address the proliferation of nuclear, chemical, and biological weapons as well as their means of delivery[2] by non-State actors.[3] Through its obligations, the resolution supplements the existing international efforts for the non-proliferation of nuclear, chemical, and biological weapons—namely the Nuclear Non-proliferation Treaty,[4] the Chemical Weapons Convention,[5] and the Biological Weapons Convention[6]—and links the proliferation of weapons of mass destruction (WMDs), terrorism, and illicit trafficking. One of the significant supplements in the resolution, with respect to the existing treaties is the universalization of export controls that were previously implemented mainly on a voluntary and national basis.[7] This also includes controls over funds and services related to export and trans-shipment that would contribute to the proliferation of related materials.[8]

The proliferation risks of nuclear, chemical, or biological weapons stem not only from actual weapons, but from dual-use goods and technology that are used in our daily life; this has led to increasing concern that legitimate trade and financial systems could be abused for proliferation purposes.[9] Countering the financing of WMD proliferation is thus crucial and should be an integral part of non-proliferation efforts by the international community. UNSCR 1540, therefore, aims at preventing the proliferation of such weapons to non-State actors by two inseparable set of requirements: by prohibiting any non-State actor from carrying out any activities related to nuclear, chemical, or biological weapons, and by controlling related materials and their related finance and services to prevent them from being diverted to weaponization.

Nevertheless, twelve years after UNSCR 1540 was adopted, the 2016 Comprehensive Review on the status of its implementation reported that financial controls on export or transshipments are "mainly related to legislation on counter-terrorism financing and money laundering and the establishment of financial intelligence centers."[10] The subsequent UN Security Council Resolution 2325 (hereafter "UNSCR 2325"), which was adopted in December 2016, also spelled out countermeasures against proliferation financing as one of the areas where more attention is required by the 1540 Committee.[11]

Although countering terrorist financing and money laundering are measures that contribute to preventing terrorists from acquiring or developing WMDs by stopping related materials or equipment that are specified by export-control regimes, considering the complexity of the procurement of sensitive goods and technology for illicit WMD programs, simply focusing on financial transactions involving controlled items subject to export restrictions will not be enough to counter proliferation financing. Proliferators tend to make use of a network of brokers and agents located overseas to procure necessary materials and many of these activities are disguised as legal trade. Proliferation financing is more than the payment for goods; it involves financial services provided in support of any part of the procurement process and not directly connected to the physical flow of goods.[12] Proliferation financing tends to be confounded with counter-terrorist financing or anti-money laundering measures owing to the absence of international understanding on what "proliferation financing" means and the lack of clear guidance for the identification and disruption of proliferation financing.[13]

Moreover, the current United Nations framework related to prohibiting the financing of materials that could be used for the development of WMDs is based mainly on sanctions on two specific countries, namely Iran and the Democratic People's Republic of Korea (DPRK), or North Korea. However, these targeted financial sanctions are list-based and focus on specific individuals and entities that have been listed by the UN Security Council or other authorities as engaged in or directly supporting prohibited proliferation activities under the equivalent resolutions. Proliferation of WMDs by non-State actors could also occur outside of these targeted countries and implementation of such targeted financial sanctions does not fully detect activities relating to proliferation financing and prevent them before they occur. The successful control of financial transactions to prevent the proliferation of WMDs by non-State actors requires three mutually reinforcing measures: anti-money laundering and counter-terrorist financing; list-based targeted sanctions; and counter proliferation financing.

While there is no universal or standard definition of proliferation financing common to the United Nations, in 2010, the Financial Action Task Force (FATF) proposed a provisional definition of proliferation financing. In many ways, this is considered a useful guide when implementing obligations related to proliferation financing under UNSCR 1540. The FATF is an independent intergovernmental body, established by the G7 Summit held in Paris in 1989. Its objectives include the development and promotion of policies to protect the global financial system against money laundering, terrorist financing, and proliferation financing of WMDs.

States' implementation of UNSCR 1540 is reviewed by the 1540 Committee, which was established as a subsidiary body of the UN Security Council, to report to the UN Security Council for its examination of the implementation of UNSCR 1540. Separately, the FATF also conducts mutual evaluations to analyze effectiveness and technical compliance with its recommendations and the effectiveness of anti-money laundering and counter-terrorist financing systems. While the roles and mandates of the 1540 Committee and the FATF differ, analyzing how these entities examine states' implementation of counter-proliferation financing measures could provide better understanding of the challenges states face in implementing proliferation-financing obligations under UNSCR 1540.

This chapter has two main sections: understanding the obligations under UNSCR 1540 and the FATF's 40 Recommendations as frameworks of counter proliferation financing, which states are required to implement; and analyzing the experiences of states, particularly that of Japan. Japan evidently puts significant effort into enforcing WMD proliferation measures, confronting the threat of nuclear weapons development posed by North Korea, but nonetheless faces challenges in carrying out broader proliferation-financing measures. Studying Japan's experience will provide more practical understanding of the challenges of implementing the proliferation-financing obligations under UNSCR 1540.

Proliferation financing under UNSCR 1540

UNSCR 1540 was adopted by the UN Security Council against the backdrop of the 9/11 terrorist attack and the discovery of the AQ Khan nuclear black-market supply network, to prevent the development, acquisition, or use of WMDs by non-state actors. All the UN member states have three primary obligations under UNSCR 1540 relating to nuclear, chemical, or biological weapons and their means of delivery: to refrain from providing any support to non-State actors seeking them; to adopt and enforce appropriate effective laws prohibiting their proliferation to non-State actors, as well as assisting or financing such proliferation; and to take and enforce effective measures to control them, including related materials, in order to prevent their proliferation, and to control the provision of funds and services that contribute to proliferation.

The obligation related to proliferation financing is stipulated in paragraph 3(d) of UNSCR 1540. The exact wording of paragraph 3(d) requires states to:

> establish, develop, review and maintain appropriate effective national export and trans-shipment controls over such items, including appropriate laws and regulations to control export, transit, trans-shipment and re-export and *controls on providing funds and services related to such export and trans-shipment such as financing,* and transporting that would contribute to proliferation, as well as establishing end-user controls; and *establishing and*

enforcing appropriate criminal or civil penalties for violations of such export control laws and regulations (emphasis added).

Although UNSCR 1540 requires the UN member states to enact effective financial controls to prevent the proliferation of nuclear, chemical, or biological weapons and their means of delivery, the resolution itself neither prescribes how to achieve such obligations, nor provides any guidance. The way to implement UNSCR 1540 obligations is, in other words, entirely up to each member state. By intentionally withholding the explicit guidance, the resolution was crafted carefully not to usurp national sovereignty.[14] Consequently, the role of the 1540 Committee was limited to examining the implementation of the resolution and reporting its findings to the UN Security Council.[15] The 1540 Committee does not have a mandate to establish legal norms, assess compliance, impose sanctions in case of noncompliance, or take other enforcement actions.[16]

The 1540 Committee developed the 1540 Matrix for each of the 193 UN member states, in order to review their implementation of UNSCR 1540. Each of the 193 UN member state's matrices are posted on the 1540 Committee website, based on which the Committee conducted the Comprehensive Review in 2016.[17] The 1540 Matrix lists breakdown elements of obligations under the resolution and identifies measures for compliance from both legislative and enforcement perspectives. Information in the 1540 matrices for each state is based on the 1540 national reports and supplemented with information obtained by governments and intergovernmental organizations. At the time of the 2016 Comprehensive Review, 176 UN member states had submitted their national reports at least once, of which 113 states submitted additional reports to their first reports.[18] The 1540 matrices are a "reference tool for facilitating technical assistance and to enable the Committee to continue to enhance its dialogue with States on their implementation of UNSCR 1540,"[19] and not for measuring their compliance in their non-proliferation obligations. The matrices, nonetheless, offer useful insight into the general trends of implementation of UNSCR 1540.

The 1540 Matrix includes 332 data fields related to the main obligations of UNSCR 1540. One field is dedicated to prohibiting the financing of the activities stipulated in paragraph 2. Data fields related to export control, the obligation under paragraph 3(d), are broken down into specific activities, such as export-control legislation in place, licensing provisions, interagency review mechanism for licenses, control lists, end-user controls, catch-all clause and intangible transfer of technology, and two fields are dedicated to the control of providing funds and services. Each activity is separated into legislative and enforcement compliance in order to check that the legislation in place is indeed enforced properly.

According to the 2016 Comprehensive Review report, the measures recorded in the above data field on the financing of illicit trade transactions related to nuclear, chemical, and biological weapons, their means of delivery and related materials are those of 109, 110, and 109 states, respectively, among 193 UN member states.[20] Having a relatively large number of measures recorded in the matrices, the contents of the measures vary greatly depending on the state. From the data fields for the Group of Seven (G7) members, who were the main driving force in creating the FATF in 1989, differences are observed in how these states implement the obligations under UNSCR 1540.

Table 12.1 shows the assessments both in the matrix data fields and FATF fourth-round Mutual Evaluation Reports for the G7 member states. Information on the 1540 Matrix data field suggests how G7 States interpret the obligation "control of providing funds" under UNSCR 1540. The data fields for Canada, France, Germany, and Japan showed that they implement such obligations through their legislations relating to money laundering and terrorist financing. Conversely, the data fields for Italy and the United States are filled with several legislations. The United Kingdom has no information on this field, which may be because it did not report to the 1540 Committee and because the 1540 Committee did not clarify the matter with that country.

The measures listed in the 1540 matrices show that there is no clear common ground for what measures are considered appropriate and effective to control proliferation financing. With these differences in the data fields, all states but the United Kingdom were given an "x," which indicates that these countries have measures in place for controls over providing funds related to export and trans-shipment. Looking only at these seven countries, it is quite evident that the 1540 matrices are not consistent in assessing what measures covering this obligation are certified as "x."

In comparison with the 1540 Matrix assessments, the table also shows the results of the FATF fourth-round mutual evaluation for those countries whose evaluations have been completed, among G7 States. While the results of the Mutual Evaluation Report will be further discussed in the following section, the table indicates that countries are assessed by the FATF with different levels of implementation depending on elements that are considered to be relevant to controlling proliferation financing.

As the 2016 Comprehensive Review indicated, many states make use of penal codes or legislation related to other financial crime risks, such as money laundering and terrorist financing, rather than adopting dedicated legislation specific to proliferation financing. The focus of counter-proliferation activities also appears to have been mainly on stopping the acquisition of equipment and materials for proliferation purposes. The follow-up resolution, UNSCR 2325, decided that the 1540 Committee shall intensify its efforts to promote the full implementation by all States of UNSCR 1540, particularly noting the need for more attention on proliferation finance measures, among other measures.[21] It continues to be a challenge for states to implement proliferation-financing obligations when there is no clear guidance or reference in the resolution.

The FATF's clarification of proliferation financing

While there is no universal or standard definition of proliferation financing common to the international regimes, in 2010, FATF published the *Status Report on Policy Development and Consultation* on combating proliferation

Table 12.1 Assessments in the 1540 Matrices and the FATF Mutual Evaluation Reports for G7 States

G7 Countries	1540 Matrix data field*1	Matrix assessment*2	FATF R2*3	FATF R7*4	FATF IO.1*5	FATF IO.11*6
Canada	Proceeds of Crime (Money Laundering) and Terrorist Financing Act, 2000, as amended, Sections 7 and 7.1	X	C	LC	SE	ME
France	Monetary and Financial Code, Articles L613-1 to L613-33-1; Customs Code Articles 60, 399, 451 and 459	X	-	-	-	-
Germany	War Weapons Control Act of 1961; Money Laundering Prevention Act of August 8, 2002 as amended (Geldwäschegesetz): financing of terrorism; Banking Act of September 9, 1998 as amended, Section 6a, Part 5a (Due diligence); Insurance Supervisory Act of December 17, 1992 as amended; Payment Services Oversight Act of June 25, 2009 as amended	X	-	-	-	-
Italy	Law no. 197 of July 5, 1991 as amended by Legislative Decree no. 56 of 2004: screening and control of all transactions; Law no. 185 of July 9, 1990, Art.27: armaments (communication of export, import and transit transactions to Ministry of Finance); Legislative Decree no.109/2007—Measures to counter financing and the activities of countries that threaten peace and international security, also in application of the EU Directive 2005/60/CE; Ministerial Decree no. 203 of October 20, 2010—Regulation on the functioning of the Financial Security Committee; Legislative Decree no. 231 of June 8, 2001; Law no. 438 of December 15, 2001, Art 1(1)	X	LC	PC	SE	SE

(continued)

Table 12.1 Cont.

G7 Countries	1540 Matrix data field*1	Matrix assessment*2	FATF R2*3	FATF R7*4	FATF IO.1*5	FATF IO.11*6
Japan	Act on Punishment of Financing to Offenses of Public Intimidation (Act No. 67 of 2002) (on terrorism financing); Penal Code (Law No. 45 of 1908)	X	-	-	-	-
United Kingdom	None		C	LC	HE	HE
United States of America	Terrorist Financing, Executive Order 13224; EAR, through IEPA, 15 CFR Parts 730–774; Bank Secrecy Act; (NW) EAR, 15 CFR Parts 730–774 (generally as an aider/abettor), see Section 764.2 (violations); Sanctions for Nuclear Proliferation, 22 USC 6303	X	C	LC	SE	HE

*1 Information provided in the data fields of "control of providing funds" in each of the country's 1540 matrices in 2016.

*2 Assessment in the country's 1540 matrices in 2016. An "x" signifies only that the reporting State asserts that it has taken relevant measures or that the 1540 Committee has found specific references to the applicable legal basis or executive measures as evidence of such steps. A blank signifies that the State has provided no information or the 1540 Committee has not established information to enable the entry of an "x" or a "?" against that particular data field.[47]

*3 FATF Recommendation 2 on national cooperation and coordination. "C" refers to "Compliant," "LC" refers to "Largely Compliant" with only minor shortcomings, "PC" refers to "Partially Compliant" with moderate shortcomings.[48]

*4 FATF Recommendation 7 on targeted financial sanctions related to proliferation, criteria are the same as *3.

*5 FATF Immediate Outcomes No.1 "Money laundering and terrorist financing risks are understood and, where appropriate, actions coordinated domestically to combat money laundering and the financing of terrorism and proliferation." "HE" refers to "High level of effectiveness" with minor improvements needed, "SE" refers to "Substantial level of effectiveness" with moderate improvements needed, and "ME" refers to "Moderate level of effectiveness" with major improvements needed.

*6 FATF Immediate Outcomes No.11 "Persons and entities involved in the proliferation of WMDs are prevented from raising, moving and using funds, consistent with the relevant UNSCRs." Criteria are the same as *5.

financing (hereafter "2010 FATF report").[22] One of the main purposes of this report was to develop policy options that could be considered in combating proliferation financing within the framework of existing UN Security Council resolutions, such as UNSCR 1540. The report proposed a provisional definition of proliferation financing as the act of providing funds or financial services which are used, in whole or in part, for the manufacture, acquisition, possession, development, export, trans-shipment, brokering, transport, transfer, stockpiling or use of nuclear, chemical or biological weapons and their means of delivery and related materials (including both technologies and dual-use goods used for non-legitimate purposes), in contravention of national laws or, where applicable, international obligations.[23]

Having proposed the provisional definition, the 2010 FATF report also recognized the importance of "balancing the burden on governments and the private sector, in particular, exporters and financial institutions (FIs), with the impact on the threat from WMD proliferation."[24] Among the vast amount of financial transactions that each financial institution deals with daily, the number of those that might be related to potential WMD proliferation risks may be small, and financial institutions cannot scrutinize every single transaction without delaying the legitimate business. To this end, the report proposed a risk-based approach be applied to identify counter-proliferation financing measures to ensure that financial institutions understand the proliferation-financing risks they face and follow the appropriate policies, procedures, and processes in place to manage such risks.

The 2010 FATF report further identified that for the purpose of effectively carrying out a risk-based approach to proliferation financing, information sharing is of critical importance. Financial institutions will only be in a position to conduct an efficient risk-management assessment if robust information and objective criteria for the identification of risks are available.[25] It would be preferable if such objective criteria for proliferation financing are clearly distinguished from those in other contexts such as anti-money laundering or counter-financial terrorism. This is because proliferators may derive funds from both criminal activity and/or legitimately sourced funds, and consequently transactions relating to proliferation financing may not exhibit similar traits to conventional money laundering.[26] The types of information that could reasonably be shared include national lists concerning high-risk entities, issuing of industry alerts by the financial intelligence unit, national typologies on how proliferators have accessed and exploited the regulated sector, feedback on suspicious transaction reporting, information on commonly used diversion routes and/or economic zones with weak export controls, and targeted de-classified intelligence.[27]

The 2010 FATF report also describes the difference between the UNSCR 1540 obligations and other types of UN financial sanctions such as those against North Korea or Iran. The types of information indicated above could be obtained through measures to implement targeted financial sanctions, which could possibly disrupt WMD proliferation networks. However, such sanctions are taking a so-called "list-based" approach, where the UN Security Council identifies the names of individuals or entities subject to asset freezes or other restrictions or introduces control lists of arms-related items or sensitive technologies established by international export-control regimes. The report suggested that such list-based targeted financial sanctions can be implemented relatively effectively by financial institutions through their use of existing screening systems. Countering proliferation financing, however, requires a risk-based approach, which could be referred to as "activity-based sanction" by the FATF, which could prevent a financial transaction even when no parties to the transactions are on the entities list, if that transaction would assist in the development of a WMD program. The 2010 FATF report also made it clear that "UNSCR 1540 primarily requires implementation of export controls, and thus no jurisdiction can rely on sanctions alone to meet these obligations."[28]

The FATF's 40 Recommendations and fourth-round mutual evaluations

In 2012 the FATF published a new set of 40 Recommendations that included two recommendations pertaining to the financing of proliferation of WMDs.[29] Recommendation 2 underscores that information sharing among policymakers, the financial intelligence unit, law enforcement authorities, supervisors, and other relevant competent authorities, at the policymaking and operational levels, are vitally important to combat the financing of WMD proliferation, as well as to combat money laundering and terrorist financing. This recommendation is wholly relevant to the implementation of UNSCR 1540. Recommendation 7 relates to the implementation of targeted financial sanctions required by UN Security Council resolutions related to proliferation.

Unlike the 1540 Committee which merely collects information on how the UN member states report on their implementation of the resolution, the FATF conducts a mutual evaluation to assess technical compliance with its recommendations and the effectiveness of anti-money laundering and counter-terrorist financing systems. The technical compliance component will assess whether the necessary laws, regulations, or other required measures are in force and effect, and whether the supporting institutional framework is in place. The effectiveness component will assess whether such systems are working, and the extent to which the country is achieving the defined set of outcomes. Each evaluation takes up to eighteen months, the process of which is composed of information analysis based on documents submitted by the assessed country; an on-site visit by the assessors; a draft report followed by a face-to-face meeting with the assessed countries on the draft; discussion during the FATF plenary meeting; and adoption of the report.[30]

The FATF's Mutual Evaluation Reports for the same G7 countries provide better understanding on how states are controlling proliferation financing. The latest reports were published for Canada in 2016,[31] France in 2011,[32] Germany in 2014,[33] Italy in 2016 (with a follow-up report in 2019),[34] Japan in 2008,[35] the United Kingdom in 2018,[36] and the United States in 2016.[37] An evaluation of the above 40 Recommendations is included in the FATF's fourth-round mutual evaluation, which began in 2013; therefore, the Mutual Evaluation Reports for France and Japan do not include evaluation on Recommendations 2 and 7. The following paragraphs introduce the results of the FATF's fourth-round mutual evaluation, particularly for Recommendation 2. Looking at the states' internal framework for information sharing is one of the useful indicators to understand how states try to control proliferation financing.

According to the Mutual Evaluation Report for Canada, the FATF assessed that Canada is "Compliant" to Recommendation 2, based on the fact that it has a number of standing committees, task forces, and other mechanisms in place to coordinate domestically on anti-money laundering and counter-terrorism financing policies and operational activities. It also assessed that Canada's counter-proliferation efforts including proliferation financing are coordinated via a formalized counter-proliferation framework, where a national Counter-Proliferation Policy Committee assesses and addresses policy and programming gaps that may undermine Canada's counter-proliferation capacity; the national Counter-Proliferation Operations Committee addresses specific proliferation threats with a Canadian nexus; and the Financial Transactions and Reports Analysis Centre of Canada (FINTRAC) is able to disclose designated financial information to the Canadian Security Intelligence Service when it has reasons to suspect that it would be relevant to investigations of threats to national security, which includes proliferation activities.

The United States was also rated as "Compliant" to Recommendation 2, with a number of interagency forums to coordinate policymaking and operational efforts to combat the financing of WMD proliferation. The Mutual Evaluation Report for the United States also identified a multifaceted institutional framework for combating the proliferation of WMDs and its financing in the United States, led by the National Security Council. As the result of the evaluation indicated, the United States regards proliferation financing as the highest level of priority, which was specifically mandated in the 2015 National Security Strategy.

On the implementation of UNSCR 1540, the United States has submitted a total of six national reports to the 1540 Committee, including one introducing effective practices. Its 2013 report provides a comprehensive description of how it controls its proliferation-financing obligation under UNCSR 1540, emphasizing the importance of establishing a strong framework that includes "preventive measures for financial institutions, strong interagency collaboration and international engagement," which align closely with the FATF's 40 Recommendations.[38] To this end, the United States has developed additional measures on effective practices to help protect financial institutions from engaging in transactions and services relating to WMD proliferation. These measures include a trade-based money-laundering advisory service relevant to countering proliferation finance, issued by the Financial Crimes Enforcement Network (FinCEN), which provides examples of suspicious indicators or "red flags" that may indicate such money laundering. At the same time, for financial institutions, the 2010 *Federal Financial Institutions Examination Council (FFIEC) Bank Secrecy Act/Anti-Money Laundering Examination Manual* established policies and procedures for bank examiners to ensure compliance with requirements and obligations mandated by FinCEN and the Office of Foreign Assets Control (OFAC).

Although the United Kingdom's 1540 Matrix filed no measures, the FATF's Mutual Evaluation Report rated it as "Compliant" to Recommendation 2,[39] based on the assessment that its counter-proliferation financing policies are coordinated under its National Counter Proliferation Strategy, of which the Foreign Secretary is responsible, and is supported by the interagency Cross-Whitehall Sanctions Group. The United Kingdom also establishes a coordination mechanism at the working level on a range of operational counter-proliferation issues.

Among the G7 countries where the fourth-round mutual evaluation has been conducted, Italy was the only country rated as "Largely Compliant" to Recommendation 2, with its main deficiency relating to the absence of a national coordination mechanism for anti-money laundering matters. The report also assessed that Italy's national Financial Security Committee is responsible for countering the activities performed by countries threatening international peace and security, as well as fund-freezing measures established by the United Nations and the European Union, which allow it to ensure coordination in proliferation-financing matters; however, this mechanism is limited to addressing matters relating to Iran and North Korea, and the law does not explicitly extend the Committee's power to coordinate and cooperate in proliferation financing-related policy and activities.

Although Italy was marked with some deficiencies, the FATF's Mutual Evaluation Reports generally showed that the above countries have internal coordination frameworks in place for information sharing on financial crime. Yet the reports did not clearly indicate how financial information is incorporated into export-licensing decisions, and equally how export-control information for proliferation-sensitive items is incorporated into mitigating financial crime in each country. One reason for this is that the FATF's 40 Recommendations are primarily for the purpose of countering money laundering and terrorism financing, and proliferation financing is handled rather as a byproduct of them.

When the movement of goods was more closely linked with the movement of funds to pay for those goods, a clear-cut jurisdiction of trade and finance ministries might have been possible. However, trade and finance activities have changed, and the activities of proliferators may no longer fall neatly within the jurisdiction of either trade or finance ministries, and payment for items will not always track neatly with the transfer of those items. Better controlling of proliferation financing requires an adequate framework, which systematically incorporates sharing financial information and export-related information.

Japan's legislative and administrative developments in regard to counter proliferation financing

While other G7 countries have undergone the FATF's fourth-round mutual evaluations, Japan underwent its third-round mutual evaluation in 2008.

Responding to the rather harsh result of that evaluation, Japan has been exerting numerous efforts to improve legislative and administrative measures in relation to the FATF's 40 Recommendations of 2012.

In Japan, the Act on Punishment of Financing to Offenses of Public Intimidation (Act No. 67 of 2002) and the Act on Prevention of Transfer of Criminal Proceeds (Act No. 22 of 2007), together with the Foreign Exchange and Foreign Trade Act (FEFTA) (Act No. 228 of 1949), comprise the major architecture for countering proliferation financing. In addition, the International Terrorist Asset-Freezing Act (Act No. 124 of 2014) provides a list of terrorists that were designated based on the relevant UN Security Council resolutions, including UNSCR 1267 and 1373.

The FEFTA is the basic law whose primary objective is to regulate cross-border transactions for the purpose of enabling the proper development of foreign transactions and the maintenance of peace and security in Japan and in the international community, and primarily addresses its obligation to freeze terrorist property. The FEFTA authorizes a competent minister(s) to take responsive measures for the maintenance of national security (Article 10), such as obligating residents and non-residents[40] to get permission for making a payment from Japan to a foreign state (Article 16), to get permission to conduct capital transactions (Article 20), as well as for importing or exporting of a means of payment (Article 19), outward direct investment (Article 23), or conducting a service transaction (Article 25).

Such responsive measures are taken: 1) when it is necessary to do so in order for Japan to faithfully perform its obligations under a treaty or other international agreement it has signed; 2) when it is particularly necessary to do so in order for Japan to contribute to international efforts toward world peace; or 3) when the Cabinet decides in accordance with article 10 of the FEFTA. Accordingly, the UN Security Council's financial sanctions are implemented under the first condition; other financial sanctions implemented by other state(s), such as G7 member states or unilateral sanctions enforced by the United States, are implemented under the second condition; and Japan's unilateral sanctions such as those against North Korea are implemented under the third condition.

The FEFTA was primarily enacted to facilitate the minimum necessary management and coordination of foreign transactions, and thus was not aiming at regulating domestic transactions. The FATF noted in its third-round mutual evaluation in 2008 that the FEFTA does not freeze funds and other financial resources, including funds derived or generated from or property owned or controlled directly or indirectly by the designated entities or persons who are nationals residing in Japan and never intended the funds to leave Japan.[41] The report also noted that "funds" in the FEFTA are generally understood as "cash and monetary instruments easily convertible into cash," and does not fully cover the aspects of terrorism support that involves assets other than funds.[42]

The Act on Punishment of Financing to Offenses of Public Intimidation (hereafter the "Terrorist Financing Act") was enforced as a domestic law to join the International Convention for the Suppression of the Financing of Terrorism in 2002, criminalizing terrorist financing and the collection of funds for terrorism.

The Act was largely amended in 2014, responding to the FATF's Mutual Evaluation Report, to add "other benefits," which includes, but is not limited to, land, building, goods, and services; to "funds" that are prohibited for provision or collection; and to enlarge the prohibition such that they cover not only the collection of funds or other benefits by terrorist plotters and the provision of funds to terrorist plotters by primary collaborators, but also those who facilitate or contribute to such activities.

The Act on Prevention of Transfer of Criminal Proceeds (hereafter the "Criminal Proceeds Act") was adopted in 2007 in order to prevent the transfer of criminal proceeds and to ensure the appropriate enforcement of international treaties concerning the prevention of terrorism financing by way of devising such measures as the identification of customers, preservation of transaction records, and reporting of suspicious transactions by specified business operators. The Act was then amended in 2011 to add verifying transactions of specified business operators, calling forwarding service providers to the list of specified business operators, accurate verification measures at the time of transactions, and strengthening punishments on the illicit transfer of passbooks. Another amendment came into effect in 2014 to include provisions regarding the responsibilities of the National Public Safety Commission in relation to the preparation of national risk assessment reports, to clarify the criteria for suspicious transactions, ensure stricter verification regarding correspondence contracts, and expand the obligation for business operators to make efforts to develop necessary systems.

With the Terrorist Financing Act and the Criminal Proceeds Act, Japan prohibits any person who provides funds and services to engage in terrorist activities, and controls financial activities to ensure such activities are not for terrorist purposes. These legislative developments serve a complementary role to the FEFTA by enlarging the financial regulation to the provision of goods and services related to terrorism.

In order to effectively enforce the above measures, in 2007, in accordance with the Criminal Proceeds Act, Japan transferred the financial intelligence unit (FIU) function from the Financial Services Agency to the National Public Safety Commission and the National Police Agency. Japan also pledged its commitment, at the G8 Lough Erne Summit in 2013, to undertake a national risk assessment of money laundering and terrorist financing. Accordingly, since 2014, Japan has published an annual national risk assessment on the National Police Agency website. In addition to these legislative and administrative efforts, in 2018, the Financial Services Agency published its *Guidelines for Anti-Money Laundering and Combating the Financing of Terrorism*, amended in April 2019, for financial institutions to enable a series of actions.[43] It requires financial institutions to continuously improve measures for anti-money laundering and combating the financing of terrorism through establishing a firm-wide governance structure involving different divisions and geographic areas and facilitating the proactive involvement of management.[44]

Japan is in the midst of its fourth-round FATF Mutual Evaluation in late 2019 and the report will be published in 2021, and at the time of writing it is still unknown how the FATF will assess any improvements in Japan. However, in terms of countering proliferation financing, there may still be room for improvement.

First, Japan's current efforts were developed based on existing laws and thus inevitably resulted in a jumble of distinctive measures, each of which has its own purposes and objectives and are under different responsible authorities. The foremost challenge stems from the fact that such existing laws were primarily for the purpose of anti-money laundering and countering financial terrorism. The laws originally focused on countering drug trafficking or money laundering by criminal organizations, in particular by *yakuza*, the organized crime syndicate originating in Japan, but not for countering proliferation financing.

Second, controlling financial activities relating to export or trans-shipment primarily under the FEFTA makes a limited contribution in countering proliferation financing, as the FEFTA does not provide effective mechanisms for using financial information in the export-licensing process. For countering proliferation financing, the FEFTA provides lists of entities and lists of export-controlled commodities which companies are not allowed do business with. This list-based approach is beneficial for implementing the UN-targeted sanctions, for instance, against North Korea. However, as the FATF report suggested, counter proliferation financing is broader than simply refusing business with the listed entities, but it also requires identifying suspicious activities and financial transactions that support proliferation. Considering alternative proposals, such as more comprehensive and dedicated legislations to control proliferation financing, may be necessary.

Third, in connection to the above two shortcomings, there is no explicit mechanism for export-control information to be shared with financial institutions, and for the governments to better identify proliferation-financing typologies and indicators of possible illegal financial activities. This is not only the case in Japan, as the same issue was raised in the United States, which was rated "Compliant" to Recommendation 2 in the FATF's Mutual Evaluation Report and the financial information may be omitted in export control.[45] It is also mentioned that financial information is also not systematically used for export-control applications.[46] In order to observe a better picture of proliferation-procurement networks, it is crucial to establish an effective mechanism to use export-control information in screening financial transactions and vice versa to use financial information, such as how the financial transaction is conducted, in export-control decision-making. Such a mechanism would also be in line with Recommendation 2. With the establishment of such an information-sharing mechanism, financial institutions could better incorporate proliferation-financing indicators into their existing monitoring system.

Conclusion: challenges to the implementation of UNSCR 1540

This chapter introduced how controlling proliferation financing differs from anti-money laundering or terrorist financing, as well as from implementing targeted financial sanctions, through the FATF's widely recognized provisional definition.

It analyzed how the UN member states interpret and implement the obligation under UNSCR 1540. UNSCR 1540 requires the UN member states to enact effective measures to control the provision of funds and services related to export and trans-shipment such as financing to prevent the proliferation of nuclear, chemical, or biological weapons and their means of delivery, but it does not prescribe how to achieve such obligations. Such lack of guidance leads to a lack of common understanding of what each member state needs to do and how to do it.

Complementary to UNSCR 1540, the FATF's provisional definition of the term "proliferation financing" is widely referred to as guidance for states in implementing the UNSCR 1540 obligations. The FATF clearly differentiates proliferation financing from money laundering and terrorist financing because proliferators may derive funds from criminal activity and/or legitimately sourced funds; consequently, transactions related to proliferation financing may not exhibit similar traits to conventional money laundering. Likewise, proliferation financing is wider in scope to list-based targeted financial sanctions and prevents a financial transaction even when no parties to the transactions are on the entities list, if that transaction would assist in the development of a WMD program.

However, the 2016 Comprehensive Review revealed that many states mix up these categories by implementing financial controls over illicit trade transactions mainly through legislation on counter-terrorism financing and money laundering. One reason could be gleaned from Japan's case, where measures have been built up based on the existing laws, the objective and structure of which may not effectively enforce measures necessary for preventing proliferation financing. The biggest shortcoming of such patchwork legislations is the lack of an effective mechanism for sharing information between exporters and financial institutions. To identify proliferation-financing typologies and indicators of possible illegal financial activities, governments require vigilant mechanisms in this regard. For the implementation of UNSCR 1540, more efforts are required by member states to raise the awareness of relevant authorities on proliferation financing to establish an effective information-sharing mechanism. This would enable jurisdictions to provide better guidance for financial institutions to appropriately prevent possible illegal transactions related to the proliferation of nuclear, chemical, or biological weapons and their means of delivery.

Notes

1 S/RES/1540, April 28, 2004. Chapter VII of the UN Charter provides the framework within which the UN Security Council may take enforcement action, and the UN member states are obliged to accept and carry out the decisions of the UN Security Council in accordance with Article 25 of the Charter.
2 Means of delivery is defined as missiles, rockets, and other unmanned systems capable of delivering nuclear, chemical, or biological weapons that are specifically designed for such use by UNSCR 1540.
3 A non-State actor is defined as an individual or entity not acting under the lawful authority of any State in conducting activities that come within the scope of this resolution by UNSCR 1540.

4   The Treaty on the Non-Proliferation of Nuclear Weapons, which entered into force in 1970.

5   The Convention on the Prohibition of the Development, Production, Stockpiling and Use of Chemical Weapons and on Their Destruction, which entered into force in 1997.

6   The Convention on the Prohibition of the Development, Production and Stockpiling of Bacteriological (Biological) and Toxin Weapons and on their Destruction, which entered into force in 1975.

7   Voluntary export control regimes of dual-use goods and technology include the Nuclear Suppliers Group for nuclear materials, the Australia Group for chemical and biological materials, the Missile Technology Control Regime for missile-related materials and technology, as well as the Wassenaar Arrangement for conventional weapons-related materials and technology including the delivery means.

8   Related materials are defined as materials, equipment, and technology covered by relevant multilateral treaties and arrangements, or included on national control lists, which could be used for the design, development, production, or use of nuclear, chemical, and biological weapons and their means of delivery by UNSCR 1540.

9   Togzhan Kassenova, "Challenges with Implementing Proliferation Financing Controls: How Export Controls can Help," Carnegie Endowment for International Peace, May 30, 2018, https://carnegieendowment.org/2018/05/30/challenges-with-implementing-proliferation-financing-controls-how-export-controls-can-help-pub-76476, accessed on August 18, 2019.

10   S/2016/1038 (2018), December 9, 2018, paragraph 99.

11   S/RES/2325 (2016), December 15, 2016.

12   Emil Dall, Tom Keatinge, and Andrea Berger, "Countering Proliferation Finance: An Introductory Guide for Financial Institutions," Royal United Services Institute for Defence and Security Studies, April 2017.

13   Jonathan Brewer, "The Financing of Nuclear and other Weapons of Mass Destruction Proliferation," Center for New American Security, January 24, 2018, www.cnas.org/publications/reports/the-financing-of-nuclear-and-other-weapons-of-mass-destruction-proliferation, accessed on August 18, 2019.

14   Richard T. Cupitt, "Nearly at the Brink: The Tasks and Capacity of the 1540 Committee," *Arms Control Today*, August 30, 2012, www.armscontrol.org/act/2012_09/Nearly-at-the-Brink-The-Tasks-and-Capacity-Of-the-1540-Committee, accessed on August 18, 2019.

15   S/RES/1540 (2004), paragraph 4.

16   Cupitt, *supra* note 14.

17   1540 Website, www.un.org/en/sc/1540/national-implementation/1540-matrices.shtml, accessed on August 18, 2019. The currently available country matrices are published in 2016. The new 1540 Matrix template was also developed after the 2016 Comprehensive Review, which is also published on the same website.

18   S/2016/1038 (2018), paragraphs 36–38.

19   1540 website, *supra* note 17.

20   S/2016/1038 (2018), paragraph 99.

21   S/RES/2325 (2016), December 15, 2016, paragraph 12. The resolution noted the areas that require more attention are enforcement measures, measures relating to biological, chemical, and nuclear weapons, proliferation finance measures, and accounting for and securing related materials, and national export and transshipment controls.

22 FATF, "Combating Proliferation Financing: A Status Report on Policy Development and Consultation," February 2010, p. 11, www.fatf-gafi.org/media/fatf/documents/reports/Status-report-proliferation-financing.pdf, accessed on August 18, 2019.

23 Ibid., p. 11.

24 Ibid., p. 9.

25 Ibid., p. 38.

26 Ibid., p. 39.

27 Ibid., pp. 42–43.

28 FATF, *supra* note 22, p. 16.

29 FATF has published sets of recommendations for four times in 1990, 1994, 2004 (combined those of 2003) and 2012, and IX special recommendations. The latest sets of recommendations are published in 2012, with regular updates. FATF, International Standards on Combating Money Laundering and the Financing of Terrorism and Proliferation—The FATF Recommendations, Updated June 2019, www.fatf-gafi.org/media/fatf/documents/recommendations/pdfs/FATF%20Recommendations%202012.pdf, accessed on August 18, 2019.

30 FATF, Procedures for the FATF Fourth Round of AML/CFT Mutual Evaluations, Updated October 2019, www.fatf-gafi.org/media/fatf/content/images/FATF-4th-Round-Procedures.pdf, accessed December 10, 2019.

31 FATF website, www.fatf-gafi.org/publications/mutualevaluations/documents/mer-canada-2016.html, accessed on August 18, 2019. This is Canada's fourth mutual evaluation report.

32 FATF website, www.fatf-gafi.org/countries/d-i/france/documents/mutualevaluationoffrance.html, accessed August 18, 2019.

33 The mutual evaluation for Germany was conducted in 2010 and the third follow-up report to it was published in June 2014, FATF website, www.fatf-gafi.org/countries/d-i/germany/documents/follow-up-report-germany-2014.html, accessed on August 18, 2019.

34 The fourth-round mutual evaluation for Italy was conducted in 2015 and the follow-up report responding to it was published in March 2019, FATF website, www.fatf-gafi.org/countries/#Italy, accessed on August 18, 2019.

35 FATF website, www.fatf-gafi.org/countries/j-m/japan/documents/mutualevaluationofjapan.html, accessed on August 18, 2019.

36 FATF website, www.fatf-gafi.org/countries/u-z/unitedkingdom/documents/mer-united-kingdom-2018.html, accessed on August 18, 2019.

37 FATF website, www.fatf-gafi.org/countries/u-z/unitedstates/documents/mer-united-states-2016.html, accessed on August 18, 2019.

38 S/AC.44/2013/17, October 21, 2013.

39 FATF website, www.fatf-gafi.org/countries/u-z/unitedkingdom/documents/mer-united-kingdom-2018.html, accessed on August 18, 2019.

40 The FEFTA defines a natural person with domicile or residence in Japan or a corporation with a principal office in Japan as a "resident" (Article 6(v)), and others are referred to as a "non-resident" (Article 6(VI)).

41 FATF, *Third Mutual Evaluation Report on Anti-Money Laundering and Combating the Financing of Terrorism for Japan.*

42 Ibid., paragraph 219.

43 Financial Services Agency (FSA), "Guidelines for Anti-Money Laundering and Combating the Financing of Terrorism," April 10, 2019, provisional translation,

www.fsa.go.jp/common/law/amlcft/en_amlcft_guidelines.pdf, accessed on August 19, 2019.

44 Ibid., p. 4.
45 Rachel A. Weise, Gretchen Hund, and Geoffrey Carr, "Export Controls and Counterproliferation Finance: Two Sides of the Same Underlying Illegal WMD Activities," *The Nonproliferation Review*, Vol. 25, No. 1–2 (2018), pp. 129–145, p. 135.
46 Ibid., p. 136.
47 1540 Website, *supra* note 17.
48 FATF, "Consolidated Assessment Rating" of fourth round Mutual Evaluation Reports, www.fatf-gafi.org/publications/mutualevaluations/documents/assessment-ratings.html, accessed August 18, 2019.

Annex I: International and domestic documents related to UN financial sanctions (as of March 2018)

Charter of the United Nations (excerpt)

We the peoples of the United Nations determined

> to save succeeding generations from the scourge of war, which twice in our lifetime has brought untold sorrow to mankind, and
> to reaffirm faith in fundamental human rights, in the dignity and worth of the human person, in the equal rights of men and women and of nations large and small, and
> [...]

And for these ends

> to practise tolerance and live together in peace with one another as good neighbours, and
> to unite our strength to maintain international peace and security, and
> to ensure, by the acceptance of principles and the institution of methods, that armed force shall not be used, save in the common interest, and
> [...]

Have resolved to combine our Efforts to accomplish these aims

Accordingly, our respective Governments, through representatives assembled in the city of San Francisco, who have exhibited their full powers found to be in good and due form, have agreed to the present Charter of the United Nations and do hereby establish an international organization to be known as the United Nations.

Chapter I: Purposes and principles

Article 1

The Purposes of the United Nations are:

1. To maintain international peace and security, and to that end: to take effective collective measures for the prevention and removal of threats to the peace, and for the suppression of acts of aggression or other breaches of the peace, and to bring about by peaceful means, and in conformity with the principles of justice and international law, adjustment or settlement of international disputes or situations which might lead to a breach of the peace;
   [...]
3. To achieve international co-operation in solving international problems of an economic, social, cultural, or humanitarian character, and in promoting and encouraging respect for human rights and for fundamental freedoms for all without distinction as to race, sex, language, or religion; and
4. To be a centre for harmonizing the actions of nations in the attainment of these common ends.

Article 2

The Organization and its Members, in pursuit of the Purposes stated in Article 1, shall act in accordance with the following Principles.

1. The Organization is based on the principle of the sovereign equality of all its Members.
   [...]
3. All Members shall settle their international disputes by peaceful means in such a manner that international peace and security, and justice, are not endangered.
4. All Members shall refrain in their international relations from the threat or use of force against the territorial integrity or political independence of any state, or in any other manner inconsistent with the Purposes of the United Nations.
5. All Members shall give the United Nations every assistance in any action it takes in accordance with the present Charter, and shall refrain from giving assistance to any state against which the United Nations is taking preventive or enforcement action.
6. The Organization shall ensure that states which are not Members of the United Nations act in accordance with these Principles so far as may be necessary for the maintenance of international peace and security.
7. Nothing contained in the present Charter shall authorize the United Nations to intervene in matters which are essentially within the domestic jurisdiction of any state or shall require the Members to submit such matters to

settlement under the present Charter; but this principle shall not prejudice the application of enforcement measures under Chapter VlI.
[...]

Chapter III: Organs

Article 7

1. There are established as principal organs of the United Nations: a General Assembly, a Security Council, an Economic and Social Council, a Trusteeship Council, an International Court of Justice and a Secretariat.
2. Such subsidiary organs as may be found necessary may be established in accordance with the present Charter.
   [...]

Chapter IV: The General Assembly

Composition

Article 9

1. The General Assembly shall consist of all the Members of the United Nations.
   [...]

Functions and powers

Article 10

The General Assembly may discuss any questions or any matters within the scope of the present Charter or relating to the powers and functions of any organs provided for in the present Charter, and, except as provided in Article 12, may make recommendations to the Members of the United Nations or to the Security Council or to both on any such questions or matters.

Article 11

1. The General Assembly may consider the general principles of co-operation in the maintenance of international peace and security, including the principles governing disarmament and the regulation of armaments, and may make recommendations with regard to such principles to the Members or to the Security Council or to both.
2. The General Assembly may discuss any questions relating to the maintenance of international peace and security brought before it by any Member of the United Nations, or by the Security Council, or by a state which is not a Member of the United Nations in accordance with Article 35, paragraph

2, and, except as provided in Article 12, may make recommendations with regard to any such questions to the state or states concerned or to the Security Council or to both. Any such question on which action is necessary shall be referred to the Security Council by the General Assembly either before or after discussion.

3. The General Assembly may call the attention of the Security Council to situations which are likely to endanger international peace and security.

[...]

Voting

Article 18

1. Each member of the General Assembly shall have one vote.
2. Decisions of the General Assembly on important questions shall be made by a two-thirds majority of the members present and voting. These questions shall include: recommendations with respect to the maintenance of international peace and security, the election of the non-permanent members of the Security Council, the election of the members of the Economic and Social Council, the election of members of the Trusteeship Council in accordance with paragraph 1 (c) of Article 86, the admission of new Members to the United Nations, the suspension of the rights and privileges of membership, the expulsion of Members, questions relating to the operation of the trusteeship system, and budgetary questions.
3. Decisions on other questions, including the determination of additional categories of questions to be decided by a two-thirds majority, shall be made by a majority of the members present and voting.

[...]

Chapter V: The Security Council

Composition

Article 23

1. The Security Council shall consist of fifteen Members of the United Nations. The Republic of China, France, the Union of Soviet Socialist Republics, the United Kingdom of Great Britain and Northern Ireland, and the United States of America shall be permanent members of the Security Council. The General Assembly shall elect ten other Members of the United Nations to be non-permanent members of the Security Council, due regard being specially paid, in the first instance to the contribution of Members of the United Nations to the maintenance of international peace and security and to the other purposes of the Organization, and also to equitable geographical distribution.

2. The non-permanent members of the Security Council shall be elected for a term of two years. In the first election of the non-permanent members after the increase of the membership of the Security Council from eleven to fifteen, two of the four additional members shall be chosen for a term of one year. A retiring member shall not be eligible for immediate re-election.

[...]

Functions and powers

Article 24

1. In order to ensure prompt and effective action by the United Nations, its Members confer on the Security Council primary responsibility for the maintenance of international peace and security, and agree that in carrying out its duties under this responsibility the Security Council acts on their behalf.
2. In discharging these duties the Security Council shall act in accordance with the Purposes and Principles of the United Nations. The specific powers granted to the Security Council for the discharge of these duties are laid down in Chapters VI, VII, VIII, and XII. [...]

Article 25

The Members of the United Nations agree to accept and carry out the decisions of the Security Council in accordance with the present Charter.

[...]

Voting

Article 27

1. Each member of the Security Council shall have one vote.
2. Decisions of the Security Council on procedural matters shall be made by an affirmative vote of nine members.
3. Decisions of the Security Council on all other matters shall be made by an affirmative vote of nine members including the concurring votes of the permanent members; provided that, in decisions under Chapter VI, and under paragraph 3 of Article 52, a party to a dispute shall abstain from voting.

[...]

Article 29

The Security Council may establish such subsidiary organs as it deems necessary for the performance of its functions.

[...]

Chapter VI: Pacific settlement of disputes

Article 33

1. The parties to any dispute, the continuance of which is likely to endanger the maintenance of international peace and security, shall, first of all, seek a solution by negotiation, enquiry, mediation, conciliation, arbitration, judicial settlement, resort to regional agencies or arrangements, or other peaceful means of their own choice.
2. The Security Council shall, when it deems necessary, call upon the parties to settle their dispute by such means.

[...]

Chapter VII: Action with respect to threats to the peace, breaches of the peace, and acts of aggression

Article 39

The Security Council shall determine the existence of any threat to the peace, breach of the peace, or act of aggression and shall make recommendations, or decide what measures shall be taken in accordance with Articles 41 and 42, to maintain or restore international peace and security.

Article 40

In order to prevent an aggravation of the situation, the Security Council may, before making the recommendations or deciding upon the measures provided for in Article 39, call upon the parties concerned to comply with such provisional measures as it deems necessary or desirable. [...]

Article 41

The Security Council may decide what measures not involving the use of armed force are to be employed to give effect to its decisions, and it may call upon the Members of the United Nations to apply such measures. These may include complete or partial interruption of economic relations and of rail, sea, air, postal, telegraphic, radio, and other means of communication, and the severance of diplomatic relations.

Article 42

Should the Security Council consider that measures provided for in Article 41 would be inadequate or have proved to be inadequate, it may take such action by air, sea, or land forces as may be necessary to maintain or restore international peace and security. Such action may include demonstrations, blockade, and other operations by air, sea, or land forces of Members of the United Nations.

Article 43

1. All Members of the United Nations, in order to contribute to the maintenance of international peace and security, undertake to make available to the Security Council, on its call and in accordance with a special agreement or agreements, armed forces, assistance, and facilities, including rights of passage, necessary for the purpose of maintaining international peace and security.
2. Such agreement or agreements shall govern the numbers and types of forces, their degree of readiness and general location, and the nature of the facilities and assistance to be provided.
3. The agreement or agreements shall be negotiated as soon as possible on the initiative of the Security Council. They shall be concluded between the Security Council and Members or between the Security Council and groups of Members and shall be subject to ratification by the signatory states in accordance with their respective constitutional processes.
[...]

Article 46

Plans for the application of armed force shall be made by the Security Council with the assistance of the Military Staff Committee.

Article 47

1. There shall be established a Military Staff Committee to advise and assist the Security Council on all questions relating to the Security Council's military requirements for the maintenance of international peace and security, the employment and command of forces placed at its disposal, the regulation of armaments, and possible disarmament.
2. The Military Staff Committee shall consist of the Chiefs of Staff of the permanent members of the Security Council or their representatives.[...]
3. The Military Staff Committee shall be responsible under the Security Council for the strategic direction of any armed forces placed at the disposal of the Security Council. [...]

Article 48

1. The action required to carry out the decisions of the Security Council for the maintenance of international peace and security shall be taken by all the Members of the United Nations or by some of them, as the Security Council may determine.
[...]

Article 50

If preventive or enforcement measures against any state are taken by the Security Council, any other state, whether a Member of the United Nations or not, which finds itself confronted with special economic problems arising from the carrying out of those measures shall have the right to consult the Security Council with regard to a solution of those problems.

[...]

Chapter VIII: Regional arrangements

Article 52

1. Nothing in the present Charter precludes the existence of regional arrangements or agencies for dealing with such matters relating to the maintenance of international peace and security as are appropriate for regional action provided that such arrangements or agencies and their activities are consistent with the Purposes and Principles of the United Nations.

[...]

Article 53

1. The Security Council shall, where appropriate, utilize such regional arrangements or agencies for enforcement action under its authority. But no enforcement action shall be taken under regional arrangements or by regional agencies without the authorization of the Security Council,

[...]

Chapter XV: The Secretariat

Article 97

The Secretariat shall comprise a Secretary-General and such staff as the Organization may require. The Secretary-General shall be appointed by the General Assembly upon the recommendation of the Security Council. He shall be the chief administrative officer of the Organization.

Article 98

The Secretary-General shall act in that capacity in all meetings of the General Assembly, of the Security Council, of the Economic and Social Council, and of the Trusteeship Council, and shall perform such other functions as are entrusted to him by these organs. The Secretary-General shall make an annual report to the General Assembly on the work of the Organization.

Article 99

The Secretary-General may bring to the attention of the Security Council any matter which in his opinion may threaten the maintenance of international peace and security.

[…]

Chapter XVI: Miscellaneous provisions

Article 103

In the event of a conflict between the obligations of the Members of the United Nations under the present Charter and their obligations under any other international agreement, their obligations under the present Charter shall prevail.

Chapter XVIII: Amendments

Article 108

Amendments to the present Charter shall come into force for all Members of the United Nations when they have been adopted by a vote of two thirds of the members of the General Assembly and ratified in accordance with their respective constitutional processes by two thirds of the Members of the United Nations, including all the permanent members of the Security Council.

Chapter XIX: Ratification and signature

Article 111

The present Charter, of which the Chinese, French, Russian, English, and Spanish texts are equally authentic, shall remain deposited in the archives of the Government of the United States of America. Duly certified copies thereof shall be transmitted by that Government to the Governments of the other signatory states.

[…]

United Nations Security Council Provisional Rules of Procedure (excerpt)

Rule 28

The Security Council may appoint a commission or committee or a rapporteur for a specified q uestion.

Foreign Exchange and Foreign Trade Act (FEFTA) (Act No. 228 of December 1, 1949) (Japan) (excerpt)

(Making and Receiving Payment)

Article 16

(1) On finding that it is necessary to do so in order for Japan to faithfully perform its obligations under a treaty or other international agreement it has signed, on finding that it is particularly necessary to do so in order for Japan to contribute to international efforts towards world peace, or if a cabinet decision as referred to in Article 10, paragraph (1) has been reached, the competent minister, pursuant to Cabinet Order, may make it obligatory for residents or non-residents seeking to make a payment from Japan to a foreign state to get permission to make that payment, and may make it obligatory for residents seeking to make or receive a payment to or from non-residents to get permission to make or receive that payment, unless the payment in question is made or received as part of a transaction or action for which it has been made obligatory for persons to get permission or approval from the same perspective as stated above.

(2) Beyond as prescribed in the preceding paragraph, on finding it to be particularly necessary to do so in order to maintain equilibrium in Japan's balance of international payments, the competent minister, pursuant to Cabinet Order, may make it obligatory for residents or non-residents seeking to make a payment from Japan to a foreign state or residents seeking to make a payment to non-residents to get permission to make that payment, unless the payment in question is made as a part of a transaction or action for which, pursuant to the following Chapter through Chapter 6, the relevant authority has made it obligatory for persons to get permission or file a notification, or as a part of a transaction or action for which, pursuant to those Chapters, the relevant authority is permitted to make it obligatory for persons to get permission or approval.

(3) Beyond as prescribed in the preceding two paragraphs, on finding it to be necessary to do so in order to ensure the reliable implementation of this Act or an Order based on this Act, the competent minister, pursuant to Cabinet Order, may make it obligatory for residents or non-residents seeking to make a payment from Japan to a foreign state to get permission to make that payment, and may make it obligatory for residents seeking to make or receive a payment to or from non-residents to get permission to make or receive that payment, unless the payment in question is made as a part of a transaction or action for which, pursuant to the following Chapter through Chapter 6, the competent minister has made it obligatory for persons to get permission or file a notification, or as a part of a transaction or action for which, pursuant to those Chapters, the competent minister is permitted to make it obligatory for persons to get permission or approval.

(4) If, pursuant to two or more of the preceding three paragraphs, it has been made obligatory for persons to get permission to make or receive a payment that, pursuant to those paragraphs, the competent minister is permitted to make it obligatory for persons to get permission for, a person seeking to make or receive such a payment may file a combined application for the permissions under those paragraphs, pursuant to Cabinet Order. In such a case, the competent minister must decide whether to give permission by taking into consideration the circumstances that have led the minister to

make it obligatory for persons to get permission to make or receive the payment under the application.

(5) Except as Cabinet Order prescribes, if it has been made obligatory for persons to get permission or approval for a transaction or action or to file notification of a transaction or action pursuant to this Act or an Order based on this Act, a person must not make or receive a payment as a part of that transaction or action without getting the permission or approval or without filing the notification.

(Restrictions on Making and Receiving Payments)

Article 16-2

If the competent minister has made it obligatory to get permission pursuant to paragraph (1) of the preceding Article, but a person has made or received a payment for which permission has been made obligatory without getting that permission, and the minister finds that the person is likely to once again make or receive a payment for which permission has been made obligatory pursuant to that paragraph without getting that permission, the minister may fully or partially prohibit the person from making payments from Japan to a foreign state (other than any such payment made through an exchange transaction that is conducted by a bank (meaning a bank as prescribed in Article 2, paragraph (1) of the Banking Act (Act No. 59 of 1981); the same applies hereinafter) or by any other financial institution that Cabinet Order prescribes (hereinafter referred to as a "bank or other financial institution"), or by a funds transfer service provider (meaning a funds transfer service provider as prescribed in Article 2, paragraph (3) of the Payment Services Act (Act No. 59 of 2009); the same applies hereinafter)), or making or receiving any payment between a resident and a non-resident (other than any such payment made or received through an exchange transaction that is conducted by a bank or other financial institution or by a funds transfer service provider, and other than the making or receipt of any other payment that Cabinet Order prescribes), but only during a period of up to one year, or, pursuant to Cabinet Order, may make it obligatory for that person to get permission to make payments from Japan to a foreign state or to make or receive any payment between a resident and a non-resident, but only during a period of up to one year.

United Nations Participation Act (UNPA) (US) (excerpt)

UNITED STATES CODE TITLE 22. FOREIGN RELATIONS AND INTERCOURSE

Chapter 7: International bureaus, congresses, and the like United Nations Organization

Sec. 287c. Economic and communication sanctions pursuant to United Nations Security Council Resolution

(a) Enforcement measures; ... Notwithstanding the provisions of any other law, whenever the United States is called upon by the Security Council to apply measures which said Council has decided, pursuant to article 41 of said Charter, are to be employed to give effect to its decisions under said Charter, the President may, to the extent necessary to apply such measures, through any agency which he may designate, and under such orders, rules, and regulations as may be prescribed by him, investigate, regulate, or prohibit, in whole or in part, economic relations or rail, sea, air, postal, telegraphic, radio, and other means of communication between any foreign country or any national thereof or any person therein and the United States or any person subject to the jurisdiction thereof, or involving any property subject to the jurisdiction of the United States. ...

(b) Penalties Any person who willfully violates or evades or attempts to violate or evade any order, rule, or regulation issued by the President pursuant to paragraph (a) of this section shall, upon conviction, be find [fined] not more than $ 10,000 or, if a natural person, be imprisoned for not more than ten years, or both; and the officer, director, or agent of any corporation who knowingly participates in such violation or evasion shall be punished by a like fine, imprisonment, or both, and any property, funds, securities, papers, or other articles or documents, or any vessel, together with her tackle, apparel, furniture, and equipment, or vehicle, or aircraft, concerned in such violation shall be forfeited to the United States. ...

International Emergency Economic Powers Act (IEEPA) (US) (excerpt)

UNITED STATES CODE TITLE 50. WAR AND NARIONAL DEFENSE

Chapter 35: International emergency economic powers

§1701. Unusual and extraordinary threat; declaration of national emergency; exercise of Presidential authorities

(a) Any authority granted to the President by section 1702 of this title may be exercised to deal with any unusual and extraordinary threat, which has its source in whole or substantial part outside the United States, to the national security, foreign policy, or economy of the United States, if the President declares a national emergency with respect to such threat.

(b) The authorities granted to the President by section 1702 of this title may only be exercised to deal with an unusual and extraordinary threat with respect to which a national emergency has been declared for purposes of this chapter and may not be exercised for any other purpose. Any exercise of such authorities to deal with any new threat shall be based on a new dec-laration of national emergency which must be with respect to such threat.

§1702. Presidential authorities

(a) (1) At the times and to the extent specified in section 1701 of this title, the President may, under such regulations as he may prescribe, by means of instructions, licenses, or otherwise—
(A) investigate, regulate, or prohibit—
  (i)   any transactions in foreign exchange,
  (ii) transfers of credit or payments between, by, through, or to any banking institution, to the extent that such transfers or payments involve any interest of any foreign country or a national thereof,
  (iii) the importing or exporting of currency or securities, by any person, or with respect to any property, subject to the jurisdiction of the United States;
(B) investigate, block during the pendency of an investigation, regulate, direct and compel, nullify, void, prevent or prohibit, any acquisition, holding, withholding, use, transfer, withdrawal, transportation, importation or exportation of, or dealing in, or exercising any right, power, or privilege with respect to, or transactions involving, any property in which any foreign country or a national thereof has any interest by any person, or with respect to any property, subject to the jurisdiction of the United States; and
(C) when the United States is engaged in armed hostilities or has been attacked by a foreign country or foreign nationals, confiscate any property, subject to the jurisdiction of the United States, of any foreign person, foreign organization, or foreign country that he determines has planned, authorized, aided, or engaged in such hostilities or attacks against the United States; and all right, title, and interest in any property so confiscated shall vest, when, as, and upon the terms directed by the President, in such agency or person as the President may designate from time to time, and upon such terms and conditions as the President may prescribe, such interest or property shall be held, used, administered, liquidated, sold, or otherwise dealt with in the interest of and for the benefit of the United States, and such designated agency or person may perform any and all acts incident to the accomplishment or furtherance of these purposes.
(2) In exercising the authorities granted by paragraph (1), the President may require any person to keep a full record of, and to furnish under oath, in the form of reports or otherwise, complete information relative to any act or transaction referred to in paragraph (1) either before, during, or after the completion thereof, or relative to any interest in foreign property, or relative to any property in which any foreign country or any national thereof has or has had any interest, or as may be otherwise necessary to enforce the provisions of such paragraph. In any case in which a report by a person could be required under this paragraph, the President may require the production of any books of account, records,

contracts, letters, memoranda, or other papers, in the custody or control of such person.

(3) Compliance with any regulation, instruction, or direction issued under this chapter shall to the extent thereof be a full acquittance and discharge for all purposes of the obligation of the person making the same. No person shall be held liable in any court for or with respect to anything done or omitted in good faith in connection with the administration of, or pursuant to and in reliance on, this chapter, or any regulation, instruction, or direction issued under this chapter.

(b) The authority granted to the President by this section does not include the authority to regulate or prohibit, directly or indirectly—

(1) any postal, telegraphic, telephonic, or other personal communication, which does not involve a transfer of anything of value;

(2) donations, by persons subject to the jurisdiction of the United States, of articles, such as food, clothing, and medicine, intended to be used to relieve human suffering, except to the extent that the President determines that such donations (A) would seriously impair his ability to deal with any national emergency declared under section 1701 of this title, (B) are in response to coercion against the proposed recipient or donor, or (C) would endanger Armed Forces of the United States which are engaged in hostilities or are in a situation where imminent involvement in hostilities is clearly indicated by the circumstances; or

(3) the importation from any country, or the exportation to any country, whether commercial or otherwise, regardless of format or medium of transmission, of any information or informational materials, including but not limited to, publications, films, posters, phonograph records, photographs, microfilms, microfiche, tapes, compact disks, CD ROMs, artworks, and news wire feeds. The exports exempted from regulation or prohibition by this paragraph do not include those which are otherwise controlled for export under section 2404 of the Appendix to this title, or under section 2405 of the Appendix to this title to the extent that such controls promote the nonproliferation or antiterrorism policies of the United States, or with respect to which acts are prohibited by chapter 37 of Title 18;

(4) any transactions ordinarily incident to travel to or from any country, including importation of accompanied baggage for personal use, maintenance within any country including payment of living expenses and acquisition of goods or services for personal use, and arrangement or facilitation of such travel including nonscheduled air, sea, or land voyages.

(c) Classified information.—In any judicial review of a determination made under this section, if the determination was based on classified information (as defined in section 1(a) of the Classified Information Procedures Act) such information may be submitted to the reviewing court ex parte and in camera. This subsection does not confer or imply any right to judicial review.

Treaty of the European Union and Treaty on the Functioning of the European Union (excerpt)

Treaty on European Union (TEU)

CHAPTER 2: SPECIFIC PROVISIONS ON THE COMMON FOREIGN AND SECURITY POLICY

SECTION I: COMMON PROVISIONS

Article 29

(ex Article 15 TEU)

The Council shall adopt decisions which shall define the approach of the Union to a particular matter of a geographical or thematic nature. Member States shall ensure that their national policies conform to the Union positions.

Treaty on the Functioning of the European Union (TFEU)

Title IV Restrictive measures

Article 215

(ex Article 301 TEC)

1. Where a decision, adopted in accordance with Chapter 2 of Title V of the Treaty on European Union, provides for the interruption or reduction, in part or completely, of economic and financial relations with one or more third countries, the Council, acting by a qualified majority on a joint proposal from the High Representative of the Union for Foreign Affairs and Security Policy and the Commission, shall adopt the necessary measures. It shall inform the European Parliament thereof.
2. Where a decision adopted in accordance with Chapter 2 of Title V of the Treaty on European Union so provides, the Council may adopt restrictive measures under the procedure referred to in paragraph 1 against natural or legal persons and groups or non-State entities.
3. The acts referred to in this Article shall include necessary provisions on legal safeguards.

Annex II: Major economic sanctions adopted by the UN Security Council under Chapter VII of the UN Charter (as of March 2018)

(Prepared by Sachiko Yoshimura, with assistance and translation by Hinako Takata)

Sanctions that target specific states, groups and individuals

Targets of UN economic sanctions	Security Council Resolutions numbers and brief Contents	Reasons for sanctions imposition
Southern Rhodesia (Zimbabwe) (lifted in 1979)	S/Res/232 (16 December 1966): Partial embargo against Rhodesia S/Res/253 (29 May 1968): Total embargo against Rhodesia	Unilateral declaration of independence by the white-minority government of Rhodesia
Republic of South Africa (lifted in 1994)	S/Res/418 (4 November 1977): Arms embargo against South Africa S/Res/421 (9 December 1977): Establishment of a sanctions committee	Policy of apartheid (racial segregation) in South Africa
Iraq (lifted in 2003, except for arms embargo and assets freeze against individuals and groups designated by the Sanctions Committee)	S/Res/661 (6 August 1990): Total embargo against Iraq S/Res/687 (3 April 1991): Inspection of weapons of mass destruction, continuation of embargo against Iraq, humanitarian exemption from sanctions S/Res/986 (14 April 1995): Introduction of Oil-for-Food program S/Res/1137 (12 November 1997): Prohibition of entry into member states' territories of Iraqi officials and armed force members S/Res/1483 (22 May 2003): Lifting of sanctions starting from Resolution 661; Continuation of arms embargo; Assets freeze on former Iraqi governmental officials	Military invasion of Kuwait by Iraq; Refusal of WMD inspection by Iraq, etc.

Targets of UN economic sanctions	*Security Council Resolutions numbers and brief Contents*	*Reasons for sanctions imposition*
	S/Res/1518 (24 November 2003): Establishment of a Sanctions Committee to designate sanction targets, replacing the Sanctions Committee established by Resolution 661 S/Res/1957 (15 December 2010): Lifting of Weapons of Mass Destruction embargo S/Res/1958 (15 December 2010): Suspension of Oil-for-Food program	
Former Yugoslavia (UN sanctions against former Yugoslavia were lifted in 1995, and UN sanctions against Bosnian Serbs were lifted in 1996)	S/Res/713 (25 September 1991): Arms embargo against Yugoslavia S/Res/724 (15 December 1991): Establishment of a Sanctions Committee S/Res/757(30 May 1992): Embargo against Federal Republic of Yugoslavia (Serbia and Montenegro), Ban of taking off/landing of aircrafts that are destined to land in or have taken off from the territory of the Federal Republic of Yugoslavia; Reduction of the level of the staff at diplomatic missions and consular posts of the Federal Republic of Yugoslavia; Prevention of the participation in sporting events of persons or groups representing the Federal Republic of Yugoslavia; Suspension of scientific and technical cooperation and cultural exchanges and visits involving persons or groups officially sponsored by or representing the Federal Republic of Yugoslavia S/Res/820 (17 April 1993): Ban of import to, and export from the areas under the control of Bosnian Serbs S/Res/942 (23 September 1994): Freezing of assets under the control of Bosnian Serb forces; Trade ban S/Res/1021 (22 November 1995): Conditions for Termination of Arms embargo	Armed conflicts in former Yugoslavia

Targets of UN economic sanctions	Security Council Resolutions numbers and brief Contents	Reasons for sanctions imposition
Somalia (still in force)	S/Res/733 (23 January 1992): Arms embargo against Somalia S/Res/1356 (19 June 2001): Exemption from the arms embargo (UN and humanitarian activities) S/Res/1519 (16 December 2003): Establishment of a Monitoring Group to investigate violation of sanctions S/Res/1744 (21 February 2007): Exemption from the arms embargo (AMISOM) S/Res/1844 (20 November 2008): Travel ban, freezing of assets, and arms embargo on individuals that threaten the Transitional Federal Institutions (TFIs) in violation of the Djibouti Agreement, that violate arms embargo and that destruct humanitarian assistance S/Res/2036 (22 February 2012): Charcoal embargo S/Res/2093 (6 March 2013): Exemption from the arms embargo (Somali security forces and UN personnel, etc.) S/Res/2182 (24 October 2014): Permission for inspection, seizure, and disposal of prohibited items in order to implement embargo; Sanctions exemption from freezing of assets on humanitarian grounds	Armed conflicts by Somali clans; Piracy by Somalia
Libya (UN sanctions were suspended in 1999, lifted in 2003. New UN sanctions were imposed in 2011.)	S/Res/748 (31 March 1992): Arms embargo against Libya; Ban on taking off/landing of aircraft to/from the territory of Libya S/Res/883 (11 November 1993): Additional economic sanctions (freezing of assets, etc.) S/Res/1970 (26 February 2011): Arms embargo; freezing of assets of individuals and groups designated by the Sanctions Committee S/Res/1973 (17 March 2011): Establishment of a no-fly zone; Ban on taking off/landing of aircraft; expansion of the target of asset freeze	Terrorist activities supported by Libyan authority; Systematic attack against civilian population during internal conflicts in Libya

Targets of UN economic sanctions	*Security Council Resolutions numbers and brief Contents*	*Reasons for sanctions imposition*
	S/Res/2009 (16 September 2011): Exemption from the arms embargo, an asset freeze, and partial lifting of sanctions (Libyan National Oil Corporation and the Central Bank of Libya, etc.) S/Res/2016 (27 October 2011): Termination of no-fly zone to protect civilians S/Res/2040 (12 March 2012): Termination of arms embargo and inspection S/Res/2146 (19 March 2014): Inspection on the high seas to regulate illegal oil export; Prohibition of providing fuels to vessels designated by the Sanctions Committee; Prohibition of engaging in transactions with vessels designated by the Committee S/Res/2174 (27 August 2014): Arms embargo against individuals and groups that prevent stabilization of Libya S/Res/2292 (14 June 2016): Permission of inspection, seizure, and disposal of prohibited items in order to implement embargo on the high seas S/Res/2362 (29 June 2017): Permission of inspection, seizure, and disposal of prohibited items in order to implement embargo	
Liberia (lifted in 2016)	S/Res/788 (19 November 1992): Arms embargo against Liberia S/Res/985 (13 April 1995): Establishment of a Sanctions Committee S/Res/1343 (7 March 2001): Lifting of sanctions measures decided by Resolution 788; Ban on import of all rough diamonds from Liberia; Travel ban on Liberian government officials; Establishment of a Panel of Experts to investigate violation of sanctions	Civil war in Liberia

Targets of UN economic sanctions	Security Council Resolutions numbers and brief Contents	Reasons for sanctions imposition
	S/Res/1521 (22 December 2003): Lifting of sanctions measures decided by Resolution 1343; Arms embargo; Travel ban on individuals designated by the Sanctions Committee; Ban on import of diamond and timber S/Res/1532 (12 March 2004): Freezing assets of former President Charles Taylor and his family S/Res/1689 (20 June 2006): Lifting the sanctions on timber S/Res/1753 (27 April 2007): Lifting the sanctions on diamonds S/Res/1903 (17 December 2009): Lifting the arms embargo on Liberian government; Arms embargo on non-governmental organizations and individuals in Liberia S/Res/2237 (2 September 2015): Lifting of travel ban and asset freeze	
Haiti (lifted in 1994)	S/Res/841 (16 June 1993): Arms embargo; oil embargo; asset freeze against Haiti S/Res/873 (13 October 1993): Re-imposition of economic sanctions against Haiti S/Res/917 (6 May 1994): Total embargo against Haiti	Coup d'état in Haiti
Angola (UNITA) (lifted in 2002)	S/Res/864 (15 September 1993): Arms embargo; oil embargo against UNITA S/Res/1127 (28 August 1997): Additional sanctions imposition against UNITA (Ban on taking off/landing of aircraft, etc.) S/Res/1173 (12 June 1998): Ban of purchasing diamonds from Angola and export ban from areas controlled by Angola's government S/Res/1237 (7 May 1999): Establishment of a panel of experts to investigate violation of sanctions S/Res/1295 (18 April 2000): Establishment of a monitoring mechanism composed of experts	Civil war in Angola

Targets of UN economic sanctions	Security Council Resolutions numbers and brief Contents	Reasons for sanctions imposition
Rwanda (lifted in 2008)	S/Res/918 (17 May 1994): Arms embargo against Rwanda S/Res/1011 (16 August 1995): Lifting of arms embargo against Rwanda's government; Imposing arms embargo against non-governmental forces in Rwanda S/Res/1013 (7 September 1995): Establishment of an international commission of inquiry to investigate arms trade in violation of sanctions	Civil war in Rwanda
Sudan (UN sanctions were lifted in 2001. New UN sanctions were imposed in 2004)	S/Res/1054 (26 April 1996): Reduction of staff at Sudanese diplomatic missions and consular posts; Travel restriction on Sudanese governmental officials and armed forces S/Res/1070 (16 August 1996): Ban on taking off/landing of aircraft registered in Sudan or operated on behalf of Sudan Airways S/Res/1372 (28 September 2001): Lifting of sanctions imposed by Resolutions 1054 and 1070 S/Res/1556(30 July 2004): Arms embargo on non-governmental organizations in Darfur S/Res/1591 (29 March 2005): Establishment of a Sanctions Committee and Panel of Experts; Travel ban and asset freeze on individuals who impede the peace process in Darfur S/Res/1945 (14 October 2010): Conditional arms trade in accordance with Resolutions 1556 and 1591 with end user documentation and assurance by states	Sudan's support for terrorist activities; Civil war in Sudan
Sierra Leone (UN sanctions relating to diamonds were lifted in 2003. Other UN sanctions were lifted in 2010.)	S/Res/1132 (8 October 1997): Arms embargo and oil embargo against Sierra Leone; Travel ban on members of military government designated by the Sanctions Committee. S/Res/1156 (16 March 1998): Lifting of oil embargo	Coup d'état in Sierra Leone

Targets of UN economic sanctions	*Security Council Resolutions numbers and brief Contents*	*Reasons for sanctions imposition*
	S/Res/1171(5 June 1998): Lifting of sanctions measures decided by Resolution 1132; Arms embargo on non-governmental military organization; Travel ban on members of former military government and RUF S/Res/1306 (5 July 2000): Import ban of diamonds from Sierra Leone; establishment of a Panel of Experts	
Federal Republic of Yugoslavia (UN Sanctions lifted in 2001)	S/Res/1160 (31 March 1998): Arms embargo against Federal Republic of Yugoslavia (including Kosovo) S/Res/1203 (24 October 1998), S/Res/1244 (10 June 1999): Exemption from the arms embargo (UNMIK, etc.)	Armed conflicts relating to Kosovo
Afghanistan/ the Taliban/Al-Qaida (After Resolutions 1988 and 1989 were adopted, different procedures have been applied to the Taliban and Al-Qaida sanctions)	S/Res/1267 (15 October 1999): Ban on taking off/landing of aircraft owned by the Taliban; Asset freeze against the Taliban S/Res/1333 (19 December 2000): Arms embargo against the Taliban within the territory of Afghanistan; Prohibition of military training; Closing of Taliban offices; Establishment of a committee of experts S/Res/1363 (30 July 2001): Establishment of a monitoring mechanism on Security Council Resolutions 1267 and 1333 S/Res/1388 (15 July 2001): Lifting of prohibition on taking off/ landing of Ariana Afghan Airlines aircraft S/Res/1390 (16 January 2002): Lifting of prohibition on taking off/landing of aircraft; Travel ban and asset freeze on Osama bin Laden and Al-Qaida entities S/Res/1730 (19 December 2006): Establishment of a focal point of de-listing requests S/Res/1735 (22 December 2006): Deciding on the types of information to be submitted for sanctions designations	Terrorist activities (allegedly) by the Taliban including United States Embassy bombings; Refusal to extradite Osama Bin Laden; Terrorist attacks in New York

Targets of UN economic sanctions	Security Council Resolutions numbers and brief Contents	Reasons for sanctions imposition
Ethiopia and Eritrea (lifted in 2001)	S/Res/1298 (17 May 2000): Arms embargo against Ethiopia and Eritrea	Conflict between Ethiopia and Eritrea
Democratic Republic of the Congo (DRC) (Still in force)	S/Res/1493 (28 July 2003): Arms embargo against armed groups and militias in DRC S/Res/1533 (12 March 2004): Establishment of a Sanctions Committee; Establishment of the group of experts to monitor sanction violations S/Res/1596(18 April 2005): Travel ban and asset freeze on individuals designated by the Sanctions Committee S/Res/1698 (31 July 2006): Extension of travel ban and asset freeze to those who impede disarmament in DRC S/Res/1807 (31 March 2008): Extension of arms embargo to non-governmental organizations and individuals in DRC (with exemption to DRC government and PKO); Asset freeze on the individuals designated by the Sanctions Committee for impeding the disarmament, recruiting, and using child soldiers and committing serious violations of international law targeting children or women S/Res/2078 (28 November 2012): Extension of designations of asset freeze and travel ban for those who violate arms embargo, impede disarmament in DRC, use child soldiers and participate in the attacks against the PKO	Civil war in DRC
Republic of Côte d'Ivoire (lifted in 2016)	S/Res/1572 (15 November 2004): Arms embargo against Côte d'Ivoire; Travel ban and asset freeze on individuals designated by the Sanctions Committee S/Res/1584 (1 February 2005): Authorization of United Nations Operation in Côte d'Ivoire (UNOCI) and French forces to monitor the arms embargo; Establishment of a group of experts	Civil war in Côte d'Ivoire

Targets of UN economic sanctions	Security Council Resolutions numbers and brief Contents	Reasons for sanctions imposition
	S/Res/1643 (15 December 2005): Import ban on diamonds produced in Côte d'Ivoire S/Res/1975 (2011): Arms embargo, travel ban, and asset freeze against individuals who impede peace and reconciliation process of Côte d'Ivoire and the activities of UNOCI S/Res/2153(29 April 2014): Lifting of the import ban on diamonds from Côte d'Ivoire	
Suspects who engaged the assassination of former Lebanese Prime Minister Rafiq Hariri (still in force)	S/Res/1636(31 October 2005): Travel ban and asset freeze on individuals designated by the international independent investigation Commission or the Government of Lebanon and registered by the Sanctions Committee as suspects who committed the assassination of former Lebanese Prime Rafiq Hariri	The assassination of former Lebanese Prime Minister Rafiq Hariri in Lebanon
Lebanon (still in force)	S/Res/1701(11 August 2006): Arms embargo against Lebanon (with exemption to UNIFIL) (Sanctions Committee or other types of subsidiary organs have not been established)	Armed conflict between Lebanon and Israel
Democratic People's Republic of Korea (DPRK) (still in force)	S/Res/1718 (14 October 2006): Embargo on WMD materials against DPRK; Export ban on luxury goods; Asset freeze on individuals designated by the Sanctions Committee; Travel ban S/Res/1874 (12 June 2009): Expanding the scope of sanctions against DPRK; Ban on transaction related to arms embargo; Authorizing member States to seize and dispose of prohibited items; Prohibition of provision of fuel for DPRK vessels S/Res/2094 (7 March 2013): Expanding the scope of UN sanctions against DPRK; Prohibition of financial support that may contribute to the DPRK's nuclear programs; inspection of all cargo if the State has credible information that the cargo contains prohibited items; denying the vessel entry to port if it has refused the inspection	Nuclear tests and military activities by North Korea

Targets of UN economic sanctions	Security Council Resolutions numbers and brief Contents	Reasons for sanctions imposition
	S/Res/2270 (2 March 2016): Expanding the scope of arms embargo; Tightening of diplomatic relations with DPRK; Prohibition of training of DPRK nationals in disciplines related to nuclear technology: Inspection of the cargo that has originated in the DPRK, or that is destined for the DPRK; Prohibition of leasing or chartering vessels or aircraft; Prohibition of using vessels flagged by the DPRK; Prohibition of taking off/landing of aircraft if the member State has credible information that the aircraft contains prohibited items; Prohibition of export of fuel; Prohibiting the opening and operation of new branches, subsidiaries, and representative offices of DPRK banks; Prohibiting financial institutions from establishing new joint ventures and from taking an ownership interest in or establishing or maintaining correspondent relationships with DPRK banks; Prohibiting financial support for trade with the DPRK	
	S/Res/2321 (30 November 2016): Expanding the scope of arms embargo; Prohibition of technological cooperation with DPRK; Limiting the number of bank accounts to one per DPRK diplomatic mission and consular post; Limiting the DPRK from using real property; Prohibition of procuring and registering DPRK vessel; Limiting the export of coal and iron from DPRK; import ban on minerals such as copper and nickel from DPRK; Ban on the sale of statutes produced by DPRK; Prohibition of export of helicopters and vessels to DPRK; Expulsion of individuals who engage in DPRK banks or financial institutions	

Targets of UN economic sanctions	*Security Council Resolutions numbers and brief Contents*	*Reasons for sanctions imposition*
	S/Res/2371 (5 August 2017): Import ban on coal, iron, seafood, and vessels from DPRK; Prohibition of opening of new joint ventures with DPRK entities or individuals S/Res/2375 (11 September 2017): Prohibition of ship-to-ship transfers to or from DPRK-flagged vessels; Limiting oil export to DPRK; Import ban on textiles from DPRK; Prohibition of providing new work authorizations for DPRK nationals; Prohibition of opening, maintenance, and operation of all joint ventures with DPRK entities or individuals S/Res/2397 (22 December 2017): Limiting export of crude oil and refined petroleum products to DPRK; Import ban on agricultural products and machinery of certain categories; Export ban on transportation vehicles and iron to DPRK; Deportation of DPRK workers (exemption from the transshipment of Russia-originated coal to other countries through the Russia-DPRK Rajin-Khasan port and rail project)	
Iran (lifted in 2016)	S/Res/1737 (23 December 2006): Embargo on materials related to nuclear and missile programmes against Iran; Asset freeze on persons or entities designated by the Security Council or the Sanctions Committee as being engaged in Iran's nuclear activities S/Res/1747 (24 March 2007): Expanding the scope of sanctions decided by Resolution 1737 S/Res/1803 (3 March 2008): Travel ban on individuals designated by the Security Council or the Sanctions committee as being engaged in Iran's nuclear activities S/Res/1929 (9 June 2010): Arms embargo against Iran; Prohibition of transactions with entities that contribute to proliferation-sensitive nuclear activities	Nuclear enrichment activities by Iran

Targets of UN economic sanctions	Security Council Resolutions numbers and brief Contents	Reasons for sanctions imposition
Eritrea (still in force)	S/Res/1907 (23 December 2009): Arms embargo against Eritrea; Travel ban and asset freeze on governmental and military leaders of Eritrea; Inspection of all cargo to and from Somalia and Eritrea S/Res/2111 (24 July 2013): Exemption from arms embargo (humanitarian supplies; protective clothing used by United Nations personnel, and humanitarian and development workers) S/Res/2023(5 December 2011): Prohibition of the "Diaspora tax" on Eritrean diaspora; Due diligence obligation to prevent financial transfer to Eritrea; Due diligence obligation to prevent funds derived from the mining sector of Eritrea	Border dispute between Djibouti and Eritrea; Piracy off the coast of Somalia
Al-Qaida (ISIL (Da'esh) is added after Resolution 2253) (still in force)	S/Res/1989 (2011) (17 June 2011): Asset freeze, travel ban, arms embargo on individuals and entities associated with Al-Qaida; Establishment of the Ombudsperson for delisting; Establishment of a Monitoring team S/Res/2161 (17 June 2014): Prohibition of transfer of explosives and raw materials that can be used to manufacture improvised explosive devices to Al-Qaida and individuals and entities associated with Al-Qaida S/Res/2178 (24 September 2014): Prohibition of nationals to travel to become terrorist fighters; Prohibition of entry of individuals for the purpose of participating in Al-Qaida and related entities S/Res/2199 (12 February 2015): Informing the Sanctions Committee within 30 days of the interdiction in their territory of any oil, oil products	Terrorist activities by Al-Qaida and ISIL (Da'esh)

Targets of UN economic sanctions	Security Council Resolutions numbers and brief Contents	Reasons for sanctions imposition
	being transferred to or from ISIL (Da'esh) S/Res/2253 (17 December 2015): Application of the same sanctions as those against Al-Qaida (asset freeze; travel ban and arms embargo) to individuals and entities supporting ISIL (Da'esh) S/Res/2368 (20 July 2017): Expanding the scope of asset freeze to financial assets or economic resources gained from the illicit trade in natural resources including petroleum and petroleum products, as well as from kidnapping for ransom and other crimes including extortion and bank robbery	
the Taliban (still in force)	S/Res/1988 (2011) (17 June 2011): Asset freeze, travel ban, arms embargo on individuals' entities associated with the Taliban and constituting a threat to peace in Afghanistan; Support of the 1267 Monitoring Team S/Res/2082 (17 December 2012): Permitting the additional freezing of accounts of individuals and entities that constitute a threat to the peace, stability, and security of Afghanistan; Exemption from the travel ban; Welcoming the government of Afghanistan's desire to assist the Committee in the coordination of listing and delisting requests S/Res/2160 (17 June 2014): Expanding the scope of asset freeze (financial and economic resources of every kind, including those used for the provision of Internet hosting, and ransom payments) S/Res/2225 (21 December 2015): Expanding the scope of asset freeze, travel ban, and arms embargo to individuals and entities that constitute threats to peace, stability, and security of Afghanistan	Disturbance of peace process in Afghanistan by the Taliban

Targets of UN economic sanctions	*Security Council Resolutions numbers and brief Contents*	*Reasons for sanctions imposition*
Guinea-Bissau (still in force)	S/Res/2048 (18 May 2012): Travel ban against individuals that impede the stabilization of Guinea-Bissau	Disturbance of peacebuilding process in Guinea-Bissau
Central African Republic (still in force)	S/Res/2127 (5 December 2013): Arms embargo against Central African Republic; Authorization of seizure of prohibited items by sanctions S/Res/2134 (28 January 2014): Travel ban and asset freeze on individuals and entities that threaten the peace of Central African Republic S/Res/2196 (22 January 2015): Exemption from the arms embargo, travel ban, and asset freeze; Seizure and disposal of items that violate the arms embargo	Civil War and violation of the ceasefire agreement in Central African Republic
Yemen (still in force)	S/Res/2140 (26 February 2014): Travel ban and asset freeze on individuals and entities that threaten peace and security of Yemen (e.g. by impeding the GCC Initiative) S/Res/2216 (14 April 2015): Arms embargo on the former President of Yemen, Ali Abdullah Saleh; Requests for inspection by neighboring States	Armed conflicts in Yemen
South Sudan (still in force)	S/Res/2206 (3 March 2015): Travel ban and asset freeze against individuals that prevent the stability of South Sudan	Violation of the ceasefire agreement in South Sudan
Mali (still in force)	S/Res/2374 (5 September 2017): Travel ban and asset freeze against those who violate the ceasefire agreement, disturb humanitarian assistance, violate humanitarian law and human rights law, use or recruit children	Violation of the ceasefire agreement and terrorist activities in Mali

Non-military measures that do not target specific states or entities

Targets of non-military measures	*Security Council Resolutions numbers and brief contents*	*Reasons for the Security Council's decisions*
Individuals and entities who are involved in terrorist acts (still in force)	S/Res/1373 (28 September 2001): Asset freeze on persons who commit terrorist acts or participate in or facilitate the commission of terrorist acts terrorist acts; Refraining from providing any form of support to entities or persons involved in terrorist acts	Terrorist attacks in New York and other places (September 11 attacks)
Non-State actors that manufacture and possess weapons of mass destruction (still in force)	S/Res/1540 (28 April 2004): Refraining from providing any form of support to Non-State actors that manufacture and possess weapons of mass destruction; Adopting and enforcing appropriate effective laws which prohibit any non-State actor to manufacture and possess weapons of mass destruction; Establishment of the 1540 Committee	Proliferation of weapons of mass destruction (especially to Non-State actors such as terrorists)

Index

Note: Page numbers in *italics* indicate figures and in **bold** indicate tables on the corresponding pages.

Ago, R. 3
Ahmadinejad, M. 88, 161
Al-Dulimi case 125–129
Al-Jedda case 123–125, 126–129
Al-Qaida sanctions 11, 12–13, 24, 29, 39, 41, 42–43, 47
Annan, K. 18, 28
Anti-Money Laundering and Countering the Financing of Terrorism (ANL/CFT) sanctions 23
application issues with UN sanctions 12–13

Berlin Decree 2
Bierstecker, T. 24
bin Laden, U. 24
blockchain 92–93
Bonn-Berlin Process 21, 27
Bush, G. W. 81

Charter, UN 1, 2, 184–194; economic sanctions and 4–5
Comprehensive Iran Sanctions and Accountability and Divestment Act 2010 (CISADA) 85
Comprehensive Sanctions Act 76–77
Court of Justice of the European Union (CJEU) 107–108; case analysis 104–107, 121–123; EU financial sanctions regimes and 97–99; introduction to 96–97; Kadi judgment 121–123; legal approaches taken by 126–129; *LTTE* case and *Hamas* case in 100–103; significance

of findings of, to Japanese courts 107; *see also* European Court of Human Rights (ECtHR)
cryptocurrencies 92–93

Democratic People's Republic of Korea (DPRK): sanctions against 145–146, 167 (*see also* European Court of Human Rights (ECtHR)); challenges in implementation of 140–145; characteristics of 140; development of 135–140; introduction to 134; nuclear and ballistic missile program and 134–135; sanctions on 7, 8, 22–23

economic sanctions, UN: application of 12–13; and coercive measures 3–9; constant criticism towards legitimacy of 53–56; difference between unilateral sanctions and 3, 34; expanding the scope of sanctions measures and growing challenges of implementation of 56–59; financial measures of 7–8; fundamental shift in use of 19–21; implementation by Japan 67–68; implementation of 10–12, 56–59, 61–62; issues with 10–13; judicial challenges against 120–129; organs and competence of 6; overview of 52–53; practice of 6–7; private sector and 111–118; relationship between individual sanctions and 59–61; scope of 56–59; smart sanctions and the Interlaken Process 8–9; UN Charter and 4–5;

see also Security Council, UN; smart
sanctions
economic sanctions, unilateral: defined
1–2, 80–81; difference between UN
sanctions and 3, 34; effectiveness of
92–93; humanitarian effects of 19–20;
institutionalization of 2–3; on Iran
159–162, **160**; legal issues regarding
implementation of 90–93; relationship
between UN sanctions and 59–61;
transition from comprehensive to
targeted 38–40; *see also* Court of
Justice of the European Union
(CJEU); Japan Foreign Exchange and
Foreign Trade Act (FEFTA); United
States, the
Effect of Awards Case 37
Elliot, K. 2
Elliott, K. 8
Emmerson, B. 123
European Court of Human Rights
(ECtHR) 120–121, 123–126; legal
approaches taken by 126–129; *see also*
Court of Justice of the European
Union (CJEU)
European Court of Justice (ECJ) 26–27
European Union sanctions on Iran 161
experts, bodies of 41–42
extraterritorial application of
sanctions 90–92

Financial Actions Task Force (FATF)
8, 23, 80, 157, 167–168; 40
Recommendations and fourth-round
mutual evaluations of 174–176;
clarification of proliferation financing
by 170–174, **171–172**
financial sector *see* private sector
compliance
Fondation Secours International 27
Foreign Exchange and Foreign Trade
Act (FEFTA) *see* Japan Foreign
Exchange and Foreign Trade Act
(FEFTA)
Fowler, R. 24

Hamas case 100–103
Hufbauer, G. C. 2
humanitarian effects of sanctions 19–20
human rights protections 90

implementation of sanctions: challenges
to DPRK 140–145; challenges to

UNSCR 1540 and 179–180; by Japan
67–78; prospects for more effective
61–62; state 90–93; by the UN
10–12, 56–59
individuals and entities, sanctions
on 22–23
institutionalization of economic
sanctions 2–3
institutional law 35
Interlaken Process 8–9, 21, 27
International Atomic Energy Agency
(IAEA) 86–89
International Blockade Committee 3–4
International Emergency Economic
Powers Act (IEEPA) 77–78, 84, 85,
195–197
International Law Commission (ILC) 3
International Sanctions 1
invoking issues with UN sanctions 10
Iran, sanctions on: asset freeze 152–156;
compared to sanctions on DPRK
140; financial measures in 150–151;
introduction to 150; monitoring
financial transactions based on
UNSCR 1929 157–159, *159*; national
159–162, **160**; proliferation financing
156–157; recent developments in
163–164; United States 86–89,
159–161, **160**; UNSCR 2231 and
162–163
ISIL sanctions 11, 12–13, 41, 47

Japan Foreign Exchange and Foreign
Trade Act (FEFTA) 84–85; as basic
legislation for UN financial sanctions
73–74; brief history of 68–71,
70; comparison of US sanctions
system with 77–78; concept of
Comprehensive Sanctions Act and
76–77; efforts to counter proliferation
financing and 176–179; grounds for
license requirement under 72–73;
implementation of UN financial
sanctions by 68–74; introduction to
67–68, **69**; limitations of 74–76, *76*;
measures to ensure enforcement of
license system under 73; significance
of EU court findings to 107; types of
regulations under 71–72
Joint Comprehensive Plan of Action
(JCPOA) 88–89, 150, 157, 161–163
judicial challenges to UN sanctions:
CJEU 121–123; European Court of

Human Rights (ECtHR) 120–121, 123–126; introduction to 120–121; legal approaches taken by courts to address 126–129

Kadi judgment, CJEU 121–123, 126–129
Karroubi, M. 161
Kim Jong Un 146

law of international organizations 43–46
League of Nations 2, 3, 5, 6, 13, 38–39; financial sanctions and 3–4
legal issues: with DPRK sanctions 140–145; with implementation of state sanctions 90–93; judicial challenges to UN sanctions 120–129; and political concerns with smart sanctions 25–30; private sector compliance 112–113
legal status of Security Council subsidiary organs 36–38
Legitimate Financial System (LFS) 82, 83
listing/delisting process and human rights 23–24
LTTE case 100–103

member states, political concerns of 27–28
Mission in Sierra Leone (UNAMSIL) 42
Mission in the Democratic Republic of Congo (MONUC) 42
monitoring bodies 42–43
Mousavi, M. H. 161

Nada case 123–125, 127–129
Nakatani, K. 3
national courts and UN sanctions 27
National Union for the Total Independence of Angola (UNITA) 23–24, 39, 41, 42
Newcomb, R. 9
North Korea *see* Democratic People's Republic of Korea (DPRK), sanctions against

Obama, B. 87–88
Oegg, B. 2
Office of the Ombudsperson 43
operational law 35–36, 37
Oudraat, C. de J. 19, 20

Pompeo, M. 163
private sector compliance 117–118; contractual protections in 115–117; due diligence in 114–115; financial sector "gold standard" of 113–114; introduction to 111–112; legal framework for 112–113

remedial law 36, 38
Rouhani, H. 88, 161–162
Royal Institute of International Affairs 1

Savimbi, J. 24
Sayadi, N. 27
Schott, J. J. 2
scope of sanctions 56–59
Security Council, UN 6–7, 18, 52–53; Comprehensive Sanctions Act 76–77; emerging legal challenges and political concerns of 25–30; financial measures of economic sanctions by 7–8; Iran sanctions and 157–159, *159*; law of international organizations and 43–46; major economic sanctions adopted by 199–213; subsidiary organs of 10–11, 34–47; *see also* economic sanctions, UN
September 11, 2001, terrorist attacks 19
smart sanctions 8–9, 18–19, 30–31, 34; current targeted 22–24; emerging legal challenges and political concerns with 25–30; formulating of 20–21; fundamental shift in use of sanctions and 19–21; on individuals and entities 22–23; listing/delisting process and human rights 23–24; political con 27–28; *see also* economic sanctions, UN
Society for Worldwide Interbank Financial Telecommunication (SWIFT) 80–81, 84, 150, 161
Stockholm Process 21, 27
subsidiary organs, Security Council 10–11, 46–47; bodies of experts 41–42; development of 40; development of financial sanctions regimes and 38–43; introduction to 34–36; law of international organizations and 43–46; legal status of 36–38; monitoring bodies 42–43; Office of the Ombudsperson 43; sanctions committees 40–41

Taliban sanctions 11, 24, 29, 39, 42–43
Treasury's War: The Unleashing of a New Era of Financial Warfare 81
Treaties of the European Union (TEU) 97
Treaty of the European Union 198
Treaty on the Functioning of the European Union (TFEU) 97, 198
Treaty on the Non-Proliferation of Nuclear Weapons (NPT) *see* Democratic People's Republic of Korea (DPRK), sanctions against
Trump, D. 163
1267 committee 29–30

United States, the: International Emergency Economic Powers Act (IEEPA) 77–78, 84, 85, 195–197; Iranian sanctions by 86–89, 159–161, 160; Japanese sanctions system compared 77–78; laws pertaining to financial sanctions in 84–86; legal system in 85–86; Participation Act (UNPA) for the UN 194–195; rationale for financial sanctions by 81–84; United Nations Participation Act (UNPA) 77
UNSCR 1540: challenges to implementation of 179–180; FATF's clarification of proliferation financing and 170–174, **171–172**; introduction to 166–168; Japan and 176–179; proliferation financing under 168–170
UNSCR 2231 162–163

Vinck, P. 27

Zarate, J. C. 81, 82